Hawaiian Blood

NARRATING NATIVE HISTORIES

Narrating Native Histories aims to foster a rethinking of the ethical, methodological, and conceptual frameworks within which we locate our work on Native histories and cultures. We seek to create a space for effective and ongoing conversations between North and South, Natives and non-Natives, academics and activists, throughout the Americas and the Pacific region. We are committed to complicating and transgressing the disciplinary and epistemological boundaries of established academic discourses on Native peoples.

This series encourages symmetrical, horizontal, collaborative, and auto-ethnographies; work that recognizes Native intellectuals, cultural interpreters, and alternative knowledge producers within broader academic and intellectual worlds; projects that decolonize the relationship between orality and textuality; narratives that productively work the tensions between the norms of Native cultures and the requirements for evidence in academic circles; and analyses that contribute to an understanding of Native peoples' relationships with nation-states, including histories of expropriation and exclusion as well as projects for autonomy and sovereignty.

We are pleased to have *Hawaiian Blood: Colonialism and the Politics of Sovereignty and Indigeneity* as one of our two inaugural volumes. J. Kēhaulani Kauanui's study investigates how blood quantum politics, first used to define "native Hawaiian" by the U.S. Congress in 1921, became a policy of colonial exclusion and erasure of sovereignty claims, whose effects are still being felt today. Kauanui traces how an indigenous attempt to reclaim lands for displaced Hawaiians was transformed into a project for the "rehabilitation" of "Natives"—ultimately defined in blood quantum as half-blooded or more—who were deemed "incompetent" and thus in need of charity. This racialization of Hawaiian identity, she argues, flew in the face of more inclusive Kanaka Maoli genealogical and kinship practices and concealed the dispossession of Hawaiians as a people and a nation.

Hawaiian / Blood

Colonialism and the Politics of Sovereignty and Indigeneity

J. Kēhaulani Kauanui

DUKE UNIVERSITY PRESS

DURHAM AND LONDON

2008

© 2008 Duke University Press

Designed by Heather Hensley

Typeset in Minion Pro by Keystone Typesetting, Inc.

Library of Congress Cataloging-in-Publication Data appear

on the last printed page of this book.

Rehabilitation

1. a. The action of re-establishing (a person) in
a former standing with respect to rank and legal
rights (or church privileges); the result of such
action; also, a writ by which such restoration is
made (In early use chiefly *Sc.*); b. Reinstatement
(of a person) in any previous position or privilege; c. Re-establishment of a person's reputation;
vindication of character; 2. a. The action of
replacing a thing in, or restoring it to, a previous
condition or status; b. Restoration to a higher
moral state; c. Restoration (of a disabled person,
a criminal, etc.) to some degree of normal life by
appropriate training; d. The retraining of a person, or the restoration of industry, the economy,
etc., after a war or a long period of military
service.

—OXFORD ENGLISH DICTIONARY

Blood Quantum

By Naomi Noe Losch

We thought we were Hawaiian.

Our ancestors were Līloa, Kūaliʻi and Alapaʻi.

We fought at Mokuohai, Kepaniwai and Nuʻuanu,

and we supported Liliʻu in her time of need.

We opposed statehood.

We didn't want to be the 49th or the 50th,

and once we were, 5(f) would take care of us.

But what is a native Hawaiian?

Aren't we of this place?

ʻO ko mākou one hānau kēia.

And yet, by definition we are not Hawaiian.

We can't live on Homestead land,

nor can we receive OHA money.

We didn't choose to quantify ourselves,

1/4 to the left	1/2 to the right
3/8 to the left	5/8 to the right
7/16 to the left	17/32 to the right

They not only colonized us, they divided us.

Thinking about Hawaiian Identity

By Maile Kēhaulani Sing

Thinking about Hawaiian identity
I start to spin in circles easily
Is identity belonging
Or is belonging identity
Do I meet the criteria
A certain textbook definition
Or is being Hawaiian my inheritance
And from my ancestors
Unconditionally given

Full, half, quarter, or eighth
It doesn't take long for
The experts to proclaim
Hawaiians are indeed
A vanishing race
Influenza, vd, and now
We've contracted
U.S. racial rhetoric
That grounds us down
To mere fractions

When my blood is measured
And my features dissected
I start to feel sick
As if infected
By reason and logic
By science and politics
All my life I have swallowed
This blood quantum theory
Like pills from the colonial pharmacy
Prescription strength invisibility
To cure this illness
Of lingering indigeneity

Hawai'i is paradise
Up for grabs
Full of aloha
And hula dance
An image of smiling natives
That everyone would love to be
The only obstacle that complicates
Is the call to discriminate
For the sake of sovereignty
Self determination fueled
By genealogical identity
Hawaiian entitlement to be free
From the thick of
American fantasy

Contents

A Note to Readers

IN THE EARLY NINETEENTH CENTURY, American missionaries applied the term "half-caste" to those of mixed white and Hawaiian parentage, but it was eventually abandoned in favor of the Hawaiian term *hapa-haole* (literally, part-white or part-foreigner) (Wright 1972: 282). Prior to that shift, during the early twentieth century, the terms "Asiatic Hawaiian" and "Caucasian Hawaiian" were used to classify and describe Kānaka Maoli who had Asian or European ancestry.* From the mid- to the late twentieth century, the term *hapa-haole* still had currency within Hawaiian communities—both on- and off-island.**

"Part-Hawaiian" eventually became more common. Fortified by the contemporary sovereignty struggle today, though, the use of the term "part-Hawaiian" (which begs the question, why not "part-white" or "part-Asian"?) has taken a back seat to using "Hawaiian" or "Native Hawaiian" for someone of any Hawaiian ancestry. Similarly, the terms *Kanaka Maoli* (real or true people), *Kanaka ʻŌiwi* (bone people), or *ʻŌiwi Maoli* (true bone) are much more common today because they emphasize Hawaiian indigeneity without referencing blood. The emergence of these terms can be attributed to the contemporary indigenous nationalist struggle and the Hawaiian language recovery movement, both of which tend to advocate for genealogical forms of articulating identity.

Throughout this book, I use "native Hawaiian" (with a lower case "n")

---

* These terms did not position "Hawaiian" as a geographical marker; "Asiatic Hawaiian," for example, could not have meant an Asian person from or in Hawaiʻi.

** Here I use the term "off-island" to describe Hawaiians living outside Hawaiʻi on the American continent. When used while in Hawaiʻi, the term "off-island" refers to individuals who are not on the particular island where they usually locate themselves (e.g., "No, Naniʻs off-island on Oʻahu [and not Kauaʻi] today."). Thus, my use of it to mean those Hawaiians who are diasporic may raise questions. But my usage recognizes the fact that many American Indian and First Nations peoples recognize their continent as Great Turtle Island, and thus another island, albeit outside of the Hawaiian archipelago. In addition, the common usage of "off-island" while *on-island* presumes a return to one island or another by the person "off-island" and thus is appropriate to acknowledge diasporic Hawaiians who continue to return time and again as part of their ongoing on-island attachments. Furthermore, there are issues regarding the political claims of off-island Hawaiians vis-à-vis the sovereignty movement (Kauanui 2007; 1998).

only when referring to the 50-percent definition in any given legal context, whereas I use "Native Hawaiian" (with a capital "N") when referring to its legal context where it is defined as anyone of Hawaiian ancestry without regard for the blood quantum rule. When not referring to a specific legal definition, I use "Kanaka Maoli" and "Hawaiian" interchangeably to describe those indigenous to Hawai'i. I do so in order to underscore the shift between the two and to remind the reader that the term "Hawaiian" does not work as a residency marker in the way "Californian" does. As Queen Lili'u-okalani put it: "When I speak . . . of the Hawaiian people, I refer to the children of the soil,—the native inhabitants of the Hawaiian Islands and their descendants"—an "aboriginal people" with a "birthright" (Lili'uoka-lani 1968: 325).

Finally, a note on the use of Hawaiian diacritical marks: *Kanaka* (without a macron) indicates the singular or the categorical plural, while *Kānaka* denotes a countable plural. Some Hawaiian words inconsistently appear with a glottal stop (e.g., *Hawai'i*) to reflect historical usage.

Acknowledgments

THIS BOOK HAS COME ABOUT AS THE result of many years of support and assistance from family and friends, as well as colleagues, archivists, and librarians. I would like to offer my *mahalo* to my father Joseph Kauanui III, as well as my stepsiblings Don F. Gates III and Kelly Chavez, and most especially my mother Carol Lee Gates whose unwavering encouragement helped me through the most difficult of times. I also wish to thank my extended families, especially my Uncle Vern Kauanui, Auntie Puanani Rogers, Kauʻi Doyle, and all of those in my *ʻohana* who have encouraged this work. I must also acknowledge my late grandmother, Blossom Pauahi Kauanui, who first explained the blood quantum policy and the Hawaiian Home Lands territory to me when I was in high school. Later when I was a graduate student, I once asked her if I should learn to hula. She laughed and said, "No! You are the writer of our family." Mahalo, Tutu.

Early on, I had encouragement for this project from Hawaiian elders who have always supported me: Kukuni Blaisdell, Paul Kealoha Blake, Hinano Campton, Sharon Wahinekaʻiu LumHo, and Healani Waiwaiole.

I would like to thank the friends, mentors, and colleagues who took time to encourage me. They read drafts, contributed critical feedback, and offered moral support at different stages—especially Noenoe K. Silva, Anne Keala Kelly, Joanne Barker, Lisa Kahaleole Hall, and Andrea Smith. As I was preparing the manuscript for initial review, both Anita Mannur and Alison Redick generously offered their support by reading draft chapters and making important editorial suggestions. Yael Ben-zvi and Jonathan Schell took time to read the introduction and offered productive critiques that pushed me further along. Several colleagues and friends offered crucial support at different points along the journey: Jennifer Denetdale, Cynthia Franklin, Eva Garroutte, Moon-Kie Jung, Shawn Kanaiaupuni, Adria L. Imada, Valerie Lambert, Jean O'Brien, Audra Simpson, Geoffrey White, Susan Gooding, Paula Wagoner, David E. Wilkins, Elizabeth Culpeper Creely, Reid Gomez and Niki Lee, Maria Elena Garcia and Jose Antonio Lucero, Dan Taulapapa McMullin,

Keta Miranda, Amberlyn Nelson, Lisa Saborío, Maivan Clech Lam, Ty Kā-wika Tengan, Elizabeth DeLoughery, Teresia K. Teaiwa, Vicente M. Diaz, David Delgado Shorter, Glen Mimura, Maivân Clech Lâm, Barbara K. Ige, Caroline Sinavaiana, and Morgan Aiwohi Torris-Hedlund.

I also had the privilege of multiple forms of financial support as this work began as a doctoral thesis and became a book: the Woodrow Wilson National Foundation Career Enhancement Fellowship, the Smithsonian Pre-doctoral Research Fellowship at the National Museum of American History, the Rockefeller Archives Center Research Grant, the Smithsonian Graduate Research Fellowship at the National Museum of American History, and the National Science Foundation Minority Pre-doctoral Fellowship. I benefited greatly from a Katrin H. Lamon fellowship at the School of American Research (now known as the School for Advanced Research on the Human Experience) in Santa Fe, New Mexico, for a year of sabbatical and leave. While in residence there, I was strongly supported by an incredible group of scholars who became friends: Jessica R. Cattelino, Circe Dawn Sturm, Jason Yaeger, Bruce M. Knauft, Lawrence Cohen, and Suzan Shown Harjo— as well as Randolph Lewis and Noah Zatz, who were there with spouses in residence.

I also wish to acknowledge the many colleagues who invited me to present aspects of this work at their home institutions: Dana Ain-Davis at State University of New York, Purchase College; Lili M. Kim at Hampshire College; Trudie Lamb Richmond at the Mashantucket Pequot Museum and Research Center; Audra Simpson and Angela Gonzales at Cornell University; Maria Elena Garcia when she was located at Sarah Lawrence College; Henry Helenani Gomes and Ellen Shimakawa at Chaminade University (twice!); Judith Raiskin at the University of Oregon; Elena Creef at Wellesley College; Jocelyn Linnekin at the University of Connecticut, Storrs; Kent Ono when he was at the University of California, Davis; and Teresia K. Teaiwa when she was based at the University of the South Pacific. Thanks also to Leti Volpp for enabling me to present part of this work at the Latino Critical Theory conference in Colorado, and Marilyn Halter who invited me to present at her workshop "The Limits of American Citizenship" in Hawai'i.

I would like to thank James Clifford, Donna Haraway, and Neferti Tadiar, who served on my doctoral committee at the University of California, Santa Cruz, in the program of History of Consciousness. I would also like to convey my appreciation to Angela Davis and the women of the Research Cluster for the Study of Women of Color in Conflict and Collaboration at UCSC.

At the Smithsonian, I would like to thank Rayna Green, Adrienne Kaeppler, Franklin Odo, and Marvette Perez for their support, especially while I was a research fellow at the National Museum of American History (NMAH). Also at NMAH, librarian Rhoda S. Ratner was always helpful, as were the specialists at the Archive Center. I would also like to thank the librarian specialists at the National Anthropological Archives at the National Museum of Natural History.

Librarian Joan Hori in the special collections at the University of Hawaii at Manoa Library has always enthusiastically helped me navigate the Hawaiian collection and provided encouragement along the way. The librarians Erhard Konerding and Kendall Hobbs at Wesleyan's Olin Library were helpful in the final stages of the copyediting.

I am privileged to teach at Wesleyan University and would like to thank all of my superb colleagues for their support—especially Claire Potter, Richard Slotkin, Joel Pfister, Henry Abelove, Elizabeth Traube, Gina Ulysse, Anu Sharma, Patricia Hill, Ann Wightman, Michael Armstrong, Elizabeth McAlister, Renee Romano, Christina Crosby, Elizabeth Emery, Allan Punzalan Isaac, as well as three former Wesleyan faculty members: Kate Rushin, Jennifer Scott, and Susan Hirsch.

I am very grateful to both Sally Merry and Noenoe K. Silva for their rigorous reviews of this work and their helpful suggestions for ways to improve the manuscript.

Mahalo nui to both Maile Kēhaulani Sing and Naomi Noe Losch for allowing me to include their powerful poetry. I am also grateful to Kauanoelehua Chang for granting me permission to have her beautiful painting appear on the cover of the book.

Brandon Clint Ledward, Ashwini Mate, Lindsey Kukona, and Sarah Diaz provided very helpful research and assistance at key times, and Will Swofford helped with the final preparation of the manuscript. Noenoe K. Silva offered her editorial labor to ensure that the Hawaiian diacritical marks appear in their proper place.

At Duke University Press, I would like to express my heartfelt thanks to Ken Wissoker and Courtney Berger for supporting this work and keeping me on task; Molly Balikov, who patiently worked with me through the difficulties of the copyediting stage; and Heather Hensley, who worked on the design. I also appreciate Florencia Mallon, K. Tsianina Lomawaima, Aleida Rita Ramos, and Joanne Rappaport for choosing this book to inaugurate their new series.

In the very last days, while tending to the minutiae, both Aileen Moreton-Robinson and Jason Villani provided warm enthusiasm and care that spurred me on.

Mahalo nui loa!

INTRODUCTION Got Blood?

TOWARD THE END OF MY TIME IN GRADUATE school in the 1990s, I traveled from California to attend a family *pāʻina* (party) in Anahola, Kauaʻi, to celebrate the birthday of my cousin's baby boy. The party was held at my uncle's house, and he was excited to host such a huge gathering to mark his grandson's first year of life. This uncle is my father's younger brother, and when I turned one year old, he helped host a *lūʻau* (feast) that my grandparents threw for me as well. My parents brought me to the island from southern California, where I was born and raised, so I could be feted by my ʻohana (family). At this more recent occasion, as I sat between my grandma and my uncle, I was confronted about my light skin color by the baby's other grandfather, who is German and Kanaka Maoli (Native Hawaiian). This was surprising for two different reasons: he himself is very light-skinned, and I had already introduced myself to him earlier to acknowledge the linking of our families. Although his son and my cousin had not married (not a problem given the prevalence of "common-law" partnerships among many Kānaka Maoli), they were, nevertheless, now ʻohana because of their children. He came right up to me and pointed his finger three inches from my nose while he demanded I tell him "how much Hawaiian blood" I have. I smiled politely, reintroduced myself, and reminded him that I was sitting in between my Kanaka Maoli grandma and uncle. Still, he insisted that I recite a fraction to answer his question of "how much?" But I refused.

I felt attacked and disrespected by his choosing my skin over kin—treating me as *haole* (white person or foreigner) and denying my connection to "our" family. I thought his insistence especially rude because he was on what I consider my home turf, even though I don't reside there, because I am part of the host family. He used the question of blood quantum as a stand-in for addressing my geographical distance as a Hawaiian living outside Hawaiʻi and to negotiate the boundary between insider and outsider, where notions of blood framed his assessment of me in determining my legitimacy and authenticity.

Before I could get into it with him, my grandma yelled, "She's got more than you! And the next time you see her, she's gonna be a professor!" Even though both assertions were true, he didn't look satisfied. And so my uncle then interrupted with something else: "She get, she get about 51 percent." I found it unsettling that my uncle felt as though he had to qualify me in some way by suggesting I had more than half Hawaiian blood quantum, but this was his way of making sure I was recognized as belonging. I turned away from both men to focus on family members who were playing music and offering special hula for the night when I heard my uncle trying to soothe him: "No worries, you know why? Our grandson, he get plenty Hawaiian blood, plenty." Here it seemed he was assuring the other man that their grandson would never be questioned in the way I had been.

Among many Kānaka Maoli, my story is typical; we are up against challenges to our racial "integrity" that aim to undercut our genealogical ties. These challenges are tied to popular notions of cultural authenticity and biological difference through the use of blood quantum, notions that have been reinforced by the law. Blood quantum is a fractionalizing measurement—a calculation of "distance" in relation to some supposed purity to mark one's generational proximity to a "full-blood" forebear (4/4, 1/2, 1/4, 1/8, 1/16, 1/32, 1/64 . . .). Blood quantum logic presumes that one's "blood amount" correlates to one's cultural orientation and identity. Thus, it is no surprise that my uncle chose to assign me 51 percent of Hawaiian blood, because the state of Hawai'i currently defines "native Hawaiian" identity by a 50-percent rule. The basis for my uncle's defense of me was a direct legacy of this racist policy, the origin of which is the focus of this book.

The contemporary legal definition of "native Hawaiian" as a "descendant with at least one-half blood quantum of individuals inhabiting the Hawaiian Islands prior to 1778" originated in the Hawaiian Homes Commission Act (HHCA) of 1921 in which the U.S. Congress allotted approximately 200,000 acres of land in small areas across the main islands to be leased for residential, pastoral, and agricultural purposes by eligible "native Hawaiians."[1] This legislation originally emerged as an attempt by Hawaiian elites to rehabilitate Kānaka Maoli who were suffering from high mortality rates—connected to the nineteenth-century depopulation brought about by colonial dispossession—as well as disease and poverty tied to urbanization. Yet paradoxically, while the earliest formulations of the proposal leading to the act were intended to encourage the revitalization of a particular Hawaiian demographic, the act simultaneously created a class of people who could no longer qualify for the land that constitutes the Hawaiian Home Lands territory. This historical division is still at play in the contemporary sovereignty movement and is manifest in the current federal legislation before the U.S. Congress threatening to transform the Hawaiian national independence claim to that of a domestic dependent nation under U.S. federal policy on Native Americans.

This book critically interrogates the way that blood racialization constructs Hawaiian identity as measurable and dilutable. Racialization is the process by which racial meaning is ascribed—in this case to Kanaka Maoli through ideologies of blood quantum. In contrast, I examine Kanaka Maoli genealogical practices and kinship and how they differ from the U.S. colonial imposition of blood quantum. Many Kānaka Maoli contest the federal and state definition of "native Hawaiian" at 50 percent not only because it is so exclusionary but because it undercuts indigenous Hawaiian epistemologies that define identity on the basis of one's kinship and genealogy. Thus, I emphasize the strategic, socially embedded, and political aspects of these indigenous practices. The blood quantum rule operates through a reductive logic in both cultural and legal contexts and undermines expansive identity claims based on genealogy. While some assume genealogy is a proxy for race, I argue that blood quantum racial classification is used as a proxy for ancestry, with destructive political consequences for indigenous peoples. I primarily focus on the legal construction of Hawaiian indigeneity in order to analyze the implications for historical claims to land and sovereignty. Providing historical context for the hearings on the HHCA, I analyze the debates that led to the passage of the legislation in order to account for how the U.S. government came to racialize Kanaka Maoli through blood quantum and why the definition of "native Hawaiian" was set at 50 percent.

The state of Hawai'i continues to use the 50-percent blood quantum rule to manage and evaluate claims to indigeneity. Once administered by the Hawaiian Homes Commission created by the U.S. Congress, the responsibility for implementing the Hawaiian Homes Commission Act of 1920 was transferred to the state in 1959. This directive was set by the U.S. federal government as a condition of Hawai'i's admission to the union in 1959, a forcible inclusion that is currently contested by Hawaiian sovereignty activists who challenge the very legitimacy of statehood. Since 1959, the state Department of Hawaiian Home Lands has administered the program and therefore verifies applicants' eligibility based on the blood rule. Although proof of Hawaiian blood quantum is required to qualify as "native Hawaiian," there has never been any territorial or state administrative mandate for documenting the fractional breakdown of ancestry on vital records.[2]

In trying to secure lease lands, applicants are required to submit primary documents to show that they qualify as "native Hawaiian." These forms of evidence can amount to up to thirty notarized documents, along with an application more than thirty pages long to substantiate a claim of eligibility. Necessary documents include certified copies of certificate of live birth, certificate of Hawaiian birth (for people who did not have a birth certificate recorded at the time of their birth but can secure a witness who can testify to the circumstances of their birth), and certificate of delayed birth. In the event that the Vital Records Division of the Department of Health does not have a birth certificate for an applicant's parents or grandparents, the department will issue a "no record" certificate, which must also be submitted to the Department of Hawaiian Home Lands. For applicants who were adopted, the Family Court in Hawai'i may be able to assist, while access to out-of-state adoption records varies from state to state. Secondary documents to substantiate one's identity as a "native Hawaiian" include certified marriage certificates, certified death certificates, and records in relation to baptism, marriage, divorce, military service, death, as well as hospital and employment records from the State of Hawai'i Archives, state courts, public libraries, and U.S. census records. Other document resource centers include the Bureau of Conveyances, Circuit Family Court, and the Kalaupapa Settlement Office (which holds records on Hawaiians held at the former "Leper Colony" who were afflicted with Hansen's disease from 1865 on), and of course, the vast Family History Centers of the Church of Latter-Day Saints.

As a result of gross mismanagement on the part of the state—violations of the congressional stipulation to administer the lands in trust—over 20,000 "native Hawaiians" remain on the waiting list, while only 8,000 have been granted leases since 1921.[3] Still, there are numerous benefits for those who do manage to secure a lease. The annual lease rent is only one dollar per year with a ninety-nine-year lease, and a lease term that can be extended for an additional hundred years to allow a lessee to pass a homestead from generation to generation. There is also a seven-year exemption from real property tax, complete exemption of tax on land, with minimal real property tax after the first seven years (in select counties). Although lessees cannot use the lease land as equity to obtain loans, they have access to low-interest government loans (subject to the whims of Congress) and can use the equity in their property to obtain loans.

A modest breach in the 50-percent rule was registered in 1992, when the state of Hawai'i passed statutes allowing "native Hawaiian" leaseholders to designate a direct descendant as a successor under the lease if they meet a blood quantum criterion of one-fourth Hawaiian blood. And in 1994, the state extended this provision to permit grandchildren of native Hawaiian leaseholders to become successors if they meet the quarter blood rule (Garcia 1997: A1).[4] U.S. Congressional amendments to the act in 1997 now allow direct descendants of "native Hawaiians" to inherit family leases so long as they can prove they are at least "1/4th Hawaiian" (B4). Prior to the 1997 congressional amendments, a grandchild of a leaseholder had to qualify as "native Hawaiian" by the 50-percent rule in order to become a successor to a lease, even though in 1982 the Hawai'i state legislature provided for a spouse or child of a leaseholder to inherit a lease if an individual can prove one-fourth Hawaiian ancestry (ibid.).[5] The 1997 amendment to the HHCA begs the question as to why these lands should not be opened up now to those who can prove one-fourth Hawaiian ancestry, as direct lessees. Also, despite this amendment, the requirement of having to prove eligibility based on blood quantum in order to secure a lease to Hawaiian Home Lands has led many Kānaka Maoli to see "50 percent" as the authenticating criterion for Hawaiian identity, the acceptance of which reveals an uneasy contradiction. On the one hand, those who abide by the rule in social contexts are acquiescing to the U.S. government's dictate as to who counts as "native Hawaiian," while, on the other hand, they disregard the U.S. government's revision of that standard. Hence, those who do not meet the 50-percent blood rule are often seen as "lesser than," where Kanaka Maoli are divided into two classes with one assuming dominance over the other.

Many Hawaiians and non-Hawaiians have become invested in blood quantum as proof of indigeneity and rely on the fractionalizing measurements of one's "blood amount" as a marker for cultural orientation and identity, even though the racial categories this logic depends on are the product of relatively recent colonial taxonomies. [6] These concerns with "measuring up" reflect a growing anxiety among Hawaiians that is all too common. In both day-to-day and legal contexts, blood is often evoked to stand in for race, indigeneity, and nationhood—and it can be used to mean any or all of these depending on the specific political agenda of any given moment.

Why 50 Percent?

There are multiple investments in changing the legal definition of Hawaiian identity, and the law itself becomes the ground upon which Kanaka Maoli are compelled to negotiate the politics of identity on American terms. As aspects of identity concerning collective property entitlements are often consequential with respect to the law, the legal definition also implicates the construction of Hawaiian peoplehood. In *Colonizing Hawai'i: The Cultural Power of Law*, Sally Merry examines the imposition of Western law in Hawai'i in the nineteenth century and how it transformed the community of Hilo (2000). Her important study specifically examines American colonialism and the racial and cultural subjugation of Native Hawaiians, where law served as a core institution of colonial control and therefore an important site of struggle implicating social relations, and thus identity.

The congressional hearings on the HHCA legislative proposal provide a critical genealogy for the 50-percent racial criterion that continues to determine land leasing eligibility. I analyze the congressional debates leading up to the HHCA between February 1920 and December 1921, before the Committee on the Territories, and include an examination of the role of Hawaiian and non-Hawaiian elites in the territory. Three sets of hearings were held between 1920 and 1921: first, the U.S. House of Representatives Hearings before the Committee on the Territories in February 1920; second, the U.S. Senate Hearings before the Committee on the Territories in December 1920, during the Sixty-Sixth Congress; and third, the U.S. House of Representatives Hearings before the Committee on the Territories in June 1921, during the Sixty-Seventh Congress. The transcripts from these hearings serve as the primary documents for my case study.

I focus on this particular period and legal context to see how the U.S. government redefined Kanaka Maoli identity through blood racialization. By analyzing the debates and discussions held within hearings, I theorize the racialization of Hawaiians through the enactment of the HHCA, examining how it undermines broader land and sovereignty claims. This book, then, accounts for the ways the blood quantum definition of 50 percent was determined as the criterion for Hawaiian land leasing eligibility within the context of U.S. colonial land appropriation and its implications for the contemporary sovereignty struggle.

The legal construction of Hawaiian identity has received little to no attention from scholars or activists. While the 50-percent blood quantum standard is common knowledge among Kanaka Maoli, no one has previously undertaken a comprehensive history and analysis of what led to this particular determination.[7] It is most common for people in Hawai'i to suggest that the 50-percent rule was created because the U.S. government thought that Kanaka Maoli would die off to the point that eventually no one would count as Hawaiian using that criterion. Because the 50-percent rule is the legacy of the colonial sugar industry in the Hawaiian Islands—where the white Americans controlling sugar plantations helped to establish a minimum blood quantum requirement so they would eventually gain control over more Hawaiian land—many Kānaka Maoli assume that they also anticipated (and even hoped for) Native demise. In other words, it is thought that, by measuring identity through 50-percent blood quantum, U.S. legislators presumed Hawaiians would eventually no longer qualify for lands. However, the expressed purpose of the Kanaka Maoli elites who first proposed the HHCA was to save the "dying Hawaiian race" by restoring them to rural life.

So, paradoxically, the 50-percent rule was in part created to encourage Hawaiian survival and physical rehabilitation, not the disappearance of Kanaka Maoli; the original concern with Hawaiian rehabilitation was figured as an intervention in the condition of an endangered people. The 50-percent rule was first used by congressional representatives who distinguished among Kanaka Maoli in order to identify those whose very existence was viewed as threatened and thought to be in need of social and biological regeneration. The stated aim of the legislation was to enable Hawaiians to escape the tenements and slums in Honolulu; back on the land, they might "till the soil and become self-supporting and raise healthy, happy families and become homeowners, new blood would be gradually infused into the race and it would thrive as it did in the days when it was in its prime" (Hawaiian Homes Commission 1922:3). A gesture toward that time of Hawaiians' "prime" entailed a valorization of the rural, where identification with the soil was part of a broader American social movement as it neatly coincided with distorted notions of Hawaiian "tradition" in relation to land.[8] A key part of the HHCA's attempt at repopulation through relocation was the link between the renewal of Hawaiian "blood" and reconnection to the soil that would tie Kānaka Maoli back to land and agriculture rather than technology and industry.

Initially, Kanaka Maoli leaders' calls for Hawaiian rehabilitation focused on indigenous mortality and reproduction, where they linked Kanaka Maoli survival to the reoccupation of Native lands. Their proposal was premised on recognition of Hawaiian citizenship under the kingdom as they dealt with unresolved land rights. But the problem was in articulating that awareness of these historical claims within the confines of American law, citizenship, and racial categories. Although billed as a proposal to allot lease lands for Kanaka Maoli rehabilitation, in the end the HHCA actually served as a policy of broad land dispossession, which accounts for why it is still looked upon with some suspicion—especially given its massive failure. The different arguments about who exactly needed rehabilitation and what constituted rehabilitation, given its broad meaning, and how Kanaka Maoli eligibility would be defined raised many historical questions—most notably the matter of how the United States came to claim the land in the first place. After the unilateral U.S. annexation of Hawai'i in 1898, the U.S. government's favored option of "returning Hawaiians to the land" rather than returning land to the Hawaiians was a typical colonial stance. It is not surprising, then, to find that Hawaiian blood quantum classification originates in the dispossession of Native claims to land and sovereignty.

The blood criterion emerged as a way to avoid recognizing Hawaiians' entitlement to the specific lands that were desired for the leasing program. I document here the discursive shift from a reparations and entitlement framework to one formulated on the basis of welfare and charity. The key players in the HHCA hearings redefined "need" in racial terms by using blood quantum as an indicator of social competency, where those defined by the 50-percent rule were deemed incapable of looking out for themselves. As Linda Gordon puts it in another context, regarding the history of welfare from 1890 to 1935 for single mothers, they were "pitied but not entitled" (1994).[9] Hence, in the quest to control Hawaiian land and assets, blood quantum classification emerged as a way to undermine Kanaka Maoli sovereignty claims—by not only explicitly limiting the number who could lay claim to the land but also reframing the Native connection to the land itself from a legal claim to one based on charity. I make the case that blood quantum was not necessarily an inevitable way of defining who would count as Hawaiian in the act and I further map the alteration of an open definition of "native Hawaiian," where at first there was *no* designated blood quantum —since the program was intended for all Hawaiians "in whole or in part"— to the end result of the 50-percent determination. In tracing the shift, this case study explores the discursive constructions of "full-blood" and "part"-Hawaiians that emerged in the debates.

Blood quantum is a manifestation of settler colonialism that works to deracinate—to pull out by the roots—and displace indigenous peoples. Because Hawaiian racial and legal definitions are intricately connected to struggles over indigeneity and political status, this book asks how the HHCA land policy relates to concepts of citizenship, native rehabilitation, and entitlement—all of which are inflected by race, class, lineage rank, and gender differences among Hawaiians. How is Hawaiian indigeneity made and unmade in the service of competing political interests of different nationalisms—those of the Hawaiian sovereignty struggle and the United States—that can support or erode sovereignty claims? In the context of the HHCA, and indeed U.S. policy in general, the logic of blood dilution through legal and popular discourses of race displaces indigeneity and erodes indigenous peoples' sovereignty claims.

Indigeneity is tied to sovereignty (Wilkins 2007: 45, 51), where the definitions of both are constantly negotiated and constructed in terms of competing interests (for example, vis-à-vis tribal nations and the United States). But in the realm of U.S. recognition of indigeneity through federal policy, a people's racial difference has to be proved as part of their claim to sovereignty. That "race," "culture," and "nation" are always inextricably linked presents a further paradox, since federal recognition of Native status is primarily framed as a political category, not a racial one (Wilkins 2007: 45–65). And because indigenous self-determination can never be untangled from discourses and relations of domination, as Native peoples struggle for greater self-determination and political power, they simultaneously challenge and reproduce some of these very same dynamics and processes. Blood quantum classification continues to have deep cultural resonance in day-to-day life as it operates in both cultural and legal contexts in terms of how one may think about race, belonging, and kinship.

With this book, I make three broad interventions. The first is within the field of Hawaiian studies and political activism, where I argue that blood quantum is a colonial project in the service of land alienation and dispossession. Blood quantum classification does not allow for the building of Kanaka Maoli political power because it is ultimately about exclusion, while it also reduces Hawaiians to a racial minority rather than an indigenous people with national sovereignty claims. Hawaiian kinship and genealogical modes of identification allow for political empowerment in the service of nation building because they are inclusive. The genealogical approach is not only more far-reaching; it is embedded in indigenous epistemologies whereby peoplehood is rooted in the land.

My second aim is to tackle the question of blood quantum within the broader field of Native studies, where there are debates about what constitutes an indigenous person and whether or not indigenous nations' use of blood quantum in their membership criteria for determining citizenship is rooted in U.S. federal policy that was premised on colonial dispossession. Critiques of tribal uses of blood quantum have been dismissed as antitribal, and defenses of blood quantum have been used in the service of gauging cultural authenticity and political commitment (discussed further in chapter 2). Here, it becomes important to delineate the legal details of these cases since some of the scholarship that has previously addressed blood politics has too often relied on factual errors.

The third intervention here is within the field of critical race theory, where land and indigeneity have been neglected in relation to the study of racial formations and the legal construction of race. Critical race theory—even though it has expanded to include Latinos and Asian Americans in addition to African Americans—has tended to offer a singular logic in explaining racial subordination in relation to whites and the construction of whiteness. By failing to consider how the racialization of indigenous peoples, especially through the use of blood quantum classification, in particular follows what Andrea Smith would call a "genocidal logic" (Smith 2006: 68), rather than simply a logic of subordination or discrimination, critical race theory fails to consider how whiteness constitutes a project of disappearance for Native peoples rather than signifying privilege. Mixed racial family histories have been routinely evoked to disqualify Natives who don't measure up for entitlements and benefits; thus this "inauthentic" status of Natives is both a desired outcome of assimilation and also a condition for dispossession.

Interrogating the construction of racial categories from the vantage point of Hawai'i provides a valuable perspective on the mutual constitutions of racial definitions and the range of variation in that process that allows for a discussion of blood constructions in which race functions as both category *and* continuum. First there is the issue of blood being perceived as a potent substance that is often seen as a social "fact" based on culture. Second, there is the concept of blood quantum as a proxy or measurement of cultural authenticity and indigenous identity where blood denotes racial and indigenous legitimacy in various contexts. Then, there is the attendant question of "how much?" While references to blood can also simply refer to lineality without referencing quotient, my focus here is on the system of classification that was specifically devised to quantify ancestry in the service of discourses of dilution, which then lend themselves to the discounting narratives of assimilation. In relation to indigenous peoples, U.S. governmental bodies have used blood quantum classifications both historically and in the present to appropriate Native lands and to promote cultural and biological assimilation to the advantage of whiteness.

This appropriation of land and resources is both historical and ongoing. Blood quantum criteria underlie recent court decisions regarding Hawaiian entitlements, and new proposals, such as federal recognition for Hawaiians to gain status akin to tribal nations, that are undermining the Hawaiian sovereignty movement and pushing questions of who counts as Hawaiian to the surface. Notably, the ruling of the U.S. Supreme Court in 2000 in *Rice v. Cayetano* has increased the crisis that now surrounds the contemporary Hawaiian sovereignty movement. In *Rice v. Cayetano,* the Court struck down Hawaiian-only voting in trustee elections for the state Office of Hawaiian Affairs. While the state's defense of the policy rested upon the history of the Hawaiian Homes Commission Act of 1920, the Court used the 50-percent blood quantum rule as one of three legal rationales to justify its decision (see the discussion in chapter 6). In addition, the ruling in *Rice* has prompted several more recent lawsuits challenging Hawaiian identity, land, and entitlements. The current situation is just one important reason why these arrangements of the HHCA are so important to understand now.

Hawaiians' Expansive Inclusivity

The configuration of Hawaiians' "lack" of blood, rooted in colonial land dispossession and disregard for indigenous sovereignty, is analogous to a problem highlighted in the work of Epeli Hauʻofa, who has examined how the Pacific has been configured to the detriment of Island peoples (Hauʻofa 1995). He summarizes the persistent image of the Pacific as "islands in a far sea," where small island states and territories are considered "too small, too poor, and too isolated to develop any meaningful degree of autonomy" (89–90). Hauʻofa argues that this belittling view is both economically and geographically deterministic and, moreover, overlooks historical processes and forms of "world enlargement" carried out by island peoples who transgress the national and economic boundaries that mark colonial legacies and postcolonial relationships. As Hauʻofa reconceptualizes an expansive Oceania, he describes this "world enlargement" as a vision in which Pacific peoples see more than just the ever-growing surface of the land as home; they also look to the surrounding ocean, its underworld, and the heavens above. On the history of Pacific Islanders, he succinctly notes, "their world was anything but tiny, they thought big and recounted their deeds in epic proportions" (90–91). Hauʻofa's work in this area enables a rethinking of Hawaiian genealogical practices in ways that counter blood quantum modes of identification and look to a global rather than a national historical framework for models of decolonization.

Thinking big and recounting deeds in epic proportions also classically describes Polynesian genealogical recitation. As this book will show, genealogy is a Hawaiian form of world enlargement that makes nonsense of the fractions and percentage signs that are grounded in colonial (and now neocolonial) moves marked by exclusionary racial criteria. Blood quantum can never account for the political nature and strategic positioning of genealogical invocation. Economically deterministic arguments describing the islands as too small, too poor, and too isolated resonate with racially deterministic arguments about people with too little, too weak, and too diluted Hawaiian "blood." In response, with regard to law, cultural politics, and self-determination, Hawaiians are emphasizing their genealogical connections to all Pacific peoples in reclaiming a place in Oceania.

The 2000 U.S. census confirmed that Hawaiians are a diverse people. That census marked the first time people could claim more than one racial designation, and approximately two-thirds claimed at least one other race or ethnicity, while about half that number identified themselves as Hawaiian only.[10] It should be noted that of those who claimed only the one racial category "Native Hawaiian," most are not solely of Hawaiian ancestry but choose it as their primary identity.[11]

Social acceptance varies for Kānaka Maoli depending on the context, but among most Hawaiians anyone of Kanaka Maoli ancestry is typically accepted as Hawaiian, regardless of racial appearance or blood quantum, because of a persistent cultural emphasis on genealogy, kinship, and ancestry. This inclusivity held strong in the face of non-Hawaiian political opposition to Native Hawaiian entitlements and the sovereignty movement thriving in the islands in the early twenty-first century. As a case in point, in 2002 the Kamehameha Schools came under fire in the federal courts for its admissions policy, which had come to privilege Hawaiians exclusively.

The Kamehameha Schools form a private K-12 institution with multiple campuses, supported by the charitable trust left by Bernice Pauahi Bishop— a nineteenth-century Hawaiian princess—for the education of orphaned and indigent children, giving preference to Hawaiians. The lands that the Kamehameha Schools are situated on are the national lands of those who descend from citizens of the kingdom. Originally the Ali'i (chiefs) had kuleana (responsibility and right) to take care of themselves through private property, and also kuleana and obligation to care for the maka'āinana (commoners). Following the Māhele of 1848 (discussed in chapter 2), the Ali'i Nui did not bequeath lands downward to their children or other heirs. They bequeathed upward to higher-ranking Ali'i in line with the traditional practice in which the highest-ranking Ali'i would redistribute the land. This left vast amounts of land in the control of Princess Ruth Ke'elikōlani, who bequeathed them to Bernice Pauahi Bishop. When Bishop died, the Bishop estate and the Kamehameha Schools were created and received the lands.

On behalf of John Doe (who was not named as plaintiff because of his status as a minor), the non-Hawaiian boy's parents charged the Kamehameha Schools with violating his civil rights because he was not admitted to the school. In the early response to Doe v. Kamehameha, defenders of the school's policy noted that the U.S. Internal Revenue Service gave the school's admissions policy a green light when it deemed the school a nontaxable charitable trust, for in one sense the school was remarkably diverse, even though it was for Hawaiians only. They pointed out that of the Hawaiian students enrolled in the 2001 school year, 78 percent identified as part white, 74 percent said they were part Chinese, 28 percent said they were part Japanese, and 24 percent identified their other ancestries, including African American, Native Alaskan, American Indian, East Indian, Arab, and Brazilian (Liptak 2003). As one Kanaka Maoli woman put it: "Every nationality goes to Kamehameha School, so it's not a racial thing" (Tanji 2003). Similarly, Governor Linda Lingle told reporters, "If you look at the ethnic make-up of the kids at Kamehameha School, they are of every ethnic background in the book. . . . I think the issue of civil rights is a red herring. It's not an issue in any case because every ethnic group is going through Kamehameha" (Staton 2003). Although race, nationality, and ethnicity are interchangeably referenced here by those involved, what is interesting in the representation of this case is the recognition that for many, *Hawaiian only does not necessarily mean only Hawaiian*. Regardless, in August 2005, a panel of the Ninth Circuit Court of Appeals ruled that the racial preferences for Hawaiians that serve as an "absolute bar" against non-Hawaiians violate the Civil Rights Act of 1991. However, in February 2006, the Ninth Circuit granted an *en banc* review of the case and vacated the August 2005 decision. In December 2006, in an 8–7 ruling, the full judiciary panel upheld the legality of the Kamehameha Schools' admissions policy based on the educational imbalances faced by Native Hawaiians that the policy seeks to address.[12] Most Hawaiians appreciate this ruling because the resources used to fund Hawaiian education at the Kamehameha Schools are part of our collective inheritance. Still, there are several other legal attacks on Kanaka Maoli entitlements and resources in the works—all of which are firmly grounded in U.S. law and principles of "racial equality" without justice (these are discussed further in chapter 6).

It may be tempting to compare Hawaiians' practice of counting anyone with Hawaiian ancestry as Kanaka Maoli with the hypodescent rule used to define blackness. This tenet, which originated in the United States, is a theory of identity and kinship which holds that a racially mixed person is assigned the status of the subordinate group (Harris 1964: 56). Marvin Harris coined the term "hypodescent" and explains that it occurs when "(a) descent governs subordinate membership in one of two groups which stand to each other in a subordinate relationship; (b) an individual who has a lineal ancestor, maternal or paternal, who is or was a member of the subordinate group, is likewise a member of the subordinate group" (108 n. 3). This system was created during the Jim Crow period to avoid the ambiguity of intermediate identity among those of African descent (56). The persistence of the customary use of the rule grows out of a long history of white enforcement but also from black affiliation and resistance.[13] Even though it is no longer legally enforced, by and large, African Americans have appropriated conventions of the rule in the service of racial solidarity in the face of anti-black racism.

Today, black identity still tends to be regarded as primary for the sake of collectivity. Kanaka Maoli identification is also about collectivity; however, that inclusion is not premised on the exclusion of one's other racial identities or ancestral affiliations. Historically, the blood logic used against indigenous peoples to disqualify them from distinction directly contradicts the one-drop rule imposed on people of African descent during Reconstruction in support of white supremacist laws. Thus, the cultural practice of counting Hawaiians all inclusively might be better described as a theory of *hyper*descent because claiming Hawaiianness can be considered a status claim to indigeneity. That is, there is a proprietary interest if not a property right.

Hawaiians' traditional form of considering who belongs and who descends from the 'āina (land) relies on bilateral descent over and above constructions of blood quantum. Hawaiians are a people who have historically treasured and relished encounters with outsiders. Indeed, marriage across racial lines was legally sanctioned by Hawaiian kingdom law in 1840 (Lind 1980:112), and Kanaka Maoli are still an inclusive people, with a long history of incorporating outsiders. Yet many point to Hawaiian racial mixedness—a result of this incorporation, often through intermarriage—as evidence of indigenous dissolution instead of a sign of cultural resilience. Only by ignoring Hawaiian genealogical practices could exogamy be viewed as a one-way road to cultural disappearance, where racial purity is confused with survival and leads to an assumption of inevitable decline. As Donna Haraway posits, "Fascination with mixing and unity is a symptom of preoccupation with purity and decomposition" (1997: 214).

This notion of "vanishing Hawaiians" was also the basis for a 1995 documentary film called *Then There Were None* by Elizabeth Kapuʻuwailani Lindsey Buyers, and a companion book by the same title by Martha H. Noyes. In the film, Buyers narrates how the Kanaka Maoli population has been transformed by foreign influences with a focus on the demise of the Hawaiian people, hence the title. She notes that sociologists at the University of Hawaiʻi estimate the extinction of "full-blooded Hawaiians" in the islands by the mid-twenty-first century. Similarly, Noyes's book begins with a portrait of the precolonial Hawaiian population. In charting a litany of historical events from the American missionary presence to the immigration of plantation workers from around the world to the overthrow of the Hawaiian kingdom, World War II, and an enduring U.S. military presence, Noyes punctuates each period with a statement that marks the dwindling "full blood population." These proclamations, each one page long, highlight the numerical decline. For example, the first marker states, "In 1778, there were between 400,000 and 1,000,000 Hawaiians in the islands. By 1822 there were only 200,000 pure Hawaiians left alive" (Noyes 2003: 11). After several more pages of pictorial history, we read, "By 1828 there were only 188,000 pure Hawaiians left alive," and then a few pages later, "By 1836 there were 108,000 pure Hawaiians left alive," and so on, until we eventually get the last summary, "By 1922 there were only 24,000 pure Hawaiians left alive." What is missing in this assessment of the state of the Hawaiian population, which reads almost like a romantic desire for extinction, is the *increasing* number of Kanaka Maoli (when one accounts for the racially mixed Kānaka Maoli) who make up the vast majority of the Hawaiian population today—all part of the legacy of the initial wave of mass depopulation. This fixation on the "full-blooded" or "pure" Hawaiian erases the survival of the Kanaka Maoli people overall by relying on unmixed Kānaka Maoli to bear the burden of representing the "true Hawaiians"—a tall order indeed. In the dynamics of this genocidal logic, the forecast of "and then there were none" predicts a complete wipeout of the "pure Hawaiians" as though they stand in for all Hawaiians. But if we look at the entirety of the Hawaiian people and refrain from obsessing over the so-called full-bloods, the population of Hawaiians will more than double in the next fifty years, while those residing in the continental United States will grow at a slightly faster rate (Malone 2005: 1).

Contrasting Positions

Ideas about Hawaiian racial identity cannot be viewed in a vacuum; in a U.S. context, the continental triangulation of black, white, and Indian racialization provides a framework for conceptualizing the Hawaiian, Asian, and white triangle formed in the colonized islands.

Dominant notions regarding American Indians and African Americans relate both to each other and to assertions of whiteness that stem from Euro-American colonization, enslavement, and other forms of domination.[14] In contradistinction to policies affecting American Indians, blood served an opposite purpose for African Americans—one that reflects their disenfranchisement, exclusion, and lack of access to U.S. national and state government. In defining African Americans, racist notions of blood served to prevent their access to full citizenship and equal protection. "Black blood" was configured to negate racial amalgamation and precluded identification as white or Native both discursively and legally.

The persistence of these contradictory logics is vividly shown in the case of President Bill Clinton, when he asserted that his grandmother was "one-fourth" Cherokee (Sturm 2004). Yet, despite this assertion, Clinton continues to be known as a former president who is white, not the "first American Indian" president of the United States. This should come as no surprise given the enduring racial notions such as "half-breed" and "blue-eyed Cherokee," as well as the expectation that American Indians should have to prove they have "indigenous blood" in order to qualify as Native. However, if Clinton had instead declared that his grandmother had been "one-fourth" African American, he would *not* still be considered a white man.

According to Brian Dippie, "The national iconography clearly reveals the distinction so sharply drawn in the 1850s between the 'submissive, obsequious, imitative negro' and the 'indomitable, courageous, proud Indian'" (1982: 92). He notes that "it remained a popular truism that while 'red' and 'white' blood blended 'easily and quickly' both resisted fusion with 'black' blood" (267). "Indian blood" was not thought to be "polluting" in the same way "black blood" was figured. Dippie points to the anxious contradictions in American policy during Reconstruction. He notes that "red-white amalgamation was being proposed in a context of racial segregation in the South, imperialism abroad, and nativism at home, all entailing deep distrust, fear, suspicion, and loathing of darker, 'inferior' peoples" (250).[15]

Ben-zvi critically examines the prominent ethnologist Lewis Henry Morgan's theory of cultural evolution throughout the nineteenth century to analyze how it was dependent on a conceptualization of racial inheritance that presupposed the disappearance of the racial category of "red" from the

U.S. national racial imagination, which maintained a binary between white and black. Her work explains the shift from a tripartite racial model to a binary one "as the simultaneous appropriation of Native American cultures into and the exclusion of African American cultures from, national culture" (2006: 203). Her important work examines these particular frames of racialization by inheritance through Morgan's evolutionary theory and the consolidation of ethnology as a national project, where his conceptualizations of inheritance, family, and hospitality served as key factors in the "disappearance" of red and its appropriation into white national discourse.

Discussing American Indian education policy after 1900, Dippie argues that "the situations of the Negro and the Indian were not really analogous . . . one was earmarked for a segregated, menial existence, the other for full participation in white civilization" (1982: 187–88). The notion of the day went like this: "The native population was small—just an infinitesimal fraction of the whole American population—and while a massive infusion of Indian blood might pollute the national type, the limited amount available could do no harm and might even do some good. Anyway, the process of red-white amalgamation was irreversible" (248).[16] Such a destiny went hand in hand with assimilation.[17] In accounting for this distinction, it is important to note that the decreasing population of American Indians made the prospects of assimilation more palatable and facilitated the project of expansion, deracination, and incorporation, while also mitigating anxieties of miscegenation.

The relationship between U.S. colonialism and indigeneity is critical to a meaningful discussion of why the relation between blood and land differed so dramatically for black people and American Indians, and for Asian peoples and Hawaiians. This difference has to do with the significance of land in the founding and subsequent expansion of the U.S. nation-state into territories that are other peoples' homelands. As Patrick Wolfe explains, settler colonial societies are premised on displacing indigenous peoples from (or *re*placing them on) the land (Wolfe 1999: 1). White Americans positioned Kānaka Maoli as inevitably disappearing Natives. For American Indians and Hawaiians, the legacies of forced inclusion within the U.S. nation-state have worked against collective assertions of political self-determination; both groups may perceive these U.S. policies as attempts to assimilate them into mainstream white American individualism. While there are differences between American Indians and Hawaiians in terms of the specificities of Native racial formations and the shifts within differing colonial contexts (especially given their different timelines and endurances), both groups experienced the unilateral imposition of U.S. citizenship. Furthermore, like "red-white amalgamation," Hawaiian racial mixing with whites and Asians was never restricted. But government representatives later deployed evidence of this racial "commingling" to undermine who could count as native Hawaiian. Governed by white supremacist racism, colonialism and genocide, and slavery, the continental U.S. racial triangulation of white-Indian-black set the stage for a corresponding and cooperative system specific in Hawai'i. An on-island racial triangulation of white-Hawaiian-Asian that developed served as a formative criterion for establishing blood quantum rules for "native Hawaiians." In the case of Hawai'i, white supremacist racism and colonialism worked together with xenophobic anti-immigration sentiments.

In locating and examining works that proposed to address Hawaiians and issues of interracial marriage, assimilation, and acculturation, I was repeatedly struck by the substantial amount of time and space allotted to issues concerning Asian immigrants in Hawai'i, including language schools, foreign citizenship, community formation, religious affiliation, and political demographics. In the blood quantum and legal debates about property and the HHCA, the matter of where the Chinese and Japanese stood in Hawai'i—in relation to both whites and Hawaiians—was prominent. Eventually, I realized that in many ways, some subtle, others crude, the racialization of Hawaiians was co-constructed in relation to Chinese and Japanese presence in the islands. As this book will show, both elite whites and Hawaiians framed the post-overthrow push to rehabilitate Kanaka Maoli in anti-Asian terms by contrasting Kanaka Maoli as U.S. citizens with the Chinese, and especially the Japanese, as "aliens." During the early twentieth century, the whiteness of American citizenship was sustained by a series of Asian exclusions, and this racialization of Asians as perpetual outsiders would play a key role in the outcome of Hawaiian blood quantum debates.[18] In Hawai'i, Asians occupied a racial place comparable to the structural relationship of African Americans to whites during Reconstruction, where they were considered an economic and political threat. The emancipation of black slaves motivated Southern whites to search for new systems of racial and economic control, and by the 1890s they passed Jim Crow segregation laws to isolate and intimidate African Americans. In Hawai'i, as in the continental United States, white Americans perceived the Japanese as a distinct danger as both a source of labor competition and a nationalist threat in the emerging world order (Gulick 1915; Adams 1924). Japanese presence in Hawai'i was deemed antithetical to the goals of Americanizing the islands, especially after World War I, a concern that had deepened by the time of the HHCA debates, when 42.7 percent of the island population was Japanese (Tamura 1994: 58).

This specific comparison between African Americans and the Japanese was not lost on the social scientist A. F. Griffiths, who acknowledged that Hawai'i had been able to "assimilate so many races" and credited the process to Christianity, a lack of social antagonism, the school system, the intermingling of children, successful immigrant labor, and the increase in property ownership, specifically by the Japanese (1915: 2–5). Griffiths also maintained that "the Negro as an Illustration" was important in analyzing the situation of the Japanese because both were viewed as a competitive threat to white supremacists' economic and political interests (6).[19] But, unlike the case for black people, the goal of dominant white Americans was not to perpetually segregate Asians; even within the confines of various forms of civic exclusion, such as the enforcement of alien land laws and antimiscegenation laws, the concern was whether it was possible to Americanize them (Lowe 1996; Ancheta 1998). In particular, the Japanese in Hawai'i were considered antithetical to the prevailing idea of what it meant to be "American" in a colonial territory that already blurred the boundaries of the nation-state, given its distance from the rest of the country and its cultural, racial, and political genealogies.

These multiple racializing logics and trajectories were formed along the forceful lines of white property interests as much as they were informed by the racial notion of what Virginia Dominguez terms "blood properties" (1986:57). They are also prime examples of what Avtar Brah calls "differential racialization," "processes of *relational multi-locationality* within and across formations of power marked by the articulation of one form of racism with another, and with other modes of differentiation" (Brah 1996: 186; original emphasis). Brah's framework enables a rejection of binary racial formulations by exploring "how different racialised groups are positioned differently *vis-à-vis* one another" (15). Brah's concept of differential racialization opens space for comparative examinations and enables a discussion of both relational and historical contexts for the racial constitution of Hawaiianness.

In his comparative examination, F. James Davis contrasts the politics of race in Hawai'i with the one-drop rule in *Who Is Black?* (1991). White Americans historically used a one-drop rule against African Americans to define them as black regardless of their identity or appearance in order to disenfranchise them. Davis cites Hawai'i as a place that offers an alternative to the one-drop rule when it comes to race and argues that Hawai'i, because it has a tradition of egalitarian pluralism, differs from the Southern context. Specifically, he states, "Race has been unimportant in class competition and there has been no systematic segregation or discrimination" (111). To support his claim, Davis points out that in Hawai'i racially mixed people, rather than being assigned membership in any one parent group, are perceived and respected as persons with roots in two or more ancestral groups (112). While this is typically the case, Davis uncritically accepts the pervasive myth of Hawai'i as a site of racial harmony by pointing to the high number of mixed-race people.

Hawai'i's history of colonization and racial domination remains entirely invisible in Davis's account. In fact, he naturalizes colonial dispossession: "There has been no systematic racial segregation and discrimination, either *de jure* or *de facto,* and people generally are scornful of anyone who exhibits racial prejudice" (1991: 111–12). Davis evokes the problematic and clichéd narrative of the Hawai'i "melting pot" influenced by the "*aloha* spirit." He further declares Hawai'i to be a site of racial equality for the racially mixed and argues that "despite the eventual wresting of political and economic power from the original Hawaiians, and some undeniable tensions among the ethnic groups, the history of the islands has generally not been racist" (111). Here, his use of the phrase "the original Hawaiians" suggests that contemporary Kanaka Maoli are inauthentic and also masks the blood quantum policy; hence, "Hawaiian" without the descriptor "original" is taken to mean *all* others in Hawai'i, thus replacing "Kanaka Maoli." Davis completely neglects to mention the use of blood quantum laws to define Hawaiianness, which seems especially curious considering that the focus of his work is on the ascendance of the one-drop rule defining blackness in U.S. history in the interest of maintaining whiteness.

The Property of Whiteness and Selective Assimilation

Examinations of Hawaiian racialization must account for forms of identification that are closely bound to land and identity, as well as to the history of property and whiteness. Providing a critical look at the concept and maintenance of whiteness, I interrogate the legal construction of racial privilege and domination as they are bound to property and citizenship. Selective assimilation has played as much of a role in the formation of whiteness as has exclusion. Because the enfranchisement of Hawaiians entailed the domestication of a previously recognized sovereign government, the project of erasing Hawaiian peoplehood through discourses of dilution was essential. The presumption of Hawaiian assimilability and deracination—in the service of settler colonialism—was critical to the blood quantum racialization of Hawaiians, and it was precisely these demands of whiteness that allowed for this selective inclusion.

Cheryl Harris argues that the very origins of property rights in the United States are rooted in racial domination (1993: 1716). In detailing the status and property of whiteness and the legal construction of white identity, she provides a critical analysis of this racial project in the context of American Indian and African American racial construction. Harris notes that although the systems of oppression that defined the status of African Americans and Native Americans differed in form, both entailed a racialized conception of property implemented by force and ratified by law (1715). Harris theorizes that the formation of whiteness was "initially constructed as a form of racial identity and evolved into a form of property" through the white domination of African and American Indian peoples (1716). Thus racial identity and property are "deeply interrelated concepts" implicated in both land dispossession and enslaved labor exploitation (1709).

In examining property value as it relates to whiteness, Harris suggests that whiteness conferred on its "owners" aspects of citizenship that were all the more valued precisely *because they were denied to others* (1993: 1744). Property is a bundle of rights applying to things; it does not simply designate the thing to which property rights apply but is constituted by the rights one can assert to those things. Specifically, Harris argues that the property functions of whiteness include the right of disposition (1731), the right to use and enjoyment, the right of reputation and status (1734), and the absolute right to exclude (1836). To this I would add the absolute right to *include*, which is implied in the absolute right to exclude, but I want to mark it more explicitly as it extends to the right to selectively incorporate indigenous peoples. Harris suggests as much when she notes that "the courts played an active role in enforcing this right to exclude—determining who was or was not *white enough* to enjoy the privileges accompanying whiteness." Later, however, she conflates the assertion of being "free of any taint of Black blood" with the "claim of racial purity" (1736). She notes that in commonly held views, the presence of black "blood" metaphorically consigned a person to being "black" whereby "Black blood is a contaminant and white racial identity is pure." Harris further adds that recognizing "or identifying oneself as white is thus a claim of racial purity, an assertion that one is free of any taint of Black blood" and that the law has played a critical role in legitimating this claim (1737). But, claiming whiteness by recognizing or identifying oneself as white is not necessarily a claim to racial purity, and saying that one is not black is not necessarily tantamount to claiming whiteness. Identifying oneself as historically white may indeed be an assertion that one is "free of any taint of Black blood," but it need not always entail the preclusion of the acknowledgment of another ancestry (for example, Clinton's Cherokee grandmother).

Constructions of whiteness—especially as they have evolved from identity into a form of property—have had to allow for a process of *selective* inclusion. This can be somewhat accounted for in the right of disposition, as well, but I want to highlight this point. Although Harris argues that for American Indians, racial domination entailed the seizure and appropriation of land in a way that racialized the conception of property (1993: 1715), she does not mention the blood racialization of American Indians in this process. Harris rigorously examines both social and legal discourses of the meanings of "bloodedness" for black people in exclusive white racial formations. Yet, while acknowledging the roots of property rights in racial domination over both American Indian and African peoples, she does not examine blood quantum policies as they were imposed on American Indians.

An inclusion of Indian racialization would have to engage with the classifications of "degrees of Indian blood" and how they interlock with notions of "Black blood." While Harris does not take this up, she does provide two accounts that enable such a consideration.[20] In the first example, Harris cites *Sunseri v. Cassagne*, a case in Louisiana in 1938. As Harris describes it, the case involved a legal suit by Sunseri, who moved to annul his marriage to Cassagne. He did this on the grounds that she had a trace of "Negro blood" (1993: 1739 n. 140). This example certainly proves Harris's point that an individual whose racial identity was at issue and was proven to have "blood

[that] was tainted" could not then claim to be "white"—and that the presence of blackness, specifically, precluded the upholding of such a claim to whiteness. However, Harris altogether neglects to discuss the detail that Cassagne had identified herself as Indian. While Sunseri disputed Cassagne's whiteness, Cassagne herself had made a claim to indigeneity, not whiteness or any sort of purity. Nevertheless, Cassagne's marriage was annulled because she was found to be "not white" by virtue of her supposedly having black ancestors—*not* because she identified herself as Indian.

In the second example, Harris discusses the Mashpee people's case, where tribal identity was dismissed by a Massachusetts court that held that the Mashpees were not a tribe at the time their lawsuit to assert indigenous land rights was filed. Harris points out how the court's ruling erased their distinctiveness, "assuming that, by virtue of intermingling with other races, the Mashpee's identity as a people had been subsumed." Furthermore, she explains, "The Mashpee were not 'passing,' but were legally determined to have 'passed'—no longer to have distinct identity. The erasure was predicated on the assumption that what is done from necessity under conditions of established hierarchies of domination and subordination is a voluntary surrender for gain" (1993: 1765).

My point here is twofold: first, Indian "blood" was disregarded by the courts in many other contexts precisely because Indianness was also more than just an identity—it potentially had its own property value and, as such, whiteness was figured as a solvent, selectively assimilating indigeneity; and second, because of the property value in Indianness, the presence of black "blood" more often than not precluded one's ability to successfully claim Indian identity for those of both black and Indian ancestry.

As I have suggested, we should consider the property functions of selective inclusion in relation to Harris's theory of whiteness as property. I liken this form of assimilation to a sort of usufructuary right for those granted "honorary whiteness." Usufruct is a contractual and sometimes juridically imposed arrangement in which the owner of a thing transfers to another person the rights of use and fruits (as in the *fruct*) derived from that use (Black 1990:1544–46). But the owner retains the right to alienate the property, similar to the right of disposition that is one of the property functions of whiteness as theorized by Harris. At the termination of the usufruct, in general, the rights of use and benefits return to the owner. Benefits can be of two types: natural and civil. Therefore, groups who are allowed mobility in assimilation do not necessarily hold property rights in whiteness; they do not have the right to exclusive use and/or possession. In other words, usufructuary rights do not grant ownership but may convey use privileges such as those accompanied with honorary white status. Consequently, selective assimilation is contingent and it demands the complicity of those wanting access to that right. The concept of usufructuary rights opens up a space to think about the selective inclusion of certain racially mixed Hawaiians as they were racialized as white in the case of the HHCA. As the following chapters reveal, enactment of the HHCA entailed problematic assumptions as to who would and should count as Hawaiian and what that would signify, determinations negotiated against the ever-present history of a stolen nation.

In considering the racialization of indigenous peoples, especially through the use of blood quantum classification, a genocidal logic of disappearance is tied to the project of selective assimilation for those Natives who still exist yet don't measure up for entitlements and benefits. But these specific rights are based on sovereignty. Thus, the "inauthentic" status of Natives is a condition for sovereign dispossession in the service of settler colonialism.

Sovereignty Politics

A series of historical events serves as critical background to contemporary Hawaiian sovereignty claims. As a people who had formed the Hawaiian kingdom—recognized as a neutral nation-state by dozens of other countries during the nineteenth century—Kanaka Maoli hold an unextinguished sovereignty claim to have the independent nation-state of Hawai'i restored under international law, as do those descendants of non-Hawaiian citizens of the kingdom (Hasager and Friedman 1994). Treaties negotiated between the Hawaiian kingdom and the United States were made after the United States and other nations recognized Hawai'i as an independent nation-state.

In 1842, King Kamehameha III dispatched a delegation to the United States, and later to Europe, endowed with the power to secure the recognition of Hawaiian independence by the major world powers of the time. Two of the members of the delegation were Timoteo Ha'alilio (a chiefly Hawaiian) and William Richards (a former missionary) (Osorio 2002: 92). On December 19, 1842, they secured the assurance of President John Tyler of U.S.

recognition of the Hawaiian kingdom's independence; they subsequently met the third member of the delegation, Sir George Simpson, in Europe and there secured formal recognition by Great Britain and France. Even though the Tyler Doctrine of 1842 asserted that Hawai'i was under the sphere of U.S. influence, several more decades would pass before the United States would assert formal colonial control in the islands (Trask 1993: 8).

Importantly, *none* of the treaties between the Hawaiian kingdom and the United States concerned land or governance.[21] The first treaty was signed in Washington on December 20, 1849. Its purpose was an agreement "to enter into negotiations for the conclusion of a Treaty of Friendship, Commerce and Navigation," a treaty of perpetual peace and amity between the United States and "the King of the Hawaiian Islands, his heirs and his successors" (United States 1849). The treaty provided for access regarding commerce and navigation, such as regulating duties and imports at favored-foreign-nation rates and allowing U.S. whaling ships access to selected Hawaiian ports. The second treaty with the United States concerned an arrangement between the postal services of the Hawaiian kingdom and the United States and was signed in 1870 (United States 1871). The third treaty, known as the Reciprocity Treaty, was signed in 1875 and was later supplemented by the Convention of December 6, 1884 (United States 1875; 1884b). The initial agreement for commercial reciprocity meant that no export duty was imposed on Hawai'i or the United States and allowed for the exchange of tax-free goods between the two nations.

The Reciprocity Treaty was critical to the haole elite because they could sell their sugar to the U.S. market duty-free (Trask 1993: 13). In 1884, the two nations negotiated a convention to renew and supplement the 1875 treaty, which allowed the United States privileged access, over other nations, to the use of Pearl Harbor. The convention, ratified in 1887, specified that the U.S. government had "exclusive right to enter the harbor of the Pearl River in the Island of Oahu, and to establish and maintain there a coaling and repair station for the use of vessels of the United States, and to that end the United States may improve the entrance to said harbor and do all other things needed to the purpose aforesaid." This element of the supplement was most controversial to Kanaka Maoli because it sacrificed the needs of the average Hawaiian for those of the sugar planters and the commercial sectors that supported them, which in turn bolstered U.S. economic leverage in Hawai'i (Osorio 2002).

Finally, in 1883 the two nations negotiated a convention between the Post Office Department of the United States and the Post Office Department of the Hawaiian Kingdom concerning the exchange of money orders to complement the treaty of 1870 (United States 1884).

The independence of the recognized nation-state of Hawaiʻi, however, was threatened by foreign elites, who eventually formed their own militia, associated with the U.S. military, called the Honolulu Rifles (Silva 2004: 122). In 1887, the Honolulu Rifles seized strategic points in the city, and mounted armed patrols forced the ruling monarch, King Kalākaua, to sign what became known as the "Bayonet Constitution," a document stripping him of his most important executive powers and diminishing the Kanaka Maoli voice in government (Kent 1993: 54–55; Trask 1993: 14–15). The king was no longer able to appoint members to the House of Nobles. The Bayonet Constitution created an oligarchy of the haole planters and businessmen by primarily empowering white Americans and Europeans. The new constitution gave U.S. citizens the right to vote in Hawaiian elections, while a large sector of the Kanaka Maoli electorate was excluded through rigorous property qualifications, with Asians entirely disenfranchised as "aliens" (Kent 1993: 55). As Jon Kay Kamakawiwoʻole Osorio points out, it "was the first time that democratic rights were determined by race in any constitution" under the kingdom (2002: 244). The oligarchy created a new cabinet with Lorrin Thurston as minister of the interior and C. W. Ashford as attorney general. Every decision would henceforth require the approval of the cabinet, now made up of foreigners. In addition, the king was prevented from dismissing the cabinet himself; that power was given to the legislature, which could dismiss any cabinet with a simple majority vote (Silva 2004: 122–26). Although since this constitution was never ratified properly by the House of Nobles, it was never legally valid under kingdom law.

Queen Liliʻuokalani attempted to promulgate a new constitution to replace the Bayonet Constitution once she succeeded to the throne after her brother Kalākaua's death. This act prompted the unlawful overthrow of the kingdom. In 1893, U.S. Minister of Foreign Affairs John L. Stevens, with the support of a dozen white settlers and the U.S. Marines, organized the overthrow of Queen Liliʻuokalani (Silva 2004; Coffman 1998; Trask 1993; Kent 1993; Liliuokalani 1964 [1898]; Fuchs 1961). In response, the queen yielded her authority under protest because she was confident that the U.S. government and President Benjamin Harrison would endeavor to undo the actions led by one of the government's ministers. Within months, Harrison was out of office and Grover Cleveland became the next president. Eventually, after sending an official to investigate the matter, Cleveland declared Stevens's action and the entire overthrow an "act of war" (U.S. Congress 1993b). He recommended that the provisional government—made up of those who orchestrated the overthrow—should step down. But they refused and Cleveland did not compel them to do so and did not assist in restoring formal recognition to the queen.

As this struggle for control was taking place, the provisional government established the Republic of Hawaii on July 4, 1894, with Sanford Ballard Dole as president. In addition to asserting jurisdiction over the entire island archipelago, the new republic seized roughly 1.8 million acres of Hawaiian kingdom government and crown lands. In an attempt to remove any doubt that the republic was not rightly "heir and successor of the Hawaiian Crown," the new constitution declared the lands "to be, free and clear from any trust of or concerning the same, and from all claim of any nature whatsoever" (Spaulding 1923: 16). It was this de facto government that ceded these same lands to the United States when it illegally annexed Hawai'i in 1898 (Silva 1998; Coffman 1998).

The United States did not annex the Hawaiian Islands by treaty. Rather, it purportedly annexed the archipelago through its own internal domestic law; the Newlands Resolution in the U.S. Congress, despite massive indigenous opposition. Kānaka Maoli organized into two key nationalist groups. The Hui Aloha 'Āina and the Hui Kālai 'Āina each submitted petitions representing the vast majority of the Kānaka Maoli; together, their petitions numbered over 38,000 signatures, at a time when only 40,000 Kānaka Maoli (including those who were racially mixed) resided in Hawai'i (Silva 2004: 151). In the two petitions, Kānaka Maoli clearly stated their opposition to becoming part of the United States "in any form or shape" (149). The U.S. Senate accepted these petitions and, in the face of such resistance, found it impossible to secure the two-thirds majority vote needed for a treaty. Regardless, under President McKinley, pro-annexationists proposed a joint Senate resolution since all that was needed was a simple majority in both houses of Congress to get it passed. And so the Newlands Resolution passed in 1898, creating the façade of annexation with no legal standing outside the United States (Omandam 1998). In addition, even the constitutionality of the annexation is questionable.[22]

Still, the U.S. resolution provided for the republic's cession of absolute title to the public land formerly known as the Hawaiian kingdom and crown lands, the same lands that would eventually be at the center of debate during the HHCA hearings between 1920 and 1921. The Newlands Resolution also specified that the existing laws of the United States relative to public lands would not apply in Hawai'i. Moreover, the resolution provided that all revenue derived from the lands would be assigned for local government use and "shall be used solely for the benefit of the inhabitants of the Hawaiian Islands for educational and other public purposes" (MacKenzie 1991: 15). The U.S. government incorporated Hawai'i as a colonial territory through the 1900 Organic Act that created specific laws to administer the "public lands" (U.S. Congress 1900). These laws again stated that these lands were part of a special trust under the federal government's oversight.

Like many other colonial territories, in 1946 Hawai'i was inscribed onto the United Nations List of Non-Self-Governing Territories. As such, Hawai'i was eligible for decolonization under international law. However, the U.S. government predetermined statehood as the status for Hawai'i. The 1959 ballot in which the people of Hawai'i voted to become a state of the union included only two options: incorporation or remaining a U.S. colonial territory (Trask 1994: 68–87). By UN criteria established just months later in 1960 through the decolonization protocols for colonies on the List of Non-Self-Governing Territories, the ballot would have included both free association and independence as choices. In addition—among those who were allowed to take part in the vote that eventually marked Hawai'i's supposed transition from colonial status—Hawaiians were outnumbered by settlers as well as military personnel.

The Hawaii State Admission Act transferred the "public lands" (the stolen crown and government lands ceded by the republic to the U.S. government) from federal to state control (MacKenzie 1991: 26). The Hawai'i state constitution provides that lands shall be "held by the State as a public trust for native Hawaiians and the general public" (article 7, section 4). Section 5(f) of the Hawaii State Admission Act details five purposes for the income and proceeds derived from the leases of these lands. These purposes include support of public education, the development of farm and home ownership, public improvements, provision of lands for public use, and "the betterment of the conditions of native Hawaiians" as defined in the HHCA (Congressional Record, United States Congress, *State Admission Act of*

March 18, 1959, 73 Stat. 4. United States House of Representatives). The 1920 HHCA was carried through statehood in 1959 when the Territory of Hawaii acknowledged the trust obligation as a condition of admission to the union. In doing so, the state also accepted the definition of "native Hawaiian" as per the 50-percent blood rule that was codified in the 1921 HHCA. Although the state acknowledges its obligation to "native Hawaiians," the courts have not delineated the public trust concept and have made it difficult for Hawaiians to pursue trust benefits (Matsuda 1988b: 139).

In the late 1960s, just one decade after statehood, the contemporary Hawaiian movement was at its nascent stage. Increasingly through the 1970s, Hawaiians island-wide protested their own social conditions as well as the displacement of other (mostly Asian) locals as a result of overnight development when multinationalization and foreign investments led to a steady boom in tourism. Developers evicted, dispossessed, and displaced many Hawaiians and other locals from lands to make way for the building of subdivisions, hotel complexes, and golf courses. Haunani-Kay Trask notes that in the early 1970s, communities resisting this kind of development identified their struggles in terms of the claims of "local" people, which included both Hawaiian and non-Hawaiian longtime residents of Hawai'i. "The residency rights of local people were thus framed in opposition to the development rights of property owners like the state, corporations, and private estates" (Trask 1993: 91). But as the decade proceeded, Hawaiians increasingly asserted their rights as indigenous and historically unique from other "locals."

Due in part to the requests of Hawaiian activists during the 1970s, the state held a constitutional convention in 1978. At this convention, the vast majority of voters agreed to the creation of an Office of Hawaiian Affairs to look out for Hawaiian interests. The OHA is organized as a state agency to be governed by a nine-member elected board of trustees and holds title to all real or personal property set aside or conveyed to it as a trust for "native Hawaiians" (defined by the 50-percent blood rule). The OHA was also established to hold in trust the income and proceeds derived from a pro rata portion of the trust established for lands that were earlier granted to the state (MacKenzie 1991: 33). Further, the OHA is restricted to using its public lands trust funds for the benefit of its beneficiaries who meet the 50-percent rule, while the Hawai'i state constitution does not establish a source of funding for "Hawaiians" who do not meet the 50-percent definition. But because the State Admission Act did not determine a formula for allocation of public lands trust income among the five specified purposes, the 1978 constitutional amendment that created the OHA did not define the pro rata share (MacKenzie 1991:33).

However, in 1980, in response to the new constitutional prerequisite, the Hawai'i state legislature set the share at 20 percent. This, no doubt, is because "the betterment of the conditions of native Hawaiians" was only one of the five trust purposes detailed in the Admission Act. The one-fifth of the revenue from these lands is to be transferred to the OHA for the benefit of Hawaiians who meet the 50-percent rule. However, due to state neglect and conflicts about the trust relationship, the state has still not transferred these revenues as stipulated.

By the 1990s, after decades of protest and a rapidly growing Hawaiian sovereignty movement, even federal representatives responded to the call for the United States to recognize the near-century-long (neo)colonial legacy that began with the 1893 overthrow. Specifically, Senator Daniel Akaka (D-HI), with support from the entire Hawai'i congressional delegation, pushed for the passage of the 1993 Apology Resolution. Besides delineating an account of U.S. encroachment and betrayal, the resolution maintains that "the indigenous Hawaiian people never directly relinquished their claims to their inherent sovereignty as a people or over their national lands to the United States, either through their monarchy or through a plebiscite or referendum." Importantly, the Apology Resolution defined "native Hawaiian" as "any individual who is a descendent of the aboriginal people who, prior to 1778, occupied and exercised sovereignty in the area that now constitutes the State of Hawaii." No reference to blood quantum was made. Hence, this recognition was extended to *all Hawaiians* in a way that accounts for lineal descendancy. The Apology Resolution has since served as a focal point for mobilization as passage of the law empowered the islands' sovereignty movement throughout the 1990s and increased Hawaiian initiatives for self-determination.

This U.S. national context is made even more complex by the international implications of the Hawaiian sovereignty struggle. A range of Hawaiian sovereignty projects currently exists. These projects span a variety of models for self-governance, including proposals for an independent nation-state—including restoring of the Hawaiian kingdom—and various proposals for working within U.S. state and federal policy. Politically, this struggle has several layers. Neocolonialism perpetuated by the state of Hawai'i is subsumed and obscured by the U.S. federal government, revealing intersections and conflicts between competing claims to sovereignty among federal, state, indigenous, and pro-kingdom governing entities.

Within these competing claims to sovereignty lies the question of which individuals legitimately have a claim—a question inflected by the 50-percent definition of "native Hawaiian." The question is further complicated by the diminishing number of Hawaiians who can claim they are "full blooded." Identity and difference are implicated by a dominant American history of defining Hawaiianness through the overdetermined logic of dilution found in racial discourse broadly imposed on indigenous peoples.

Overview of the Chapters in This Book

As a close reading of the HHCA hearing transcripts needs a genealogical frame, in chapter 1, "Racialized Beneficiaries and Genealogical Descendants," I focus on the differences between the Hawaiian genealogical model and the blood quantum model. Even though blood has evolved as a metaphor for ancestry in Hawaiian contexts, as an administrative procedure it is qualitatively distinct from Hawaiian genealogical practices, which work in substantially different ways and to dissimilar ends. Blood modes are exclusive while genealogical ones are usually inclusive. As a classificatory logic, blood quantum fragments ancestry by dividing parts of a whole and severing unions by portioning out blood "degree." Focusing on Hawaiian kinship practices and genealogical reckoning as they might have been practiced from 1900 to 1920, I explore how cultural models of determining indigeneity could have prevailed in the HHCA discussions had the framework of sovereign entitlement to the lands been sustained. This chapter is integral to my analysis of the hearings, because I make the case that blood quantum was not necessarily an inevitable way of defining Hawaiianness through the HHCA.

In chapter 2, " 'Can you wonder that the Hawaiians did not get more?' Historical Context for the Hawaiian Homes Commission Act," I offer important background on the issues of depopulation, rehabilitation, and land entitlement, as well as those of race, indigeneity, and citizenship. Kanaka

Maoli suffering in the early twentieth century had its roots in land and political dispossession, which helps to explain why Hawaiian elites formulated a solution to the problem in the homesteading proposal which led to the HHCA. Another key issue is the Māhele land division of 1848, whereby the Hawaiian kingdom first privatized land, because it relates to contestations over Kanaka Maoli land entitlement that emerged in the HHCA hearings. I also explore the theory that the HHCA was modeled after the General Allotment Act of 1887, which has been incorrectly cited as the first U.S. policy to use blood quantum against American Indians. Finally, I examine the issue of U.S. citizenship in relation to Hawaiians as it differed for the Chinese and Japanese, a distinction that informs the blood discourses of Kānaka Maoli as assimilable into whiteness or Asianness and is tied to contestations over indigeneity and Americanization in the territory.

In chapter 3, "Under the Guise of Hawaiian Rehabilitation," I detail the first hearing on the rehabilitation proposal before the House Committee on Territories. In February 1920, two different parties traveled from Hawai'i to Washington, D.C. to present their proposals for use of the soon-to-be-freed-up lands before Congress. In the early stages of the debate on the proposal, there was no discussion of blood quantum, let alone criterion. The Hawaiian elites who mobilized around the rehabilitation proposal justified it by arguing that Kanaka Maoli were entitled to the lands that would be used for homesteading. This is to say, within a framework of social justice and legal claims, there was no need to distinguish among Hawaiians when it came to discussing eligibility—all were entitled, by definition. By the end of this round of debates, a fractional definition of one-thirty-second blood quantum for "native Hawaiian" emerged.

In chapter 4, "'The Virile, Prolific, and Enterprising': Part-Hawaiians and the Problem with Rehabilitation," I detail the second hearing on the proposals, this time before the Senate in December 1920, where participants hotly debated the notion of who really counted as Hawaiian. They drew sharp distinctions between "full-blooded" and "part" Hawaiians. This chapter focuses on how differences *among* Kanaka Maoli were cited to challenge the one-thirty-second blood definition. In doing so, they opened the entire issue of defining Hawaiian by questioning who exactly was considered to be *in need* of rehabilitation. Moreover, they eventually went so far as to insist that the rule defining Hawaiian should be set at "full blood." In considering a criterion limited to "full blood" Kānaka Maoli, the participants from the Territory of the Hawaiian Islands focused on repopulation as the key form of rehabilitation, which served to take the focus off of indigenous entitlements to the land in question. In turn, different constructions of Hawaiianness corresponded to the shift away from recognition of indigenous entitlement toward the privileging of white property interests in the lands. The rehabilitation plan was eventually justified as a form of government charity for Kānaka Maoli, rather than being based solely on their right to the lands.

Written in two parts, chapter 5, "Limiting Hawaiians, Limiting the Bill," delineates the process by which the bill was revamped in Hawai'i in early 1921, after it failed to pass in the U.S. Senate. First, I examine how the failure of HR 13500 in the U.S. Senate resuscitated the question of opening cultivated lands for the Hawaiian homestead program in the bill because only a small amount of poor quality land was identified for Kanaka Maoli leasing, while the business elite—also known as the "Big Five," the name given to a group of reigning corporations—was positioned to claim the majority for itself. The Big Five was considered an oligarchy and was aligned with the Hawai'i Republican Party. Together these powerful corporations insisted on holding on to the prime lands. To make the proposal palatable to the powerful business sector, Hawaiian elites negotiated changes informally with the dominant class of white Americans that reflected plantation and ranching interests at odds with rehabilitative homesteading. As part of these concessions, the blood quantum determination was settled at 50 percent for the definition of "native Hawaiian." The second part of the chapter examines the third hearing before the House Committee on Territories in June 1921, where the Hawaiian elites explained what happened in the territory with the blood quantum determination. This, the last of the debates on the measure, entailed justifying the compromise of the 50-percent rule. In these discussions, more blatant pushes to exclude Asians and affirm white property rights surfaced—all in the service of maintaining the territory as an American outpost.

In chapter 6, "Sovereignty Struggles and the Legacy of the 50-Percent Rule," I focus on the implications of the blood quantum rule on contemporary Hawaiian sovereignty politics. Since the HHCA, blood quantum classifications of Hawaiianness have consistently been used to enact, substantiate, and then disguise the further appropriation of land while they obscure and erase sovereignty claims and conceptions of identity as a relation of genealogy to place. I study the details of the U.S. Supreme Court case *Rice v. Cayetano* in 2000 in order to show how the 50-percent blood rule was a central factor in the Court's opinion. The implications of the ruling have proven pivotal for Hawaiian sovereignty politics because they have intensified the sense of urgency among different Kanaka Maoli political groups (including the state agencies which oversee federal funding for Native Hawaiians and Hawai'i's congressional delegation) to pursue their varying agendas and political visions for resolving the outstanding sovereignty claims heretofore unadjudicated. Also, I offer an account of the campaign for federal recognition—which itself relies on the existence of the HHCA—and the way that model relies on a limited form of indigenous self-governance and how the history of the 50-percent rule looms in the background of the proposal. Finally, I investigate the implications of the U.S. Apology Resolution and the segment of the Hawaiian sovereignty movement opposing federal recognition in favor of independence from the United States and how they reckon with questions of inclusion and belonging for a potential citizenry under their envisioned nation-state.

Racialized Beneficiaries and Genealogical Descendants

AT A GATHERING AT 'IOLANI PALACE in 1998 to promote the restoration of Hawaiian sovereign self-governance for the hundred-year anniversary of the U.S. annexation, a high-profile Hawaiian woman with blond hair and blue eyes talked with two other Hawaiians, both darker than she. From afar, a white woman who was visiting from California noted how the two darker-skinned Hawaiians seemed to defer to the blond and suggested that it was internalized racism on their part. "They seem to be paying her special attention because she's white," she said. Her friend, who is Kanaka Maoli, also watching the incident from a distance, explained that they were paying respectful attention to the fact that the blond is of higher-ranking lineage than either one of them; they deferred to her because of her Hawaiianness, *not her whiteness.*

An examination of Hawaiian genealogy and kinship practices has the potential to open up meaningful ways of engaging indigenous concepts of identity. Many Kānaka Maoli typically refer to both their lineage *and* kinship system as "genealogy" and use the term interchangeably with the Hawaiian term *mo'okū'auhau*. One of the many meanings of *mo'o* is a succession or series, while *kū'auhau* is defined as pedigree, lineage, old traditions, genealogies, historian, and to recite genealogy. *Mo'o* can mean lineage as well as succession, while *kū'auhau* can be used to describe one who is skilled in genealogy and traditional history (Handy and Pukui 1972: 197). *Mo'o* is also the word for lizard and lizard-like supernatural beings. The imagery of the *mo'o* lizard with visible vertebrae and *kua mo'o* (vertebrae backbone, or to link something together) "is apt and obvious as a simile for sequence of descendants in contiguous unbroken articulation," where one traces his or her genealogy in steps, just as one can follow the vertebrae of the spine (Handy and Pukui 1972: 197; Kaeppler 1982: 85). It is interesting to note that the word *'auhau* is used to mean an assessment, tribute, levy, or tax, which indicates the reciprocal relationship between the common people, the chiefs, and the land. I provide these definitions not in the hope of finally translating *mo'okū'auhau* into English but rather to suggest that the word Hawaiians use for genealogy does not inherently carry racial, genetic, or blooded meanings. However, the significance of *mo'okū'auhau,* by virtue of its very untranslatability, represents the extent to which genealogy carries a very specific historical and cultural weight in the Hawaiian context, which is embedded in a series of meaningful traditions and historical circumstances that are reflected in its persistence into the culture and language today.

As a colonial imposition, the blood quantum model of identity is a demeaning alternative to Hawaiian kinship and genealogy as inclusive and expansive indigenous models of belonging. Moreover, governmental uses of the blood quantum mode aim to alter and displace the indigenous form of identification. The concepts and practices of *mo'okū'auhau* must be reconceptualized as a uniquely indigenous way of knowing and understanding lineage expressed through a variety of practices that include allegory and symbolism, as well as actual descriptions of kinship relations that in and of themselves are metaphors for the Kanaka Maoli cosmos and religious system. Even Hawaiian tattooing is a visual manifestation of social relationships among people, the gods, and the universe that changed over time (Kaeppler 1988: 157). Kaeppler argues that instead of being strictly decorative, "tattoo was primarily a protective device and a function of genealogy" (157). Mary Kawena Pukui noted that tattoos marked individuals' social location as part of a village, as devotees of the same god, or as descendants of a common ancestor (cited in Kaeppler 1988: 166).

As an epistemology framework, the Hawaiian cultural system of genealogy undermines the logic of blood quantum. Lilikalā Kameʻeleihiwa notes that genealogies "are the Hawaiian concept of time, and they order the space around us" (1992: 19). They are also a mnemonic device by which the *moʻolelo,* or the exploits of the chiefs, are recalled (22). In other words, genealogies frequently serve as a device intended to aid in cultural memory. They are metaphorical in that they are both allegorical and symbolic, but they are also literal since Hawaiian kinship is based on a system of common descent.

Hawaiian society was and continues to be based on principles of bilateral descent, where descent groups are formed by people who claim each other by connections made through both their maternal and paternal lines. Hawaiian kinship terminology does not distinguish male and female lines; all the relatives within a generation receive the same kin-term without regard to collateral versus lineal or matrilineal versus patrilineal distinction. According to Jocelyn Linnekin, "since rank was bilaterally determined, descent could be traced upward in a myriad of ways, the details varying contextually depending on what was advantageous in a given situation" (Linnekin 1990: 94). This is not to say that gender was not a salient factor; rank itself is thoroughly gendered.

In terms of structural power and significance within chiefly society and among *maka'āinana* (the common people), Hawaiian women figured crucially in the strategies by which men effectively raised their own status and ensured higher rank for their children (Kame'eleihiwa 1992: 36; Linnekin 1990: 95). "This symbology does not only pertain among the chiefs; a similar complex of meanings surrounds women among the commoners, for whom access to land is the analogue to chiefly status ambitions" (Linnekin 1990: 110). Because Hawaiian women were (and still are) key to rank differentiation, they were in a sense "a pivot point between chiefs and commoners—the means by which the social rank of one's descendants can either rise or fall" (108–9). Both symbolically and politically, Hawaiian women were "points of access to power and are associated with achieving and demonstrating *mana*" (107–8). Moreover, through their association with high *kapu* (that which is sacred), and with inherent rights in the land, Hawaiian women signified access to rank and political authority, while also using rank and *mana* for their own ends. With the arrival of the Calvinist missionaries from New England came a transformation of Hawaiian norms, where female subordination was encouraged and naming practices eventually privileged the paternal side (Grimshaw 1989; Merry 2000). Yet today Hawaiian women assert themselves by drawing on cultural precedents of female power (Kame'eleihiwa 1999).

There is a difference between Kanaka Maoli kinship and genealogical practice in contrast to blood quantum classification that modifies and dislocates indigenous forms of recognition. In this chapter, I argue that in the context of the battle over Hawaiian sovereignty and land, a genealogical approach is incompatible with the blood quantum method of determining identity, even though blood quantum is often thought to be a numerical translation of genealogy. I explore how genealogy is evoked in contemporary Hawaiian contexts and present an overview of Hawaiian origins, genealogy, and kinship in contrast to the system of blood quantum classification. To highlight the differences and incommensurability, I examine two moments in Hawaiian history where race and genealogy intersected in ways that reflected the growing influence of Euro-American conceptions of race: the battle in 1874 between Queen Emma and King Kālakaua over the election to the kingdom throne, and the efforts of a Kanaka Maoli party sent to Washington, D.C. in 1897 in an attempt to stop U.S. annexation and restore Hawaiian independence after the illegal U.S.-backed overthrow. In conclusion, I focus on the ways that Kanaka Maoli identity persists today despite the intrusion of blood quantum schema, whereby kinship is the basis of everyday social identity and genealogical introductions establish relationships and make for social intrigue. As one Hawaiian friend put it, "Genealogy is our national pastime."

Contemporary Genealogies

In the present-day context, Hawaiians continue to invoke their lineage at specific moments appropriate to their own social positioning. In other words, genealogy is about quality, not quantity. For this reason, genealogies are impossible to quantify because they are about status and relationships, not arbitrary blood measurements. Hence, the codification of ancestry through blood quantum classification serves as an erasure of indigenous multiplicity. The distinction between genealogy and blood quantum is like the difference in accounting for cultural versus economic capital, or *mana* versus money. Through verbal introduction, people attempt to see how close they can get to others, dead or living. Hawaiians identify themselves through their *'ohana*—extended families—affiliations, and island locations. They use genealogical relationships to establish a collective identity through the social nexus of *'ohana*. Kame'eleihiwa argues that recognition of shared genealogy also helps Hawaiians make a collective distinction between Hawaiians as a people and non-Hawaiians (1992: 2–3).

Today when Hawaiians, upon meeting each other, ask other Kānaka Maoli who their *'ohana* are, it is a call to identify themselves through both paternal and maternal lineal connections and a challenge to locate themselves genealogically. Since this may include hierarchical rank-status, genealogy can divide as well as connect. But more often these exchanges mark proximity. Such invocations are always contextual, political, and specific, depending on where the reciter is at that particular moment and in whose company she or he speaks. Given the history of massive depopulation that followed from exposure to Westerners, Kānaka Maoli still seek out ways to identify each other, as survivors would, especially since the U.S. census of 2000 counted only 401,162 people who claimed Hawaiian ancestry (Ishibashi 2004).

Even in cross-cultural contexts, Hawaiians may invoke something common in two different people's lineage in order to attempt a connection. For example, at a sovereignty event called "the Alaska-Hawai'i Connection," my auntie Puanani Rogers, who is an independence activist on the island of Kaua'i, evoked the *kolea* bird (golden plover) in her welcome for Faith Gemmil, a Gwich'in activist who was featured in the program, because the *kolea* migrate back and forth from Hawai'i to Alaska each year.[1]

Hawaiian concepts of genealogy do not necessarily preempt the many ways that blood may be used as a metaphor for ancestry or how Hawaiians continue to identify both their genealogical links *and* their blood quantum. Genealogical questions may sometimes be coupled with blood quantum–based questions such as "Where is your *'ohana* from?" "The same Naki as the ones on Molokai?" "How much Hawaiian you got?" or "What's your blood quantum?" But a family tie remains the overriding form of identifying others: "She's Verna's granddaughter." "He's a Waiwai'ole, you know, the ones on Kaua'i now." Even though some Hawaiians have taken on the blood quantum system of classification, Hawaiians consistently prefer genealogy over blood degree in deciding who counts as Kānaka Maoli, because genealogy is the means by which one gets to kinship, whereas with blood quantum, the conversation tends to stop once the fractional answer is produced (for example, "I'm three-quarters Hawaiian" or "just one-thirty-second Kanaka"). Blood quantum is an attempt to size up someone in order to determine if they are "Hawaiian enough," and it works to deracinate (uproot), whereas genealogical connections are inherently about *rootedness* by putting the recognition of ancestors back in "ancestry"—and, therefore, connecting Hawaiians to the *'āina* (land). As Lilikalā Kame'eleihiwa notes, these genealogical relationships "reveal the Hawaiian orientation to the world about us, in particular, to Land and control of the Land" (Kame'eleihiwa 1992: 3).

What are the consequences when genealogy is assumed to be the same as blood notions and racial identity? And how might we better understand Hawaiian discourses of identification in relation to genealogy and notions of blood? First, in contrast to genealogies, which connect people to each other and to the land, blood quantum is a classificatory scheme using "blood degree," calculated by biological definitions, in order to determine generational closeness to a forebear who is supposedly racially unmixed. It is a fractionalizing measurement based on the assumption that one's "blood amount" indicates one's cultural orientation, as if culture is not something that is learned. Such processes of blood identification codify complex relationships and compel people to submit proof in ways that do not account for the acknowledgment of multiple interpersonal ties that cross the span of generations and lateral affiliations. These processes thus reduce the multiplicity and fluidity of the indigenous genealogical practices to a static, one-dimensional measurement. In this way, U.S. governmental policy works to racialize our genealogies and attempts to erase our indigenous identity and its attendant sovereignty rights.

This is not to say that Hawaiian forms of genealogical reckoning are unfamiliar with biological notions and connections. That genealogy includes biological connections does not mean, however, that it is the same as blood quantum classification. Kinship relations, with ancestry or descent forming the dominant component of belonging, are more important for Hawaiian society, despite being sometimes accompanied by the pervasive discourse of blood quantum.

Even as genealogical practices have changed over time and adapted to new historical circumstances, Hawaiians today still place a premium on their lineages and focus on those who share that lineage. They may still evoke genealogy with regard to rank, but it is not necessarily determinative of leadership or always with authority. Haunani-Kay Trask argues that while some Hawaiians may be genealogically empowered to hold leadership positions, "genealogy is not a sufficient condition for leadership" (Trask 1993: 122). Here the contingency of genealogy must be noted; genealogies may still open up possibilities but do not fix status or leadership. Kameʻeleihiwa interprets Hawaiian traditions in a way that potentially serves to circumvent hierarchical practices of genealogical invocation. She recalls that Davida Malo, a Hawaiian scholar of the 1840s, once taught that all Hawaiians were *Aliʻi* but that some forgot their genealogy and became commoners. Writing between 1866 and 1871 Samuel Kamakau also noted that some chiefly Hawaiians simply chose not to live as *Aliʻi* (Kamakau 1991 [1964]: 6). Kameʻeleihiwa suggests, "That means that we all have the genealogical right to rise up and become political leaders" (1992: 324). Whether or not Hawaiians feel enabled to do so, genealogy is still dominant in everyday exchange.

Hawaiian Origins, Genealogy, and Kinship

ORIGINS

If one were to ask any Hawaiian to account for the origins of Kānaka Maoli as a people, there would surely be a wide range of responses. As Noenoe Silva argues, Hawaiian origin genealogies include archetypal figures layered on top of each other and genealogies can be understood as both literal and metaphorical (Silva, personal communication, 2004). They serve as genealogies for real people living today and they account for our *akua*, gods, who, in some cases, migrate on voyaging vessels and, as visitors, are referred to as *malihini*, or strangers. There is not one accepted founding cosmological narrative of the Hawaiian world. The Kumulipo is a prominent genealogy of the universe that came to rule the Hawaiian origin genealogies, but there are a number of other possibilities to choose from. Indeed, even the name of the Kumulipo suggests this: it is "*He* Kumulipo," *a* Kumulipo (in Hawaiian), not *the* Kumulipo.[2] In one of the dominant versions of the Kumulipo, Wākea (Sky Father) and Papahānaumoku (Earth Mother, literally she who births the islands) are primordial humans (Silva 2003: 117–18). As Kameʻeleihiwa asserts, they were half-siblings by the ʻŌpūkahonua lineage and mated to become parents of the islands as well as Hoʻohōkūkalani, their first human offspring (Kameʻeleihiwa 1992: 23).[3] The union between Wākea and Papahānaumoku was considered a Nīʻaupiʻo (incestuous) mating, from which divine power is derived (Kameʻeleihiwa 1992: 25). The metaphors for this kind of mating offer insights into how Kanaka Maoli regarded lineage without using blood metaphors. For example, the incestuous genealogies are all likened to a coconut frond, where *piʻo* means "arching," and where a child born of such a union was a *nīʻaupiʻo* (coconut frond arched back upon itself) (Handy and Pukui 1972: 108; Davenport 1994)

In an origin narrative told by Kamakau, a Hawaiian historian writing from the 1840s to the early 1870s, Hulihonua (male) and Keakahulilani (female) are said to have been the first man and woman in the ancient past (Kamakau 1991 [1964]: 3). He notes that parents were in charge of their own family groups, where "for the twenty-eight generations from Hulihonua to Wākea, no man was chief over another" until Kapawa, twenty-five generations after Wākea, who was the first to be set up as a ruling chief, and from then on the Hawaiian Islands became a chiefly ruled society (3).

Where the significance of the connection between the planes of the cosmos and the society is neither merely metaphoric nor metonymic, this is a system of common descent (Sahlins 1985:141). As Kameʻeleihiwa notes, the essential lesson of the Kumulipo "is that every aspect of the Hawaiian conception of the Hawaiian world are one indivisible lineage" (1992: 2). Although Papa and Wākea came to dominate the genealogy accounting for Hawaiian people's origins, some Hawaiians have different interpretations of the lineage.

GENEALOGY

Precolonial Hawaiian civilization was a hierarchical class society based on both ascribed and achieved status. The two main classes which constituted the Hawaiian social order were the chiefly *Aliʻi* and the commoner *Makaʻāinana,* with *Kaukau aliʻi* serving as a buffer in this successive hierarchy (Young 1998; Kameʻeleihiwa 1992: 37). The *Aliʻi* were a floating class, tenuously related to the people on the land and dependent on them for support (Linnekin 1990: 76; Kameʻeleihiwa 1992: 26). Kameʻeleihiwa writes,

> Those at the top were *kapu,* or sacred, and possessed *mana.* Those at the bottom were *noa,* common or free from *kapu* and, by extension, without the necessary *mana,* or power, to invoke a *kapu*—although even a common fisherman, if successful, had some *mana.* Those in between were on a sliding scale, having less *mana* the farther down the triangle they slipped and the farther they fell from high lineage. These differentiations in status were designated by birth. There tended to be, however, a constant shift away from *kapu* because [male] *Aliʻi Nui* found it difficult to mate only with high female *Aliʻi Nui.* Those intermarrying with *Aliʻi* of lesser rank produced *kaukau aliʻi* who, in turn, could descend with the same facility to *makaʻāinana* rank (1992: 46).

The *Makaʻāinana*'s primary affiliations were determined through territorial considerations as inhabitants of the same *ahupuaʻa* (divided land area). Because kinship was not exclusive, well-defined, tightly knit local groups with recognized leaders did not emerge, but each *ahupuaʻa* had its own *konohiki* (land steward) (Kameʻeleihiwa 1992: 29; Sahlins 1985: 22).

Kamakau notes that there were many degrees of chiefs within Hawaiian society and lists eleven different gradations (1991 [1964]: 6–7). He also mentions those in-between classes such as the *ali'i maka'āinana,* chiefs in the countryside living as ordinary people without the attendant restrictions of the chiefly class. Today many Hawaiians refer to the *Maka'āinana* as the people who were the "eyes of the land," as in *maka* (eye) *'āina* (land) *na,* while Handy and Pukui gloss the term as people *on* the land, as in *ma* (on) *ka* (the) *'āina* (land) *na* (Handy and Pukui 1935: 4). The *Ali'i* and the *Maka'āinana* are said to be descended from the same ancestors: Wākea and Papa. Davida Malo suggested that the Hawaiian people were derived from that couple and there was no distinction between them until later, when there was a separation of the chiefs from the people (Malo 1951 [1838]: 52). There was also a class known as *kauā* who were born outcasts from their ancestors' time. However, once the Hawaiian religious system of the *'ai kapu* was broken in 1819, *kauā* were released (Kamakau 1991 [1964]: 9).

Handy and Pukui explain that within the *Ali'i* class, genealogy was a carefully guarded "historical science" handled by *'Aha Ali'i* (councils of chiefs), where order and right in the matter of succession, formal marriage of those who were high ranking, and claims to relationship with the high born had to be proven genealogically (1972: 196–197). They preserved these genealogies by monitoring physical paternity, but even when the patrilineage was unclear, there was a way to accommodate contested fatherhood (Handy and Pukui 1972: 56). For example, *punalua* describes the relationship between first and secondary mates who are not family relations in cases where one man had two female partners or one woman had two male partners. Handy and Pukui suggest that the purpose of the *punalua* was to safeguard children born from such triangles, as all three adults would be responsible for caring for the children. Also, *punalua* typically received each other as siblings and accorded each other the same treatment as one would a relative (Handy and Pukui 1972: 56). The child could also claim either genealogy or both.

Just as Hawaiian genealogical identity does not fit into established colonial blood quantum schema, as Linnekin has noted, "Hawaiian social organization does not neatly fit into established anthropological categories" (1990: 115).[4] The reason Kanaka Maoli can still evoke a myriad of genealogical connections today is because there were no exclusive boundaries between defined sets of relatives or bounded descent groups associated with land. Because Hawaiian land tenure was highly contingent and entailed a succession of caretakers, genealogical rank was a critical part of that succession

(Linnekin 1990: 85). Instead, there was social flexibility, with no determinate kinship groups or rigidly prescribed relationships—a suppleness that persists today. Linked to this flexibility and mobility is the fact that the proportion of chiefs was greater than the number of ancestral lines to which they could trace (Linnekin 1990: 94; Sahlins 1985: 19). Given that they were all related to each other somehow, the multitude of genealogical possibilities also made for the structural instability of the Hawaiian chieftainship since social arrangements were in constant flux (Linnekin 1990: 94; Sahlins 1985: 20). As Marshall Sahlins put it, "Lineage is not so much a structure as it is an argument" (1985: 20). This premise explains how genealogy as an epistemology of Hawaiian identity is in conflict with blood quantum narratives that rely on a colonial logic of fixedness. Based on his ethnohistorical research reconstructing Hawai'i at the time of Captain Cook's arrival in 1778, Sahlins argues that Hawaiians did not trace descent so much as ascent, where they selectively chose their way upward, by a path that notably included female ancestors, to a connection with some ancient ruling line (20).[5] Thus, Kanaka Maoli society was sustained hierarchically through chiefly rank rather than using gender as its primary divider.

Certainly concepts and practices of genealogy and rank have changed over time.[6] Kame'eleihiwa notes that although by the 1870s Hawaiians had made a definite shift to Western models of governance, wherein genealogies outside of the ruling monarchs may have seemed irrelevant, "Hawaiians continued to cling to our great genealogical debates as if the lineages of the Ali'i Nui [great chiefs] were proof that the race still existed as a great nation" (1992: 20). Hawaiian-language newspapers had been publishing genealogies as early as 1834 (20). Kame'eleihiwa argues that the "editors . . . had a political purpose for publishing genealogies, for genealogies are a means of glorifying one's ancestors and one's past . . . [if] the ancestors are glorious, so too are the descendants, especially when compared to the Americans" (20–22). Also, Silva points out: "Although the genealogies were also used as attempts to say to the disrespectful Americans that the ali'i should be respected because of their illustrious genealogies, that attempt failed because American cultural identity depended on the rejection of the idea of rule by European aristocracy—rule by virtue of illustrious ancestors is anathema to the American discourse of democracy. That the ali'i themselves equated themselves to European royalty exacerbated the inability of each side to understand the other" (Silva, personal communication, email April 12, 2006). Clearly, Hawaiians' emphasis on genealogy kept on continuously and never abated, but there were other reasons to publish the genealogies that were also political.

During his reign (1874–91), David Kalākaua had *He Kumulipo* written down to bolster or prove his right to rule (Silva 2004: 92). In 1880, he also established the Papa Kūʻauhau Aliʻi (Board of Genealogy of Hawaiian chiefs) to gather, revise, and record genealogies. Noenoe Silva explains that one of the main objectives of the board's work was to identify *Aliʻi Nui* and verify their genealogical claims, which could then help identify those who could serve in the Hale Aliʻi (the House of Nobles) (94–95). These projects "were done for specific political reasons and not simply as knowledge for knowledge's sake"; they were motivated by the desire to "keep the rule of Hawaiʻi in Kanaka Maoli hands" (94–95). As Silva explains, "The identification of the aliʻi nui and transcription of mele and moʻokūʻauhau worked to define the nation as lāhui Kanaka and began the development of national narratives. This functioned to interrupt the discourse that said that 'progress' meant becoming more like the United States—that is, ruled by Euro-American immigrants. Viewed in this way, these activities can be seen to be direct resistance to colonization" (95). Furthermore, as Silva argues, *He Kumulipo* must be understood as a political text as well as a genealogical account of our origins in the cosmos "because of how it figures in the national consciousness of the lāhui and, thus, how it continues to function as resistance to colonization and the attendant project of colonization" (97–98).

By 1896, even the Hawaiian-language newspaper *Ka Makaainana* (The Commoner) began publishing genealogies. As the editors of *Ka Makaainana* pointed out, "It is said, the one who does not know the genealogy is a rustic from the back country, and the one who knows, he is a chief or a person of the court" (cited in Kameʻeleihiwa 1992: 21). This suggests that all Hawaiians, regardless of rank, had an investment in knowing their genealogy, especially during this period after the illegal overthrow in 1893 and prior to the unilateral "annexation" by the United States in 1898, when the Kanaka Maoli population in Hawaiʻi numbered only approximately 40,000 (Schmitt 1968: 74).[7]

KINSHIP

Three primary factors determine Hawaiian kinship: relationship, duty, and status. Hawaiian kinship is made up of grandparents, grandchildren, blood ties, spouses, paternity, adoptive parents, plural mating, adoptive platonic marital relations, engrafted relationships, sons and daughters, nephews and nieces, brothers, sisters, and cousins, parents, uncles and aunts, relatives through marriage, fostering, adopting, and categories of friendship (Handy and Pukui 1972: 40–73). Regarding relationship horizontally, the family is stratified by generations—grandparents, parents, children—but vertically, sex cuts through the generations. For example, historically, male children were claimed by the father's side and female children by the mother's side (Handy and Pukui 1972: 42). Status is determined by genealogical seniority, not by generation, age, or sex (43). "Within a generation, all males have one term for each other, likewise females: males and females have distinct terms for each other" making up systematic segregation (43). Inclusive terms for generation can be explained as a logical consequence of regarding the extended family as a unit while recognizing genealogical sequence (43). For example, in Hawaiian tradition, all males of the parents' generation were called *makua kāne* (father) by the children, all females of the parents' generation were called *makuahine* (mother), and all of those in the grandparents' generation were called *kupuna* (grandparent). The generations were (and still are) genealogical strata, not age groups—and regard for seniority is the logical corollary of the principle of genealogical sequence.

Biological relationships were defined and ordered in terms of three factors: generation, genealogical seniority, and gender (Handy and Pukui 1972: 43). Historical terms used to designate biological relatives include *pili* (to adhere), *pili koko* (blood ties), *wehenaʻole* (cannot be untied or unwrapped), *ʻiʻo ponoʻī* (own flesh), and *pili kana* (closely related) (48). Kanaka Maoli also had another way of identifying biological relatives with the saying *kuʻu iwi, kuʻu ʻiʻo, kuʻu koko* (my bones, my flesh, my blood) (65). One could "cut" the blood tie and then all privileges and obligations would cease and no more mutual help or voluntary assistance in time of need would be provided (49). Also, one could become an accepted member of the family by attaching him or herself to the *ʻohana*, known as *pili kāmau* (to add on) (65).

There are three secondary categories of relationship whose basis is social rather than biological (Handy and Pukui 1972: 44). The first category by which nonbiological relatives were (and continue to be) incorporated is adoption—*hoʻokama* (to make a child). The second category is fostering—*hānai* (to feed). Hawaiians of different genealogical lines of descent were incorporated through *hānai*. But *hānai* often entailed blood kin where a child was given to another relative besides the birth parents, such as to grandparents, aunts, or uncles (167).[8] The third category is marriage, called *awaiāulu* (to bind securely, fasten, as of the marriage tie) or *hoʻāo* (to stay until daylight), a traditional way of registering interest in an enduring intimate relationship (Pukui and Elbert 1986: 26, 74, 34). The intimate relationships between *kāne* and *wahine* are sometimes referred to in the literature as "marriage" but that term does not correspond to Kanaka relationships. In addition, there were same-sex sexual relationships such as that of the *aikāne* (a male lover) of an *Aliʻi Nui* (Kameʻeleihiwa 1992: 47). There were also *māhū*—alternately defined as hermaphrodites and homosexuals (Pukui and Elbert 1986: 220). In contemporary Hawaiian vernacular, *māhū* is typically used to describe someone who is a transgender female or an effeminate gay man. Both the *māhū* and *aikāne* relationships exist side by side with *kāne* and *wahine* but they do not affect genealogies. The fact that unrelated persons could be incorporated in these ways into *ʻohana* does not undercut the fact that Hawaiian society still works by ancestral links and privileges genealogy.

Colonialism, Blood Quantum, and Euro-American Kinship

The differences between a blood quantum system of classification and Hawaiian kinship and genealogical links need to be examined in relation to both contrasting notions of cultural identity across cultures and the historical process of colonialism. Blood quantum enforced by the law is a colonial imposition. With regard to cultural identity and boundary formation, Alan Howard (1990) contrasts the nineteenth-century colonial framework that structured interactions with Oceanic peoples with Oceanic perspectives and cultural systems. Howard explores the relationship between cultural paradigms and historical events in identity formation. Because cultural paradigms are never static in that they have a generative aspect to them, he argues that identity must be analyzed contextually.

Howard identifies four main assumptions of the European colonial perspective. First, genetic inheritance is the main transmitter of a person's vital substance. Here, primary characteristics are inborn; one's social worth is determined by race, which is seen as an immutable attribute; experience ostensibly alters one's fundamental character only superficially (Howard 1990: 264). It might seem that the emphasis on breeding and bloodlines as critical determinants of difference is comparable to the Kanaka Maoli passion for genealogy. But Hawaiian lineage is not solely determinative in terms of one's status as designated by birth. As Kameʻeleihiwa notes, one could elevate one's *mana* (status) through deeds and talents, as well as one's selection of a higher ranking mate, known as a form of *'imihaku* (to seek a chief) (1992: 46).[9] Second, in the (colonial) European paradigm, race, culture, and language strongly cohere with one another, where a set of features is said to compose a distinctive racial type (264). Third, where race, language, and culture do not cohere, the character of individuals is primarily determined by genetic inheritance. Here racial identity is figured as a matter of degree with subcategories like "half-caste" and "octoroon" imposed to keep boundaries clear (265). Finally, when racial mixing occurs, the character of individuals is most strongly affected by the "lowest" racial type in their genetic makeup, where "inferior racial stock" is perceived as a contaminant that cannot be fully overcome, where the notion of the "throwback" (the threat of atavism) is ever present (Howard 1990: 263–65). This last supposition arguably undergirds the theory of hypodescent used in the United States to define African Americans as black regardless of their European or American Indian ancestry, which brings us to an aspect of the European colonial paradigm for which Howard does not account.

In settler colonial societies, depending on the context, the so-called inferior racial stock is not always regarded as a pollutant. For example, as Brian Dippie's work shows, in the United States the national iconography clearly reveals the distinction sharply drawn in the 1850s between the "submissive, obsequious, imitative negro" and the "indomitable, courageous, proud Indian" (1982: 92). Consistent with blood quantum practices, it "remained a popular truism that while 'red' and 'white' blood blended 'easily and quickly' both resisted fusion with 'black' blood" (267). Dippie summarizes the notion of the day: "The native population was small—just an infinitesimal fraction of the whole American population—and while a massive infusion of Indian blood might pollute the national type, the limited amount available could do no harm and might even do some good" (248).

Despite his omission of this point, Howard's theorization of contrasting paradigms between Oceania and colonial European cultural worldviews is key to tracing the distinctions between a blood quantum system of classification and Hawaiian kinship and genealogy as the basis for Kanaka Maoli identity. In contrast with Western colonial perspectives, Howard has drawn out some underlying similarities regarding identity amid the diversity among Pacific peoples.

With regard to Oceanic perspectives, Howard identifies three main assumptions. First, a person's vital substance is transmitted genealogically but is supplanted by the food from which one gains sustenance. Taro is a prime Hawaiian example of this. Taro is closely linked to the origin of the Kanaka Maoli people, as it was the main source of food for Hawaiians (before rice overtook taro production in the wake of policies enacted by the sugar economy from the mid-nineteenth century into the early twentieth, which diverted water from the taro beds to the plantations, as well as the departure of the Chinese from the plantations). Moreover, genealogically, the taro itself is considered to be the elder sibling of the Kanaka Maoli people. In one Kumulipo, Wākea (Father Sky) and Papahānaumoku (Earth Mother) were temporarily split by Wākea's desire for their daughter Hoʻohōkūkalani. Wākea impregnated Hoʻohōkūkalani but she gave birth prematurely (Kameʻeleihiwa 1992: 23).[10] They named the fetus Hāloanaka (quivering long stalk) and buried him, and from there grew the first taro plant (24). The second offspring from their union was a son named Hāloa, in honor of his elder sibling, who was the first Hawaiian *Aliʻi Nui*—considered the ancestor of all Kanaka Maoli people (24). When one eats taro, therefore, one is eating Hāloa. To "eat Hāloa" is, in fact, an expression in the Hawaiian language for eating taro (Silva, personal communication, April 12, 2006).

Second, according to Howard, there is the assumption that a person's character, and by extension a group's character, is a product of one's specific relational history. Relational history exemplifies Hawaiian genealogical reckoning as strategic, always partial, and shifting depending on one's current set of relationships and perspectives. They are contingent and allow for mobility because they are not overly determined by one's birth.

The third assumption is that places have character by virtue of their histories. In other words, people who are raised in a place or assimilate to a group by occupying it acquire its character (Howard 1990: 265–67). Here, one's cultural identity is often tied to a specific locality (267). For the case of Kanaka Maoli, researchers have found that in questions of identity, place plays a critical role through Native Hawaiian traditions and customs that "weave together physical, spiritual, and social ties to the land and sea" (Kanaʻiaupuni, Malia, and Liebler 2005: 691). Furthermore, place is a key force in the interplay of internal and external influences on contemporary Kanaka Maoli identity processes, where Native Hawaiians' genealogical connection to Hawai'i as the ancestral homeland is one unique characteristic to which no other group holds claim (691).

Thus, in Oceanic contexts, generally speaking, there is an emphasis on kinship and notions of common substance; both are usually considered to be contingent rather than absolute (266). Oceanic concepts of a person's character tend to be assessed in terms of one's current set of committed relationships, not those into which one was born. Whereas in the colonial frameworks a person's vital substance comes from genetic inheritance, in the Pacific Islands context, one's substance is acquired through genealogical inheritance and sustenance from feeding in any given set of relationships.

Unfortunately, while Howard's theory of the cultural paradigms is critical to my efforts to show how the blood quantum system of classification is rooted in colonial European cultural paradigms, his own reading of the contemporary politics of claiming indigeneity among indigenous minorities seems misguided. He asserts:

> At the opposite end of the spectrum from the Kainantu who are . . . unreflective about cultural identity, are contemporary Australian Aborigines, Hawaiians, and New Zealand Maori. As a result of European colonization they have been relegated to minority group status in their own homelands, where they are in the position of political and economic under classes. Concerted, self-conscious efforts are being made in these part-societies to reformulate traditional identities. In the face of political fragmentation, activists in each instance are seeking to redefine their heritage in a manner that will allow them to be more effective participants in the larger political arena. . . . But these people are in a bind. The most obvious way to achieve unity is to adopt European notions of ethnicity to accept biological assignment in principle, but to invert the value loadings. . . . Thus anyone with indigenous ancestors would qualify for membership in the ethnic community. Membership would be unequivocal. Unfortunately, this does not work in practice, in part because the people who are most indigenous culturally are least likely to accept group assignment in racialist (or biological) terms. If, however, a leader adopts traditional assumptions about identity, he or she is likely to receive support from only one faction—those who identify with the specific history (and current political interests) that the leader represents. (Howard 1990: 267–68)

It is true that indigenous Pacific peoples who continue to endure settler colonial societies in Oceania as minorities in their own homelands are working toward political empowerment and unity that may entail a reformulation of traditional identities. But these are most often projects of reclamation framed as part of cultural decolonization. Where I agree with Howard is that indigenous peoples such as those he mentions, including Hawaiians, may not see themselves in terms of blood quantum and race, but here he assumes that an exclusion of non-Hawaiians (those without Hawaiian ancestors, and therefore ancestry) by political activists is an acceptance of biological assignments and the adoption of European notions of ethnicity (instead of a way to claim Hawaiian identity for Hawaiians).

In a Hawaiian context, to assume that "the people who are most indigenous culturally are least likely to accept group assignment in racialist (or biological) terms" (Howard 1990: 268) is problematic. Hawaiians' inclusion of "anyone with indigenous ancestors" as part of the Kanaka Maoli community can be considered a traditional assumption about identity given the genealogical approach; to do so need not entail any adoption of "European notions of ethnicity to accept biological assignment in principle," (267) especially given the legacy of colonialism, depopulation, and the stakes of sovereignty within contemporary nationalist struggle—especially for the indigenous underclass in a settler state. Still, the bind Howard points to is salient in this context, where political support is fragmented and leaders may receive backing from one faction depending on their own criterion for community membership and collective action.

David Schneider's formative work on (Euro) American kinship is crucial to understanding the ideologies Hawaiians face when asserting their own genealogical understandings of themselves. In his research with mostly middle-class white adults in Chicago, Schneider found that blood is the first criterion for defining and structuring who counts as a relative in concepts and practices of (Euro) American kinship (Schneider 1968: 23). The blood relationship as it is defined in (Euro) American kinship is formulated in concrete biogenetic terms, where kinship is whatever the biogenetic relationship is (23). In other words, in dominant "common sense" understandings, it is believed that "both mother and father give substantially the same kinds and amounts of material to the child, and that the child's whole biogenetic identity or any part of it comes half from the mother, half from the father"

(23). More recently, this "two-halves" biogenetic equation has become much more complicated and problematized given the mutations of bioscientific categories in the mid- to late twentieth century from race to population to genome code (Haraway 1997). In her account of biological kinship studies in the twentieth-century United States, Donna Haraway traces the symbolic and technical status of blood from the equation between blood and kinship and race (with blood and gene understood as one) perceived in the first decades of the twentieth century to the midcentury conceptual shift, wherein blood is reconceived as the key fluid studied for genetic frequencies (Haraway 1997: 222). As the gene began to displace blood/race in discourses of human diversity, blood was eventually seen as "merely the tissue for getting DNA samples" (222). Nonetheless, the reliance on racial notions of "full-blood" American Indians (or Native Hawaiians) is still necessary for blood quantum racialization, and this colonial logic vis-à-vis indigenous peoples in the United States has yet to be displaced by these developments in bioscientific categories; the "common sense" notions outlined by Schneider still prevail by and large:

> Two blood relatives are "related" by the fact that they share in some degree the stuff of a particular heredity. Each has a portion of the natural, genetic substance. Their kinship consists in this common possession. If they need to prove their kinship, or to explain it to someone, they may name the intervening blood relatives and locate the ascendant whose blood they have in common. It is said that they can trace their blood through certain relatives, that they have "Smith blood in their veins." But their kinship to each other does not depend on intervening relatives, but only on the fact that each has some of the heredity that the other has and both got this from a single source. (Schneider 1968: 23)

Here, distance and blood are perceived as subdividable things (25–26). The three categories of relatives are built out of two elements: relationship as natural substance and relationship as code for conduct (29).

In the Euro-American system, genealogical distance "may be roughly measured by how many intervening categories of relatives there are, or how many generations one must go back before a common relative is found" (Schneider 1968: 73). For example, "1/2048th Lakota" is considered ten generations "removed" from a "full-blood Lakota" in biogenetic standards. In dominant American kinship, there is "a tendency to forget distant collaterals and distant ascendants, but the boundary in either the past or the present is fuzzy and there are interstitial areas which are so faded at any given moment as to be barely visible. The distant ascendants are dead and no relationship obtains with them. Without a relationship, there can be no reason to retain them . . . unless of course, they are famous, in which case they may be remembered though descendants along collateral lines, lacking fame, will not be known. The distant collaterals are 'too far away' " (72). Correlating to this biologistic theory is the idea that the significance of kin relationship depends completely on the proximity of the ancestral connection. As Eva Marie Garroutte argues, "It is precisely this belief about the importance of genealogical distance that gave birth to the notion of blood quantum as a measure of exact degree to which the strictly physical kinship substance was depleted" (Garroutte 2003: 123). Garroutte goes on to cite Jack Forbes, who points out how ridiculous this notion is within indigenous epistemologies, where, in many tribes,

> Persons are descended in the female line from a "first" ancestor, usually a being with an animal or plant name. If for example, one is a member of the "turtle" matrilineal lineage, one might find this situation: 500 generations ago the first "turtle" woman lived, and in each subsequent generation her female descendants had to marry men who were non-turtles, i.e., with other lineages in their female lines. A modern-day "turtle" person, then, might well be, in quantitative terms, one-five-hundredth "turtle and four-hundred-ninety-nine-five-hundredths non-"turtle," and yet, at the same time, be completely and totally a turtle person. (Forbes quoted in Garroutte 2003: 125)

How does Hawaiian kinship diverge from Euro-American kinship on the matter of genealogical distance? For one thing, it can often be in the interstices where many Kānaka Maoli can locate and sustain their richest family relationships, where there is no such thing as "too far away." But in another sense, Hawaiian kinship can resemble the (white) American system Schneider theorizes, where Kanaka Maoli may selectively claim a famous ancestor by generation and rank. But that does not necessarily mean that there need not also be relationships to those others in between, or no reason to remember or "retain" the rest.

As briefly discussed above, a typical 'ohana (extended family) includes the *mākua* (parents and relatives of the parent generation), the *kūpuna* (grandparents and all relatives of the grandparent generation), and *keiki* (the children) (Handy and Pukui 1972). Writing in the late twentieth century, Mary Kawena Pukui noted, in discussing Hawaiian *'ohana* (extended families), that "members of the *'ohana,* like taro shoots, are all from the same root.... With Hawaiians, family consciousness of the same "root of origin" was a deeply felt, unifying force, no matter how many offshoots came from offshoots. You may be 13th or 14th cousins, as we define relationships today, but in Hawaiian terms, if you are of the same generation, you are all brothers and sisters. You are all *'ohana*" (Pukui et al. 1972: 167). Here there is no assumption that the importance of kin relationships depends on the proximity of biological connection, no such thing as "distant relatives." With regard to what some would see as "distance," Pukui relies on the metaphor of the taro shoots to assert that family consciousness is strong "no matter how many offshoots came from offshoots." The symbol of taro is extremely important here given that the Hawaiian term for extended family, *'ohana,* signifies the family as offshoots of the same stock. Etymologically, *'Ohā* is the root or corm of the taro plant. Like a scion, *'Ohā* can also mean a sprout (Handy and Pukui 1972: 3). Here there is a rootedness—being grounded in the *'āina* (land)—that comes with kinship, which is based on genealogical ties, whereas deracination (uprooting) is the basis of the blood quantum model of identity.

With the colonial cultural encounter between Europeans, mainly the English, and later Euro-Americans, we can see these different systems of establishing cultural identity and social position with regard to genealogy and race. By 1849, the term *hapa haole* came into common usage to describe Hawaiians with European ancestry, even though it was not a category on the census.[11] *Hapa* can describe length, fractions, and amount, while *haole* means foreigner, signifying Europeans and Euro-Americans and simply white, and *hapa haole* means a person who is "part white and part Hawaiian" (Pukui and Elbert 1968: 58). By 1850, only about five hundred hapa haole existed in Hawai'i (Lind 1955: 22). By 1853, "nearly a thousand persons, or slightly more than one percent of the total population were listed in the census as "Hapahaole" or "Part Hawaiian" (22). As Clarence E. Glick wrote in "Interracial Marriage and Admixture in Hawaii," "Even in 1853, the distinction between Hawaiians and part-Hawaiians was imprecise. The 983 'half-natives' listed [on the census] must be regarded as persons who had the social position of 'half-native' rather than as the entire number of part-Hawaiians" (1970: 278). Those among Hawaiian elites who benefited from the social positions of their white fathers identified as hapa haole, which implied a degree of privilege and status, regardless of (or in addition to) their mothers' genealogical status (280). Those children were "not regarded as a distinct racial or social group, although they were frequently referred to as *hapa haoles*" (280).

During the seventy-five years after foreign contact began in 1778, many children of Hawaiian mothers and foreign fathers, mainly of European descent, were reared as Hawaiians and absorbed into the indigenous group. For example, early on, European men became advisors to chiefly men and their female Hawaiian relatives to seal the outsider men's loyalties. Hence their children were integrated into the Hawaiian elite. Glick also describes a process of absorption facilitated by the widespread practices among Hawaiian women of adopting and rearing children by younger natural mothers. "As a result of continued absorption of part-Hawaiians into the Hawaiian group since 1853, those now claiming to be 'full-Hawaiians' include a large number of persons with admixture of other ancestries" (1970: 279). In other words, "full Hawaiians" may actually be "part Hawaiians." This means that Hawaiian identity at the time was primarily reckoned and recognized through cultural norms, not biological/racial logics. Between 1778 and 1850, many children were of mixed ancestry but were absorbed within Hawaiian communities. Some were not even aware of their mixed ancestry, especially if they were adopted by other Hawaiians (279). By 1866, "Natives and Half-castes" were divided in the census data (Marques 1894: 257–58; Schmitt 1968: 74). Glick further specifies that the term "half-caste" was used from 1866 to 1890 in the last census of the independent Hawaiian kingdom.

Sally Merry notes that "by the end of the nineteenth century, a new language of nationality became more important as the Kingdom was overthrown and replaced by a republic based on the political structures and legal arrangements of the United States" (Merry 2003: 129). Under the Republic of Hawaii—illegally formed just over a year after the 1893 overthrow—census takers tabulated the nationality of the Hawai'i-born children of foreign-born parents using the parents' nationality and did so as a marker of race (Schmitt 1968: 62–63). This was the first time that people born in

Hawai'i were listed under their parents' nationality, since, under the kingdom, this distinction remained unmarked; all were simply kingdom nationals. As Merry explains, "Following the U.S. model, *nationality* became a code word for race, referring to a discrete racial identity with presumed attached cultural characteristics marked by country of origin" (129). Once the United States took Hawai'i as a territory (colony), the censuses of 1910, 1920, and 1930 attempted to differentiate between "Caucasian-Hawaiians" and "Asiatic-Hawaiians" (Glick 1970: 278). Here we have social categories expressed in racial terms—all classifications that were meant to distinguish racial difference in the service of the American colonial project.

Two *Mo'olelo*

Two very different stories from the late nineteenth century provide insight into the changing Hawaiian notions of genealogy and race with the intensified influence of Europeans and white Americans. The first is a piece of campaign lore which comes from the history of Queen Emma Naea's 1874 campaign to become the Hawaiian monarch, which she lost to David Kalākaua. This history is recounted by Jonathan Kay Kamakawiwo'ole Osorio in *Dismembering Lāhui: A History of the Hawaiian Nation to 1887.* He discusses the elections within the context of how Hawaiians believed in the kingdom's legitimacy because it symbolized their struggle as a people, and their promotion of "Hawai'i for Hawaiians" in the face of haole (white) economic ascendancy (Osorio 2002: 146–47). My focus centers on how questions of race and genealogy emerged in Queen Emma's fight for the throne. The second story comes from an editorial published in the Hawaiian nationalist newspaper *Ke Aloha Aina* on October 23, 1897, and later translated into English in 1998 by Keao Kamalani and Noelani Arista in *'Ōiwi: A Native Hawaiian Journal,* where it appeared as a primary document without commentary. The original 1897 editorial was written in response to community concerns over which Hawaiian leaders would represent Kanaka Maoli political interests in Washington, D.C., and how the decision was made on the basis of blood quantum regarding the individuals who had previously played this diplomatic role. These two stories, examined side by side, provide insight into Hawaiians' shifting regard for race and genealogy as they intersected, complicated, and co-implicated each other.

In the first *mo'olelo,* Queen Emma decided to campaign for the head of the monarchy when King Lunalilo died without naming an heir to the throne. There was an election to determine who the Hawaiian monarch would be. Queen Emma ran against David Kalākaua, who was the son of a female high chief named Keohokālole, a descendant of the kapu chiefs of Moku o Keawe (Hawai'i Island), and male high chief Kapa'akea, an active member of the Privy Council during the reigns of Kamehameha III and IV. Although Kalākaua won the election of 1874, there was a fight at the time over his genealogy because he was not of the Kamehameha lineage.

Supporters of Queen Emma claimed she had a higher genealogy than Kalākaua because of her link to the Kamehamehas. Her father was George Naea, and her mother was Fannie Kekelaokalani Young, the daughter of an *Ali'i* (chief) woman named Ka'ō'ana'eha—whose father Keli'imaika'i was brother to Kamehameha I—and an English man named John Young.[12] Young, Queen Emma's grandfather, had been a close advisor of Kamehameha I, who made him governor of Hawai'i. Although of mixed European and Hawaiian ancestry, his son John Young, Jr., who like his father was called Keoni Ana (the Hawaiianized version of his name), was raised and groomed just as any other Hawaiian *Ali'i* child, and eventually became part of the House of Nobles and served as a consul to Kamehameha III.[13] As Kamakau explains, "among all the foreign ministers there was one of their own blood whom the Hawaiians trusted, and he was John Young son of Keoni Ana who was said to be born of the daughter of Ke-ali'i-maika'i Ke-po'o-ka-lani. Her mother was Ka-li-o-ka-lani, hence, Young belonged to the chiefs and was looked upon with special favor by the king" (Kamakau 1991 [1961]: 407–408). Hence, the claim that Queen Emma's genealogy was higher than Kalākaua's was based on her claim to the Kamehameha line, which was not at all diminished by the fact that she had an English grandfather. Importantly, in this case, her European ancestry was not seen as something that weakened her high-ranking Hawaiian lineage, which bolstered her claim and popularity. Her mixedness was not seen as negative in any way nor a discount of her Hawaiianness; she lost the election for completely different reasons—namely, her gender and her anti-American and anti-missionary political stance made her a problematic choice for haole members of the legislature. In contrast to her, they saw Kalākaua as potentially pro-American since he had wavered on the issue of a Reciprocity Treaty with the United States rather than opposing it outright (Osorio 2002: 152–54).

It was Kalākaua's genealogy that was presented as his weakness by many Kānaka Maoli because he was not a Kamehameha (Osorio 2002: 157). Though some disparaged Queen Emma's genealogy, the attacks came from a distant relative of Kalākaua named Koiʻi, who claimed that she was not descended from Keliʻimaikaʻi (Kamehameha's brother), but from Kalaipaʻihala, a half brother of Kalaniʻōpuʻu (276–77). In other words, her haole ancestry had no bearing on how Kanaka Maoli regarded her as a Kamehameha, and thus more suitable for the throne than Kalākaua.

In the second moʻolelo, a nationalist editorial reveals a shift in understanding among Hawaiian leadership with regard to race and political representation. On October 23, 1897, Ke Aloha Aina—a Hawaiian-language newspaper that promoted Hawaiian independence and opposition to U.S. annexation—published an editorial, "The Leaders Belong to the People and the People Belong to the Leaders," by Edward L. Like and Emma ʻAʻima Nāwahī (1998 [1897]: 4–5).[14] The piece focuses on the purported mixed reception of Hawaiian leaders chosen to represent the Hawaiian Kingdom in Washington, D.C., in their quest for justice and restoration of Queen Liliʻuokalani, as detailed in another Hawaiian newspaper editorial from a paper called Kuokoa. The editorial also suggested that the writer of the original article was the chief editor of Kuokoa, a defender of annexation, who was "striving with all his might on behalf of his master to demolish the confidence of the people in sending representatives for themselves because of their love for the land in which they were born" (1998 [1897]: 98). Furthermore, the editorial writers suggested, "such talk is like placing their fishing lines on the fence, looking for something for us to disagree about" (98).

The executive council of the ʻAhahui Kālaiʻāina—one of three key royalist organizations—had chosen their president David Kalauokalani, James K. Kaulia, and their secretary J. M. Kāneakua to serve as representatives to Washington. When those names were announced, "it silenced some people and brought pain to others" (Like and Nāwahī 1998 [1897]: 95). To defend their choices, Nā ʻAhahui Alakaʻi—a coalition of leaders made up of Hui Kālai ʻĀina (the same as ʻAhahui Kālaiʻāina) and Hui Aloha ʻĀina, another nationalist organization which fought U.S. annexation—offered an overview of past delegations that had traveled to Washington on their behalf.

The first was in 1839, when Haʻalilio was sent as a representative for the kingdom for the purpose of securing recognition of Hawaiʻi's independence.

William Richards (a former missionary) was also sent as part of the delegation, which on December 19, 1842, secured the assurance of President John
Tyler of U.S. recognition of the Hawaiian kingdom's independence. Subsequently Ha'alilio and Richards met the third member of the delegation, Sir
George Simpson (former commander of Fort Vancouver), in Europe and
secured formal recognition by Great Britain and France on November 28,
1843 (Silva 2004: 36). The editorial noted that Ha'alilio's trip was a success,
which was attributed in part to his being an "Ali'i Hawai'i kokopiha"—a
"full-blooded Hawaiian chief" (Like and Nāwahī 1998 [1897]: 97). Notably,
the editorial did not mention the role of the two non-Hawaiians in any
negative way, as they were considered loyal to Ha'alilio's efforts.

The second trip detailed in the editorial was made by the team of a German named Paul Neumann and Prince David Kawananakoa, who was said
to serve under Neumann "like a secretary" but was of no benefit in securing
the attention of the U.S. president (Like and Nāwahī 1998 [1897]: 97).

The third party was composed of H. W. Widemann, Samuel Parker, and
John Cummins, none of whom was able to meet with the president. In their
consideration as to "why in the world did the President not agree to see the
many delegates of the Queen," the editorial writers focused on Parker and
Cummins, the two Kānaka Maoli of the team (Widemann was a German
who married a Hawaiian). The editorial described both of them as "he koko
hapa Hawai'i"—"half-blooded Hawaiian": Cummins was "a half-blooded
Hawaiian and a sugar plantation owner in league with the people who
overthrew the monarchy" and Parker was "mixed-blood of the foreigners
who visited Hawai'i and he has mixed with those who overthrew the government" (Like and Nāwahī 1998 [1897]: 97). The editorialists surmised that "it
might have been one or more of these reasons that kept them from meeting
and discussing with President Cleveland in their capacity as representatives" (98). As an alternative to Cummins and Parker, these members of Nā
'Ahahui Alaka'i proposed for the next trip:

> What we are saying is, Be careful in the selection. Do not choose
> people in league with those who overthrew the kingdom and certainly
> not those who dip their hands in the same plate as these people, lest
> the fish look suspiciously upon the rotting bait. The leaders of the
> nation will get a full-blooded Hawaiian such as Ha'alilio so that they
> won't be rejected by America when questions of lineage are asked. The

answer will not be, "My father was from a whaling ship and picked a companion in Honolulu, stayed there and married my mother and had me." The people will recite their lineage from Kumulipo and Welaahilaninui, the forefather of the Hawaiian people. (98)

Of course, any Kanaka Maoli with a haole father and Hawaiian mother could still recite their lineage from Kumulipo and Welaahilaninui, but the editorialists focused on the chosen Hawaiian representatives' high-ranking paternity for important reasons. For one, their reference to a racially mixed Hawaiian stating (hypothetically) "My father was from a whaling ship" also suggests that there are relevant issues of rank and class at play—where a Hawaiian narrating his paternity in this way would be naming his father as a common laborer. Clearly, the writers were anticipating what sort of Hawaiian it would take in order to prevent the U.S. representatives from diminishing the Hawaiian's position as a diplomatic representative, whether along racial or class lines—in this case a probable combination of the two. At stake here was the U.S. attempt to annex Hawai'i; a treaty of annexation was proposed in the U.S. Senate at the time; they were discussing who was to deliver the Kū'e petitions and do the lobbying (Silva 2004).

Still, here we see American racial discourse influenced Hawaiian norms regarding race mixing—quite a shift from the case of Queen Emma. Indeed, in both of these stories, the potential takeover by Americans in one form or another is the central concern. The writers were concerned with American perceptions of racially mixed Kanaka Maoli and whether or not those men were authoritative *as Hawaiians,* especially given the political purpose of their trip. In both examples of Parker's and Cummins's haole paternity, the editorialists could have instead suggested that each man respectively emphasize his genealogical links through his mother's lines to legitimize his connection to Kanaka Maoli, especially in the case of Cummins, who was widely recognized as *Ali'i Nui.* But the editors were more worried that in a white American social and political context—where one's paternity is more determinative of one's social standing—any Hawaiian with mixed parentage could be disregarded.[15] The editorialists suggested a candidate for the future who could name an illustrious Hawaiian fore*father* and connect himself to the Kumulipo. Thus, neither man was seen as best suited to travel to Washington to speak about the broad-based Kanaka Maoli opposition to the treaty of annexation. Instead, the editorialists cited Ha'alilio as a model for the sort of Hawaiian who should have been chosen, in an open attempt to conform to the European masculinist conventions of statehood, where representation of nation in terms of "civilized manhood" was critical. Related to the issue of conforming in order to gain access into the exclusive nineteenth-century family of nations, it was also important for the kingdom to present itself as Christian (Silva 2004: 36). This transformation had been ongoing since 1820, where the definition of family was fundamentally transformed (Merry 2000: 255).[16] Merry argues that "these processes of refashioning the family and sexual subjectivity paralleled other efforts to constitute a nation according to European understandings of that entity" (256).

The anxieties about Parker and Cummins did not emerge simply because their fathers were white; each man was seen as suspicious because each was moneyed through his plantation ties and was politically problematic due to his alliances with those who overthrew the Hawaiian government. In other words, the editorialists used a critical focus on blood as a means to criticize the politics of the men in question. It could not have been their racially mixed background alone that troubled the members of the Hui who evaluated the previous representatives, because some of the Hui members themselves were racially mixed.[17]

These two different *moʻolelo* from the nineteenth century—that of the battle between Queen Emma and Kalākaua in 1874 and the question of Hawaiian leadership in 1897—offer insight into Kanaka Maoli regard for genealogy and race. What these two stories have in common is that genealogy played a crucial role in Hawaiian political representation. In the case of Queen Emma, her European ancestry was a nonissue due to her Kamehameha lineage that made her more suitable to Hawaiians as a reigning monarch than Kalākaua. In addition, one can also see how her anti-American stance, quite different from Kalākaua's, played a large role in why Kānaka Maoli backed her bid for the throne. But in the case of which Kanaka Maoli representatives would represent the independence claim in Washington, the European ancestry of Kānaka Maoli was made into an issue depending on their political role in the community. A political leader's high-ranking lineage was reason for loyalty, despite European ancestry (for example, Richards and Sir George Simpson), if she supported the interests of Hawaiian independence, whereas a Hawaiian with mixed ancestry might be seen as questionable, even if he was of high rank, because his whiteness was then highlighted by his political disloyalty when he was believed to have betrayed the Hawaiian nation. In other words, to be recognized took more than simply having a strong lineage; one had to prove one's loyalty to the people.

Conclusion

One cannot overestimate the primacy given to genealogy among Kanaka Maoli today, even in the face of the persistent 50-percent rule and the over-determined logics of dilution that aim to discount Hawaiian indigeneity. The blood quantum rule is not only abstract and somewhat arbitrary; it is, in practice, restrictive. Percentages fragment by dividing parts of a whole, severing unions, and portioning out blood "degree." Genealogical practices of identification differ greatly from those that rely on blood quantum although they are often conflated or thought to be one and the same in commonsense notions of "blood." While Euro-American kinship norms and criteria have become commonplace among some Kānaka Maoli, especially in the face of state control over Hawaiian land, many are insisting that recentering Hawaiian genealogical practices and kinship norms is an integral part of decolonization. Genealogies connect people to one another, to place, and to land: they are about relatedness. Genealogical emphasis on "blood flow," within Hawaiian social forms and institutions, allows for the flux of continual change. Where blood quantum categorization is always about the individualization of particular bodies, genealogical reckoning enlarges the collective and the social. This politics of kinship is integral to the cultural and legal claims advanced by Kanaka Maoli and is manifest in the contemporary sovereignty movement.

Given the overview of Hawaiian genealogical models presented in this chapter, it will become clear that the HHCA did not have to racialize Kanaka Maoli using a blood quantum criterion. While blood quantum has become normative, it deserves to be denaturalized in order to show how the HHCA could have unfolded in an entirely different way. Had there been an abiding focus on Hawaiian land entitlements, rather than a shift to a welfare discourse of Hawaiian neediness, genealogical descent could have remained as *the* way to determine Kanaka Maoli eligibility for homesteading in the service of Hawaiian rehabilitation, since as descendants of the kingdom Kānaka Maoli could claim an equitable right to the land as their inheritance. But neither the island representatives serving the interests of the sugar corporations nor the U.S. government intended to bolster Hawaiian claims, especially those that would call occupation by the United States into question.

As we turn to the story of the passage of the 50-percent rule in the HHCA, we will see the way that race emerged as a means of corroding Kanaka Maoli claims to the land in question. In the debates, these categories became more rigid, due to the context of disputes over land, property, taxation, welfare, and U.S. federal policy's role in obliterating Kanaka Maoli forms of genealogical identification and contributing to their deracination. In the debates surrounding the act and Hawaiian claims to the land that would be used for rehabilitation, the blood quantum plan overtook the Kanaka Maoli genealogical approach, and, as we will see, this displacement resulted in part from a shifting focus on blooded notions of competency pertaining to "full bloods" versus "part-Hawaiians."

2   **"Can you wonder that the Hawaiians did not get more?"**

Historical Context for the Hawaiian Homes Commission Act

> Hawaiians only live for to-day and know nothing of competition. Take those people
> and place them among a bunch of Eastern Yankees, and take the Chinese and Japa-
> nese who are Far Eastern Yankees. Place the Hawaiians among those people; can
> you wonder that the Hawaiians did not get more?
>
> —John H. Wise, speech to the House Committee on Territories, February 1920

TERRITORIAL SENATOR WISE'S APPEAL to the House Committee on Territories in February 1920 was his attempt to justify a land-leasing proposal he
helped design under the direction of the Hawaiian Civic Club—an organization made up of middle- to upper-class Hawaiians—of which he was a
leading member. A year earlier, Wise first introduced the Hawaiian Rehabilitation Bill in the Territorial Senate on February 19, 1919 (Vause 1962: i;
Curry 1920: 1–2). In Washington now, before the members of the House
committee, Wise pleaded for the leasing scheme to benefit Kanaka Maoli,
pointing to their dispossession in Hawai'i, which had resulted from their ig-
norance about competition from whites and Asians (Japanese and Chinese).
Moreover, his assertion that Hawaiians only "live for to-day" resonated with
how haole racialized Kanaka Maoli as simplistic and short-sighted and also
evoked the explanations about "primitives" found within the prevailing
social Darwinism of the day. Oddly, at the end of Wise's rhetorical question,
he positions Hawaiians as "placed among" the others. Yet Kānaka Maoli
were not "placed"; they had already been *displaced* in their own homeland.

This chapter provides and explores the historical background for the
HHCA debates on the Hawaiian rehabilitation proposal. Central to these
discussions, besides the condition of Kanaka Maoli and their need for rehabilitation, was the history of Hawaiian land holdings, dispossession, appropriation, and management. The roots of the Hawaiian Homes Commission
Act took hold in an on-island Hawaiian-led political movement for Native
rehabilitation shortly after 1910, which was spurred by Hawaiian depopu-

lation and land dispossession in the nineteenth century and struggles for survival in the early twentieth century. Besides the ongoing white American national hostility against Chinese laborers, evinced in federal legislation such as the Chinese Exclusion Act of 1882, anti-Japanese sentiment also played a strong role in the outcome of the blood racialization of Hawaiians through the HHCA.

Representatives on the House Committee on Territories were responsive to Senator Wise's plea on behalf of the territorial commission members because they saw the empowerment of Hawaiians as a strategy to quell Japanese ascendancy in the islands. For example, Representative Charles F. Curry, who chaired the first HHCA hearing, was well known to be anti-Japanese in his home state of California, where a joint immigration committee had recently been launched to pursue U.S. exclusion of the Japanese. Curry encouraged the territorial proposal for Hawaiian empowerment by arguing that he feared the Japanese would outcompete Hawaiians as well as eventually outvote them in elections once the island-born Nisei came of voting age (Murakami 1991: 46). Thus, in the HHCA debates, invocations of Hawaiians as "citizens" and "Americans" (as opposed to Asian "aliens") provided a context for determining who counted as Native and raised the key issues of identity and entitlement in contrast to both the Chinese and Japanese in Hawai'i.

The rehabilitation movement was led by two prominent Hawaiian organizations that shared the aim of Native rehabilitation: the 'Ahahui Pu'uhonua o nā Hawai'i (Hawaiian Protective Association) and the Hawaiian Civic Club. Their common objective was that the U.S. government fulfill what they believed was an American social and moral responsibility to help impoverished Kānaka Maoli who were socially and politically disenfranchised. The homesteading proposal thus began with a desire by elite Hawaiians to rehabilitate common Hawaiians who were suffering from high mortality rates, unemployment, and poor living conditions in tenement housing, especially those living in urban Honolulu (Vause 1962; Murakami 1991). Those proposing the rehabilitation plan for homesteading feared that Hawaiians would continue to die off unless some of the lands being used for sugar cultivation were freed up for them (Akana 1992; Curry 1920; Murakami 1991; Parker 1989; U.S. Congress 1920b).

These were precisely the same lands the sugar plantation owners wanted to retain but whose leases were soon to expire. In the 1880s, during the reign of King Kalākaua, the kingdom government negotiated thirty-nine long-term leases to sugar corporations whose interests covered 26,653 acres of the best agricultural land on four major islands. Nearly half of these lands were crown lands once reserved for the Hawaiian monarchy but subsequently leased from the occupying territorial government. Importantly, none of these leases contained a withdrawal clause that could have allowed for cancellation if the lands were needed for some other "public" purpose according to the territorial government (Murakami 1991: 45). But even without such a clause, the lands were set to become available for general homesteading (not specific to Kanaka Maoli) once the leases expired (45). In all, government leases to over 200,000 acres of public lands were set to expire between 1917 and 1921—a definite threat to the sugar elite (Vause 1962; Kent 1993: 76; Parker 1989; Murakami 1991: 44).

The economic interests in sugar were enormously profitable and forceful throughout the United States, but especially in the island colonies.[1] In Hawai'i, a business alliance known as the Big Five dominated economic and political life. The Big Five consisted of Brewer and Company Ltd., Theodore H. Davies Ltd., American Factors Ltd., Castle and Cook Ltd., and Alexander and Baldwin Ltd. With the exception of Davies, who was British, all these corporations were run by American missionary descendants (though American Factors Ltd. was German-controlled as H. Hackfeld and Company until 1918). The Big Five monopolized the sugar trade and acted as agents for thirty-six out of thirty-eight sugar plantations (Kent 1993: 70–72). Consequences for the common Hawaiians were shaped by the massive concentration of land ownership in the large plantations, estates, and ranches that came to economically and politically dominate Hawai'i's landscape (Murakami 1991: 44). For the sugar elite, profits depended heavily on continued access to vast acres of dirt-cheap public-lease lands. One plantation, for instance, held ninety-five thousand acres at two cents an acre per year (Kent 1993: 75–76). As Lawrence Fuchs noted, "By 1909, half of the privately owned land of Hawaii was controlled by haole corporations, one sixth by individual haoles, another sixth by the haole directors of Bishop estate, and the remaining sixth by individual part-Hawaiians, Hawaiians and Asians" (Fuchs 1961: 253).

The tension between Kanaka Maoli rehabilitation goals and those of the haole sugar elite set off an intensive lobbying trip to Congress by the legislative commission in order to get the land laws of the territory changed, which would take an amendment of the Organic Act. The 1900 Organic Act, which organized the Hawaiian Islands into the U.S. colonial territory, allowed for the previously existing land laws under the Republic of Hawaii to govern the use of the so-called public lands ceded to the United States. But the Organic Act also included two new restrictions. First, the term of any agricultural lease was limited to no longer than five years. Second, no corporation, including any sugar plantation, could acquire and hold more than one thousand acres of land, subject to vested rights (Murakami 1991: 45). In other words, the plantation economy would eventually have to give way to a more diversified economy with room for small farmers. In 1908, the U.S. Congress amended the act to extend the lease limit, and in 1910, the U.S. Congress amended the Organic Act to provide that any twenty-five persons upon petition to the Commissioner of Public Lands in the Territory of Hawaii could obtain title to agricultural homesteads (Murakami 1991: 45). The sugar elite were threatened by this amendment because the new terms could be combined with the withdrawal provision and thus break their grip on the best agricultural lands they leased from the territory (45). After all, the concentration of leases in their hands had been the primary reason for the failure of earlier attempts at homesteading for the general public in Hawai'i.

With the leases for thousands of acres of land set to expire at the time, the two parties went to Washington to try and secure access to the land for very different reasons—one for Native rehabilitation and the other for sugar expansion, which created a dichotomy of political interests within the legislative commission. From the very beginning, then, in the HHCA, these two opposing efforts were problematically intertwined with each other, which set the course for the drastic revisions to the original proposal. With their different agendas, the two members of the territorial legislative commission each took it upon themselves to inform U.S. congressional representatives about the Hawaiian people and their history. At each step of the process, the goal of rehabilitation said to be at the heart of the land proposal for poor Hawaiians was differently interpreted as multiple competing interests and motives among the Kanaka Maoli elites and the sugar business advocates surfaced. Besides the interests of the Big Five, Hawaiian Island territorial politics revolved around three axes of power: the delegate to Congress, the governor (an appointed, not elected position), and the territorial legislature (Okihiro 1991: 13). To maintain their political hegemony, the Big Five had to control the legislature and sway Congress and the president, because the territorial governor's power was limited. As a result, sectors of Hawai'i's white elite—including the Hawaiian Sugar Planter's Association (HSPA), the Honolulu chamber of commerce, and the industrialist Walter F. Dillingham[2]—arranged to elect their candidate as the delegate to Congress and established offices in Washington for their lobbyists, whose power frequently eclipsed that of the territory's delegate (Okihiro 1991:13). For example, on June 18, 1919, the Honolulu Chamber of Commerce passed resolutions defining its position in regard to Congressional Delegate Jonah Kalaniana'ole Kūhiō, who had announced that he would not permit people or organizations of the territory to present their views to officials or before committees of Congress except through him. But the chamber resolved that they would not back down in D.C.; they would certainly pursue measures where their own presentation and advocacy would be "most effectual" (*Honolulu Star-Bulletin* 1919f).

Delegate Kalaniana'ole and Senator Wise were the Hawaiians who played a central role in the rehabilitation legislation and in the hearings for the HHCA. In Washington, as in Hawai'i, Delegate Kalaniana'ole was recognized as the successor to the throne had the monarchy survived (see figure 1; U.S. Congress 1920c: 40).[3] Kalaniana'ole was born in 1871 to a high chief of the last principal chief of the island of Kaua'i. After completing St. Mathews School in San Mateo, California, Kalaniana'ole attended the Royal Agricultural College in England. Upon returning to Hawai'i to find Queen Lili'uokalani overthrown, he took part in an armed insurrection to restore the monarchy and was subsequently charged with treason, for which he spent a year in jail (see figure 2)—however, the full story of the prince's participation was never told until after his death.[4] In early 1902, the burgeoning Republican Party in Hawai'i recruited him to defeat congressional delegate Robert William Kalanihiapo Wilcox, who served in Congress from November 6, 1900, to March 3, 1903 (and who also had an earlier history of revolutionary activity) (Nose 1967). Not only did Kalaniana'ole defeat Wilcox; he was elected to Congress for ten consecutive terms.

Wise was born in 1869 to a Hawaiian mother of high-ranking lineage

Figure 1. Prince Jonah Kalaniana'ole Kūhiō as Mō'ī of the Order of Kamehameha in full regalia, ca. 1920. HAWAII STATE ARCHIVES, KALANIANAOLE PHOTOGRAPH COLLECTION.

Figure 2. Prince Jonah Kalaniana'ole Kūhiō in 1895, during his imprisonment for treason. HAWAII STATE ARCHIVES, KALANIANAOLE PHOTOGRAPH COLLECTION.

Figure 3. Hawaii Territorial Senate, 1919. HAWAII STATE ARCHIVES, TERRITORIAL LEGISLATURE
1900–19.

(Nawaʻa) and a father of German ancestry. In 1893, just months after the
U.S.-backed overthrow of the Hawaiian kingdom, Wise graduated from the
Oberlin Theological Seminary in Ohio. Upon his return home to Hawaiʻi,
he joined the Board of Missions but soon resigned when he became aware of
their support and participation in the overthrow (*Honolulu Star-Bulletin*
1937b). In 1895, Wise, like Kalanianaʻole, participated in a coordinated attempt to restore Queen Liliʻuokalani to her throne. Although the plan failed,
both men served a year in prison for committing treason. But by 1900 Wise
overcame this political stigmatization within the new U.S. colony and served
as Hawaiʻi's delegate to the Democratic national convention, going on to
work in the territorial government. By 1915 Wise was elected as senator
without even needing to campaign (see figure 3).

Wise's and Kalanianaʻole's push for Native rehabilitation and entitlement
to lands entailed a dual argument—legal and moral claims—for American
social obligation to long-suffering Hawaiians. They discussed Kānaka Maoli
in relation to their prior status as citizens of the kingdom, with special
attention to *makaʻāinana* (commoners) and whether they still had claims to
particular lands in Hawaiʻi under the U.S. system. They specifically questioned whether, as American citizens, those who were *makaʻāinana* would
still be entitled to lands from which they had been dispossessed in a land

privatization scheme under Kamehameha III in 1848, the Great Māhele. These were the same lands identified for the homesteading proposal in 1920 that the haole who control the sugar industry wanted to hold onto. They justified land reclamation as a form of reparation for Hawaiians who were of nonchiefly commoner ancestry and were rendered even more landless after the 1893 U.S.–supported overthrow of the kingdom and the subsequent unilateral U.S. annexation in 1898 than they had been when the kingdom first privatized communal land holdings in 1848.

Hawaiian advocates for the HHCA saw a clear connection between leasing particular lands to Kanaka Maoli and their rehabilitation goals; they considered their lobbying as an intervention in the condition of an endangered people, their people. As an editorial in the *Honolulu Star-Bulletin* put it: "The wisdom of the movement is recognized by men and women of leadership among the Hawaiians, who in casting about for ways and means to improve the future of their people, see in this prospective hegira the opportunity for social uplift, for the fostering of physical regeneration, industry, application and promotion of higher morals, as well as affording a life of better standards, better living conditions, and an all around better environment than will ever be found in the congested tenement districts of the city" (*Honolulu Star-Bulletin* 1919c). The suffering of Kānaka Maoli in the early twentieth century had its roots in land and political dispossession, which helps to explain why the Hawaiian elites focused on land recovery as a solution to the problem.

As a way of providing context for the HHCA debates, this chapter details the scope of Hawaiian depopulation which informed the proposal for rehabilitation, and the nature of the Māhele land division of 1848 as it related to contestations over land which emerged in the HHCA hearings. It is no coincidence that many Hawaiians today call the HHCA the "second Māhele," since it enabled another wave of widespread land dispossession. But the HHCA has also been seen as a Hawaiian version of the General Allotment Act (GAA) of 1887, which broke up reservations and privatized tribal land holdings, especially since the GAA has often been (mis)understood as the first use of blood quantum policy by the U.S. federal government.

Finally, this chapter examines racial discourse and the legal issues of U.S. citizenship in relation to Hawaiians as it differed for the Chinese and Japanese during the early twentieth century. I argue that a process of selective assimilation of Kanaka Maoli, as an indigenous people, was remarkably different from the exclusion of Asians in Hawai'i when it came to both the U.S. franchise and potentials for land acquisition during the period of the HHCA debates. White Americans' racialization of Chinese and Japanese as "aliens" emerged in contrast to their racialization of Hawaiians as Native—a distinction focused on Kanaka Maoli as assimilable, and thus "indigenous blood" as dilutable. Race, law, and citizenship in Hawai'i were structured and sustained along a racial triangulation of haole-Hawaiian-Asian devised as white-Native-alien. Claire Jean Kim has theorized the "racial triangulation of Asian Americans" in relation to the U.S. black/white racial binary, where whites have valued Asian Americans as "superior" to African Americans, albeit while racialized as unassimilable (Kim 1999). Here, I propose a different racial triangulation in the Hawai'i context, in which Asian groups were racialized in contrast to Native Hawaiians vis-à-vis the haole, even as they were seen as distinct from each other.

The Māhele of 1848 and the Contestation over Land

To fully comprehend the stakes and legal contestations involved in the HHCA, an examination of the 1848 privatization of communal land is crucial; the lands for the HHCA were to come from crown properties originally allotted in the Māhele. The HHCA hearings reflect a struggle over whether the former kingdom lands were part of the U.S. public domain or a land base that Hawaiians were entitled to as their own. Senator Wise asserted that the crown lands were never really vested in the U.S. federal government, except in trust for the common people, the Kanaka Maoli (U.S. Congress 1920c: 33). At the hearings, those from the pro-Hawaiian camp explained that since the Māhele was such a disaster for the *maka'āinana,* leasing opportunities through the HHCA would enable the United States to be more responsible to the people than the Hawaiian monarchy had been. In other words, the focus on the Māhele linked the moral and legal issues raised in the HHCA debates.

By the mid-nineteenth century, Hawaiians and their descendants became largely a landless people, in part the effect of their unfamiliarity with the Western rules of land tenure, through the Māhele land division (Matsuda 1988a: 137; Kame'eleihiwa 1992). The Māhele was the first time the Hawaiian government had privatized lands which had always been held in common

(Kameʻeleihiwa 1992). Lilikalā Kameʻeleihiwa documents (white) American participation in this land-division process, which took place less than three decades after Hawaiians' conversion to Christianity around 1820. Also, many of those who immediately profited from the land-tenure transformation were the Calvinist missionaries-turned-businessmen whose recommendations were crucial in promoting the change (Kameʻeleihiwa 1992: 15). In the capitalist venture, the Hawaiian chiefs joined white American and European merchants, who constituted the bulk of the foreign population in Hawaiʻi at that time, and recognized in the Māhele an opportunity to acquire land of their own.

The Māhele was also brought about by the belief that many Hawaiians could be saved from extinction through the acquisition of land in fee simple, which would help them in reestablishing a life of farming (Yamamura 1949: 233–34; Linnekin 1990; Kameʻeleihiwa 1992: 297). Jocelyn Linnekin notes that as "emigration came to be perceived as a problem in the 1840s, foreign residents and missionaries pressed for the establishment of individual land titles, arguing that private property would result in pride of ownership and would motivate commoners to remain on the land" (198). The publicly stated purpose of the land division was to create a body of landed commoners who would then prosper by means of their small farms (Kameʻeleihiwa 1992: 297). In a speech before the Royal Agricultural Society in 1850, Judge William Lee, a New York attorney who became the kingdom's chief justice, declared the importance of the Māhele for Hawaiian commoners:[5] "Until the last year the Hawaiian held his land as a mere tenant sufferance, subject to be dispossessed at any time it might suit the will or caprice of his chief . . . I thank God that these things are now at an end, and that the poor *Kanaka* [Hawaiian] may now stand at the border of his *kalo* [taro] patch, holding his fee simple patent in his hand, bid defiance to the world" (Lee cited in Yamamura 1949: 234). Lee's declaration involved an inverted logic, however, because under the communal system *everyone* had access to land.

Prior to the 1848 division, land-tenure patterns were characterized by values and practices of reciprocity rather than private ownership (Matsuda 1988a: 135). Before the Māhele, Hawaiian land tenure was managed through a hierarchy of distribution rights that was contingent on chiefly politics with a succession of caretakers (Linnekin 1990: 85; Kameʻeleihiwa 1992). The *Mōʻī* (paramount chief of each island) allocated *ahupuaʻa* (traditional land sections) to lesser chiefs, who entrusted the land's administration to their local land stewards, the *konohiki*. The *konohiki* administered land access for *maka'āinana* (commoners), who labored for the chiefs and fulfilled tributary demands.

The Māhele created three categories of landholder: the monarch, the government, and the chiefs. Under the Māhele, the king first divided the lands of the kingdom between himself and the chiefs and *konohiki* (land stewards). He then separated the government lands from the crown lands, reserved for the monarch and his descendants. The king surrendered part of his original share in the lands that became the government lands and reserved the smaller portion for his own use as the crown lands (Hobbs 1935: 46). Kamehameha III administered these lands through his agents as might any citizen under the system of private property ownership; they were sold, mortgaged, or leased at will, and the revenues resulting were diverted to his personal use (Hobbs 1939: 64). But what about the *maka'āinana?*

With few exceptions, there tends to be a large consensus in the scholarly work on the Māhele regarding the benefits for the *maka'āinana.* The predominant take on the matter is that by the end of the division, the common Hawaiians received only 28,658 acres of their allotted 984,000 acres (Lâm 1975: 103; Lâm 1989: 262–63; Kame'eleihiwa 1992: 295; Kelly 1980). The prevailing literature asserts that less than 1 percent of the total land acreage passed in fee simple to Hawaiian commoners with little more than 8,000 fee simple titles going to the commoners under the Kuleana Act of 1850. The awards made by the Land Commission to *maka'āinana* were called *kuleana* (to have interest) awards. Out of 14,195 applications made for *kuleana* awards in 1848, of approximately 80,000 Hawaiians at the time, only 8,421 claims were awarded (Kame'eleihiwa 1992: 295). Most scholars explain this small number by suggesting that few Hawaiian commoners registered their land claims, especially since they were required to pay for the survey of the lands they set out to secure, and those who did found that theirs were frequently lost to fraud, adverse possession, tax sales, and undervalued sales to speculators (Chinen 1994 [1958]: 31; Kame'eleihiwa 1992: 295; Lâm 1989: 262; Matsuda 1988a: 137; Kelly 1980).[6] Others have speculated that many were uninterested in small plots of rural land, especially when they required wide-ranging gathering rights to maintain a traditional subsistence lifestyle (Matsuda 1988a: 137). By traditional precedent, carried over into the Māhele guidelines, abandoned or uncultivated lands would revert to the *konohiki* of the *ahupua'a* (Linnekin 1990: 201). Hence, *kuleana* lands were allowed to slip back by default into the hands of either the government or the chiefs of the surrounding land (Linnekin 1990: 201). But the Māhele did not, in itself, alter the rights of the *maka'āinana* in the land because it did not convey any title to land (Lâm 1989: 259; Chinen 1994 [1958]: 20).[7]

Still, the ultimate effect of the Māhele was to create and introduce private ownership of land and commodification of labor and to accelerate the dislocation of Natives (Matsuda 1988a: 137). As Linnekin notes, "It is ironic that emigration was thus used as a justification for the individualization of title, for the land division was perhaps the single event most responsible for land abandonment (1990: 198–99). Moreover, and perhaps more importantly, in the HHCA debates, both Wise and Kalaniana'ole cited 28,000 acres when they discussed massive Kanaka Maoli dispossession under the Māhele.

In the debates of the HHCA, the lands under discussion for homesteading and sugar expansion were part of the crown lands under the kingdom (as divided in the Māhele). In 1898, the Republic of Hawaii (under Sanford B. Dole) ceded them to the United States at annexation. But there was also a contest over the nature of these lands and who had claim to them under the crown—a legal dispute with implications for the HHCA hearings. The relationship between the origins of the crown lands and entitlement was forged through a gendered process, entangled in a net of inheritance, property, and matrimony. The case called into question whether the lands were held in common for the people or property of the monarch to dispose of as he or she wished.

After King Kamehameha III's time of leadership, the legal stability of the crown lands was forged through the conflict about property and dower rights. King Kamehameha IV, the successor, administered these lands through agents in much the same manner as his uncle, as a private citizen with individual title. Queen Emma, his consort, joined him in making deeds. She waived her right of dower in such lands (Hobbs 1939: 65). However, with the accession to the throne of Kamehameha V (who was brother of the late monarch) a dispute arose over the crown lands. The deceased King Kamehameha IV left no will to make specific disposition of the property to his surviving consort or to his successor in office. As a result, Queen Emma laid claim as heir of the late king to one-half of the crown lands and to a dower right in the other half (ibid.). However, the attorney general opposed her claim, holding that the crown lands constituted "a royal domain annexed to the Hawaiian Crown" that would descend from each holder of the crown to the successor in office. The court also held that Queen Emma could not lay claim to the lands by both right of descent and right of dower and in that case her right to dower (as widow) would be lost in her superior right to inherit as an heir (ibid.).

Litigation ensued between Kamehameha V and Queen Emma and the case went before the court. The judge ruled that the reigning sovereign "might enjoy the revenues accruing from them during his lifetime, and might sell, mortgage, or lease them at will, the proceeds becoming his private property" (Hobbs 1939: 67). The opinion also stated that on the death of the monarch, any remaining lands were to pass to his (or her) successor in office, subject, of course, to the same dower rights as any private lands (67). In a step to offer a solution so that the queen's interest would be settled, the court granted her six thousand dollars a year from the public treasury in lieu of her interest in the crown lands (66–68). The court further held that the lands then in the crown-land areas should remain "henceforth inalienable and shall descend to the heirs and successors of the Hawaiian crown forever" (70). Until this particular case, no precise consideration had been given to the exact legal status of the crown lands, as it had been widely assumed that the crown lands would remain with the monarch (65–66).

This historical context regarding this land base is essential to fully understanding the HHCA debates. The elite Kānaka Maoli in the Hawaiian Protective Association and the Hawaiian Civic Club first proposed rehabilitation through land reclamation as a form of reparation for those in dire straits who were likely to be *maka'āinana* and therefore had been disproportionately dispossessed through the Māhele division when the lands were allotted to the crown, and had subsequently been further removed after the U.S.-backed overthrow of their monarch, the establishment of the provisional government, and the Republic of Hawaii in 1894. The republic then ceded these lands to the United States when it unilaterally annexed Hawai'i against the consent of Kanaka Maoli, and they became the "public lands" of the colonial territory in 1898. In the HHCA debates, both Wise and Kalaniana'ole argued that Hawaiians at large had a vested interest in these same lands. They maintained that these lands were held for the benefit of the people by the sovereign and had been stolen through the overthrow and later ceded to the United States at the time of annexation, without Hawaiian consent.[8] Even though the legality of U.S. control over those lands was subtly contested, neither the congressional nor territorial representatives agreed on whether the lands were part of the public domain or a Hawaiian inheritance. Their lack of agreement seems to have led to a revised approach taken by the Hawaiians involved in the debates, who underscored the connection between land access and a *moral obligation* to aid Hawaiians—hence, their focus on rehabilitation.

Depopulation, Rehabilitation, and Homesteading

The goal of Wise and Kalaniana'ole was to secure some of the soon-to-be-freed lands for the benefit of Hawaiians who were struggling to survive. Issues of Hawaiian rehabilitation were central to the HHCA initiative, at least in its early stages. At the time, shortly before 1920, the Hawaiian birthrate was below the U.S. national level, and infant mortality was eight times as high as the U.S. national average. At that same time, the death rate of Hawaiians was higher than that of any other American minority (Parker 1976). However, the U.S. government failed to establish any health program to counter this crisis (92–93). Although the Indian Affairs Commission in the Department of Interior was responsible for Hawaiian affairs at that time, the federal government virtually ignored the Hawaiian population until 1920 (Wright 1972: 31; Parker 1976: 92–93).[9] Even then, the initiative came from Hawaiian leaders in the territory, not from the federal government.

In the years leading up to 1920, two Hawaiian organizations composed of middle- to upper-class Hawaiian men—most of whom were also of high genealogical rank—took the lead in forming a rehabilitation movement (McGregor 1990: 5). As noted, these were the 'Ahahui Pu'uhonua o nā Hawai'i (the Hawaiian Protective Association), formed in November 1914, and the Hawaiian Civic Club, which originated in November 1918 (Vause 1962: 14; McGregor 1990: 1–5). The Hawaiian Protective Association was created with the express purpose to plan for the "Hawaiian's future salvation," where the people would be uplifted through educational and social work and encouraged to become homeowners (Akana 1992 [1921]: 82). This was the organization that devised the plan for land reclamation for Kanaka Maoli rehabilitation. McGregor notes that two hundred Hawaiians helped to found the 'Ahahui Pu'uhonua o nā Hawai'i and identifies those that made up their leadership body (1990).[10] As Hawai'i's delegate to Congress, Kalaniana'ole hosted the first meeting, where he, along with Senator Wise, the Reverend Akaiko Akana, Honolulu mayor John Lane, and attorney Noa Aluli, was selected to draft a constitution for the 'Ahahui (1990: 1). These Hawaiian men were among the most prominent in all of Hawai'i.

The 'Ahahui Pu'uhonua o nā Hawai'i envisioned a homesteading plan to rehabilitate Hawaiians upon the "ceded lands" that were formerly crown and government property. As Wise declared, alluding to the Māhele, "The most unfortunate day for the Hawaiians was when the law gave them the right to dispose of their land . . . the race belongs to the soil, and when the Hawaiians abandoned the land and came to live in the tenements, and under other unnatural conditions, in the towns, they began to die. Unless they can be gotten back to the soil, they are a doomed people" (*Honolulu Star-Bulletin* 1918b). Their aim was thus to enable Hawaiians to escape the tenements and slums. The Hawaiian Civic Club, which included some of the same members as the 'Ahahui Pu'uhonua o nā Hawai'i, was formed to create a forum to discuss and promote Hawaiian welfare and culture. Kalaniana'ole and others decided to organize a club to draw together middle- to upper-class Kānaka Maoli to work on the tenement issue in response to the Honolulu Ad Club (made up of haole) and its public campaign to repair or destroy the dilapidated buildings (McGregor 1991: 4–5). Their initiative resulted in the founding of the Hawaiian Civic Club, with Judge William Heen (a Chinese-mix Kanaka) elected as president, and Reverend Akaiko Akana (also Chinese Kanaka) as vice president (Akana would eventually go to Washington to intervene in the debates about the HHCA proposal when the businessmen representing the sugar interests in the territory traveled there to vehemently oppose the bill). The Hawaiian Civic Club's first order of business was the passage of the HHCA in order to rehabilitate Hawaiian suffering from the ongoing effects of colonization (McGregor 1990: 5).

Rapid Hawaiian depopulation was far from new in the islands. These conditions were a continuation of an earlier, massive population collapse. In total, Hawaiians suffered a depopulation rate of at least 83 percent within the first forty-five years of contact (Stannard 1989: 45–49; Kame'eleihiwa 1992: 141). From an estimated population of 800,000 when Captain James Cook arrived in 1778 (Stannard 1989: 45–49), a mere half-century later the 1823 census for the kingdom reported 142,000 Kānaka Maoli (Roberts 1969: 91). Hawaiians were decreasing in such great numbers that, from 1832, "return to the land" movements were seen as a means of preventing the depopulation of the Hawaiian people (Vause 1962: 2). From that time, rehabilitation efforts continued, albeit sporadically.

From 1848 to 1893, the number of Hawaiians was again devastated by some 50 percent, from 88,000 to 40,000, making them a numerical minority in Hawai'i (Kame'eleihiwa 1992: 311). This decline reduced Kanaka Maoli in ways that made them more subject to settler colonialism. White nativists even appropriated their indigenous identities and began naming themselves the *kama'āina* (children of the land)—where earlier on they self-identified as "white" or "Caucasian" (Wood 1999: 37–48).[11]

As early as 1868, Hawaiian kingdom government funds were appropriated to import Pacific Islander laborers with an eye toward rehabilitating Hawaiians through intermarriage (Hobbs 1935: 51). Judith Bennett (1976) provides insight into the 1870s push to revive the declining Hawaiian population, even as it was linked to the planters' goals of seeking new workers to replace Hawaiian laborers. She argues that besides the planters, others among the political and economic elite of Hawai'i saw the need to replenish the dying Hawaiian population but that their motives were often more "global and patriotic" (Bennett 1976: 3). Advisors to King Kalākaua, such as Walter M. Gibson and others, were "intent on preserving the indigenous population by injecting a cognate or kindred people into the Hawaiian community and thus sustaining the numerical power base of the monarchy" (ibid.).[12] They identified other Pacific Islanders—specifically the Gilbertese—whom they counted among the closest groups racially, culturally, and geographically. But as Bennett argues, the "hope that these people could help the recovery of the declining Hawaiian population was a vain one" (22).

There had also been earlier attempts to provide opportunities for Hawaiians to homestead. Under the Republic of Hawaii, which superseded the kingdom, the Land Act of 1895 utilized the so-called public lands for this purpose (Hasager 1997: 167). The 1895 land law provided for general homesteading with 999-year leases and various occupancy, alienation, and descent restrictions. It is important to note that people had to make a living off the land as well as reside there. Hawaiians obtained over half of these leases (Murakami 1991: 44–45). However, their tracts averaged less in value per acre than those held by non-Hawaiians (Parker 1976: 95). Many Hawaiians soon lost these homesteads because they could not meet the lease restrictions, while others sold their interests to non-Hawaiians for nominal sums (Murakami 1991: 44–45).

Soon after the U.S. takeover, the "ceded lands" became a source of conflict between the sugar planters and Kanaka Maoli since Governor Frear blocked Hawaiian attempts at homesteading there in 1911 (McGregor 1990: 8). One of the key problems with the general homesteading program became evident in the Waiākea lands in a Hilo, Hawai'i Island, case which centered on a conflict over a plantation-homesteader agreement (*Honolulu Star-Bulletin* 1918c). In another example of the force of sugar power as a barrier to general homesteading at the time, the Kekaha Sugar Company on Kaua'i Island purchased outright the lease of the Knudsen estate for more than $200,000. The original government lease was negotiated "way back in the time of the Kamehamehas" and was set to expire on June 1, 1920 (*Honolulu Star-Bulletin* 1918a). Then-governor Pinkham had declared earlier that as soon as the Knudson lease expired, the Kekaha lands would be opened up for general homesteading. The arrangement placed the sugar company, as sublessee, in a position to deal directly with the territorial government, which found the money hard to turn down.

By the time of the first HHCA hearing in 1920, the territorial government and various private organizations had tried several movements to return Hawaiians to the land. According to Vause, however, the HHCA's version of "rehabilitation" was already considered meaningless because few leaders in the islands believed that another homesteading scheme would solve the problem. Rather, they identified social disorganization as the real problem among Hawaiians. The post–World War I period proved a difficult time in Hawai'i, and particularly for Hawaiians. The price of Hawaiian staple foods such as fish and poi (pounded taro corm) almost doubled and a disproportionate number of Hawaiians were suffering in urban tenements and squatter camps (McGregor 1990: 5). In addition, there was increased competition for jobs between Kanaka Maoli and Asians.

The "anti-Asiatic" movement in Hawai'i worked to restrict both Chinese and Japanese labor migration and eventually organized to keep both groups out of preferred occupations (Jung 2006: 79). For example, a 1903 territorial law excluded those ineligible to become U.S. citizens from being employed as mechanics or laborers for public works (Jung 2006: 79). In another example, the Hui Poʻolā (Hawaiian Stevedores' Union) was concerned with the increase of Japanese and Chinese on the waterfront. The Hui Poʻolā organized a movement to drive Chinese and Japanese stevedores from the harbor in a "Hawaii for Hawaiians" campaign. At a meeting held by the Hui on April 4, 1919, Clarence L. Crabbe, a Hawaiian superintendent of the Oceanic Wharf at Pier 6, shouted, "Drive the Japanese out" and called attention to the fact that 80 percent of the laborers were Japanese while only 20 percent were Kanaka Maoli (*Honolulu Star-Bulletin* 1919b). At the same meeting, the veteran stevedore D. K. Kaeao encouraged a rejuvenation of former times when Hawaiian waterfront workers had prestige: "Then, we had everything . . . now, alas, we have nothing. Even our jobs are going away from us" (ibid.). Another lament was made by Benjamin Wright of the Honolulu Ironworks, who declared that Kanaka Maoli "had lost their flag, their lands, and had nothing left to give but their vote" (ibid.). He warned the Hawaiians in attendance, "And now the Japanese are coming in herds to take your jobs away." Many among Hawaiians and whites also feared that the Japanese would begin competing for general homesteading leases if the Organic Act was not amended. These local concerns over job competition and labor activism would eventually dovetail with the U.S. Congress's alarm over Japan's influence in Hawaiʻi, and such concerns found a receptive audience in Congressman Curry, who chaired the HHCA debates.

Responding to the severe conditions among Kanaka Maoli, both the ʻAhahui Puʻuhonua o nā Hawaiʻi (Hawaiian Protective Association) and the Hawaiian Civic Club worked to aid the Hawaiian people at large. Moreover, they articulated their concerns in racial terms that were specific to Kānaka Maoli. Marylynn Vause characterizes the actions of these key Hawaiian leaders as manipulative, arguing that it was through two key issues that "Hawaiian leaders attempted to inculcate 'racial consciousness' in the Hawaiians" (1962: 4). She cites the early formulation of a "racial issue" as a response to both the increase in cost for specifically Hawaiian food staples and the growing competition "between Hawaiian and non-Hawaiians, particularly Japanese, for jobs" (4). Further, Vause problematically attributes these conditions entirely to the postwar timing and argues they were "exploited" by the Kanaka Maoli leadership. That the leaders focused on these particular issues as a rallying call for Hawaiian unity seems clear. But these key figures in the movement were already operating from a particular form of racial consciousness given the nature of their organizing, the membership body of the two organizations, and the focus on recovering lands for Hawaiian people in dire straits. Hence, to say they "formulated" the condition of Kānaka Maoli as a "racial issue" suggests they invented it as such rather than responded to it.

The call for Hawaiian rehabilitation went beyond concerns about reproduction by linking Hawaiian survival to the reoccupation of land, a claim to land based on the history of the kingdom and the dispossession of the Kanaka Maoli after the U.S.-backed overthrow. Had the U.S. representatives —including congressional delegate Kalaniana'ole—fully reckoned with this history, they would have had to question the U.S. annexation altogether. The multiple ways they steered away from calling U.S. sovereignty into question were crucial to the formulation of the proposal and help to explain the layered contradictions that surfaced in the hearings. The problem the Hawaiian elites faced was in articulating these historical claims within the confines of American law, citizenship, and racial categories, for the U.S. framework of unilateral incorporation did not allow room for this multi-layered recognition, which would have necessitated acknowledging that Hawai'i was a stolen nation.

Federal Legacies

Concepts of property, competence, and degree of blood were all central to the formation of the HHCA in 1920. While such modes of individualization did not entail the dissolution of Hawaiian political entitlements that had been dismantled earlier, after the unlawful U.S.-backed overthrow of the kingdom, they nonetheless led to a particular kind of subjection for Hawaiians. In the HHCA, blood quantum classification in relation to land allotment did not anticipate or facilitate the withering of wardship, as in the case of the General Allotment Act. While the HHCA was the first source of blood quantum as applied to Hawaiian people, it is clear that such classifications were already well in place elsewhere as an administrative technique by the time the HHCA passed, and Congress had already imposed land allotment on American Indian tribes.

On first examination, it might seem that the HHCA was modeled on the General Allotment Act, as Linda Parker suggests (Parker 1989: 153). But the two acts differ in important ways. The General Allotment Act (ch. 119, 24 Stat. 388)—commonly known as the Dawes Act—was signed into law by President Grover Cleveland on February 8, 1887 (Dippie 1982: 172). Allotment signaled a shift in the U.S. federal policy from isolation of American Indians to absorption into a dominant white American mainstream (Wilkins 2007: 116–17; Dippie 1982: 173). It broke up communal tribal land holdings through the privatized allotment of individualized title in fee simple and trust patents. The act entailed the individualized distribution of tribal lands into private tracts of various amounts: female or male heads of household received 160 acres, single persons were entitled to 80 acres, and all others received 40-acre allotments (Wilkins 2002: 110–111).[13] Privatization of Indian lands was "considered essential for the rapid assimilation of Indians into Euro-American culture" (Wilkins 1997: 65).[14] Allotment was easily seen as a means to an end: the assimilation of the Indians into white society. In this equation there would be no future shortage of land for the Indians because after they were absorbed there would be no Indians in the conventional sense (Dippie 1982: 175; Utley 1984: 215). Here, the notion of racial absorption for American Indians went hand in hand with the justification of tribal land dispossession. At the time of the passage of the General Allotment Act, tribes controlled nearly two billion acres of land, but by 1924 the act and its amendments relating to the sale of "surplus" lands, lease arrangements, and other policies had reduced the amount of Indian-owned land to 150 million acres (Wilkins 2007: 169).

Integral to the Dawes Act were the values of individualism, self-sufficiency, and high regard for private property (Dippie 1982: 263). Allotment and assimilation would advance the goal of (individual) Indian self-sufficiency (179). Brian Dippie explains, "Amalgamation was the assimilation program at its most literal, and it made perfectly good sense within the tradition of the Vanishing Indian" (269). As Frederick Hoxie notes: "Once the tribes were brought into 'civilized' society, there would be no reason for them to 'usurp' vast tracts of 'underdeveloped' land. And membership in a booming nation would be ample compensation for the dispossession they had suffered. But most important, the extension of citizenship and other symbols of membership in American society would reaffirm the power of the nation's institutions to mold all people to a common standard" (Hoxie 2001: 15). Theodore Roosevelt explicitly spoke to this aim in his message to Congress on December 3, 1901, where he declared: "The General Allotment Act is a mighty pulverizing engine to break up the tribal mass. It acts directly upon the family and the individual. Under its provisions some sixty thousand Indians have already become citizens of the United States. . . . The effort should be steadily to make the Indian work like any other man on his own grounds" (Wilkins 2007: 117). Later, critics would charge that the Dawes Act was cold-bloodedly predicated on the assumptions of future Indian decline. Yet the authors of the legislation believed that allotment in severalty would arrest the population decline (Dippie 1982: 175). Still, the act made no provision for possible increases in the Native population, which is why after a reservation had been allotted, there was "surplus" land to sell to white settlers. This process, in which land parcels were allotted, needed a determinate population of individuals. Such a "fixed" population meant that land could then be distributed once and for all. Clearly, the Dawes Act was internally inconsistent and ill-conceived, as the HHCA would later prove to be as well.

Whereas the General Allotment Act worked to systematically break up tribal land holdings, Hawaiian lands had already been privatized in 1848. Allotment under the HHCA proved to be a different form of Native assimilation. Unlike the explicit push to *detribalize* Indians through the Dawes plan—with individual land title vulnerable to alienation—the initial aim of the HHCA proposal was to rehabilitate urban Kānaka Maoli by *returning* them to land "for their own good." Only through individually leased plots, and not through the cultivation of traditional Hawaiian communal land tenure and collective social structures, were they encouraged to have children and therefore to rehabilitate through biological reproduction. The HHCA was not necessarily about assimilation; for one thing, the lands allotted by the HHCA created concentrated Kanaka Maoli communities that, at least in the early period, were almost entirely Hawaiian. Even though the legislation promoted American (Calvinist) values of individualism, the HHCA did not serve as a form of societal integration like the Dawes Act. Instead, it institutionalized a form of racial segregation for "native Hawaiian" lessees who occupied the allotted territories that make up Hawaiian Home Lands on the margins of society.

Because the HHCA does not allow for ownership of the homestead lands, it also created a form of dependency in the leasing scheme. Stress on preventing land alienation amounted to another form of paternalism. And the way to assimilate the "native Hawaiians," or so it was thought, was to make them farmers over individualized land bases that would be *inalienable* because these farmers were deemed incompetent and at risk of losing the land. Kānaka Maoli who did not meet the 50-percent blood quantum rule were considered already competent in their American citizenship and, as such, able to secure private property.

Some scholars have argued that the U.S. blood quantum classification used against American Indians originates in the General Allotment Act. For example, Ward Churchill and Glen T. Morris locate the dictate of blood degree in the General Allotment Act, by which, they suggest, "full blood" Indians were deeded with trust patents, over which the government exercised complete control for a minimum of twenty-five years, while "mixed blood" Indians were deeded with patents in fee simple, "over which they exercised rights but were forced to accept U.S. citizenship in the process" (Churchill and Morris 1992: 14).[15] Lenore A. Stiffarm and Phil Lane Jr. make an argument in line with Churchill and Morris: "Under provision of the 1887 General Allotment Act, all full bloods were tightly restricted to small land parcels and, as legally defined 'incompetents,' expressly denied control over them for a minimum of twenty-five years. On the other hand, mixed bloods were often allotted much larger parcels, often in better areas, and with immediate full control over their property" (1992: 41). M. Annette Jaimes also argues that blood quantum identification was adopted by Congress as part of the General Allotment Act (1992: 126). But she casts allotment by blood in very different terms, suggesting that "each Indian, identified as being those documentably of *one-half or more Indian blood,* was entitled to receive title in fee of such a parcel; all others were simply disenfranchised altogether" (126). She goes further in suggesting that tribes have racist enrollment requirements based on blood quantum that are derived from the General Allotment Act (122–27).

John LaVelle has exposed these misreadings of the General Allotment Act eligibility as a distortion of law, policy, and history in the service of the derogation of tribal nations (1999: 252–54). Examining the actual text of the act, LaVelle—unlike Jaimes and the others—explicitly states that it does not contain any mention of blood quantum at all, and he specifically charges Jaimes and Churchill with perpetuating an antitribal ideology by fabricating the requirement in order to foment popular hostility toward tribes (254).

LaVelle asserts that they falsely accuse the tribes of complicity in the destructive policy of the General Allotment Act by disparaging tribes that use blood quantum to determine eligibility for citizenship within Native nations (260). Whereas Jaimes has argued that the use of blood quantum and its federal origins has usurped the sovereignty rights of tribes, LaVelle instead highlights the fact that "Congress made eligibility for allotments under the act depend exclusively on the tribes' own independent membership determinations" (259). Even in subsequent legislation on the act in 1894, 1901, and 1911, actions for allotments referred to Indians "in whole or in part of Indian blood" (259). LaVelle exposes what he has assessed as a "hoax" and further challenges the notion that tribal nations that use blood quantum to determine eligibility for membership are reproducing colonial policies. While revealing the lack of proof and faulty evidence in other scholars' publications, LaVelle's work claims to untie the use of blood quantum from the ongoing federal project of indigenous dispossession. Yet blood quantum has its origins in a colonial process that is undeniable given that U.S. governmental agents used it in the service of hastening indigenous assimilation.

As LaVelle also notes, the Burke Act of 1906, which amended the General Allotment Act, set up a process whereby the "Secretary of the Interior may, in his discretion, and he is hereby authorized, whenever he shall be satisfied that any Indian allottee is competent and capable of managing his or her affairs, at any time to cause to be issued to such allottee a patent in fee simple" (U.S. Congress 1906b). This stipulation led to a scheme to determine allottees' competency linked to percentage of Indian blood—typically marked at one-half—and the Indian Office used this policy from 1917 to 1920, then later employed a case-by-case approach to determine competency (LaVelle 1999: 259). This means that a criterion of 50-percent blood quantum was circulating as a normative standard within U.S. federal administrative practice at the same time the HHCA hearings were held to determine the provisions for Hawaiian land leasing.

Joanne Marie Barker also traces blood degree requirements to the administrative processes of allotment. She describes the Burke Act's intent to "phase out" Indian dependency while slowly moving Indians into U.S. society through the auspices of private property ownership (1995: 75). In their earliest form, blood quantum criteria were not utilized for purposes of exclusion but as an evaluative index to determine an allottee's competency within the applications for fee patents—to determine qualifications for managing private property ownership (Barker 2003: 28–29). Discussing the assumption that an invocation of blood quantum was a valid way to evaluate competency, Barker shows how dominant U.S. scientific theories of social evolution intersected with allotment practices (1995: 78–79). She goes on to show how even "by 1887 [the year of the Dawes Act] the equation between blood-culture-identity and so the ability to quantify it, had been naturalized as an accepted scientific truth and so could be institutionalized in policy and administration" (81). Barker explains that competency "was evaluated at two stages: during the first issuance of patents to allottees, and when the allottee applied for a fee patent [at the end of the trust period of the 1906 act]" (75–76). Eventually, "blood quantum became a kind of 'bottom line' criterion as the administrative burdens of allotment increased" (76).[16] Moreover, Barker argues that those "figurations construct an Indian that is salvageable and redeemable, but only as that Indian is made governable" (91).

These attendant issues of "governmentality" are visible in other contexts specific to Native racialization. Examining the making of modern citizens among the Lakota people from 1880 to the mid-1930s, Thomas Biolsi (1995) argues that blood quantum is a technology of individuated subjection. He asserts that, generally, "the existence of tribes as political and legal entities and of federal trust authority over individual Indian wards were seen as temporary states that would gradually wither away" and that "blood quantum registration was an administrative technique that anticipated, measured and even facilitated this process" (40). Biolsi contrasts the blood principle used against American Indians with the hypodescent rule imposed on African Americans. Different from rules such as those operating under Jim Crow laws, "blood quantum was associated not with the separation of the races, but with assimilation" (41). He argues that rather than defending "discrete boundaries," blood quantum was useful for projects of assimilation that blurred racial boundaries. Blood quantum registration was a matter of *gradient*—one that inevitably generated the interpenetration of "races both conceptually and practically" (40–41). These different ways of defining and creating racial categories, depending on whether the aim was segregation or limited forms of assimilation, demonstrate the contradictions in U.S. legal policies based upon widespread assumptions that identity is determined in the "blood" (Dominguez 1986: 89).

Assimilating Hawaiians and Alienating Asians

The relationship between white Americans' paternalist treatment of Kanaka Maoli and the strong anti-Asian sentiment in the islands played a formative role in the operative logic within the HHCA debates. Participants in the HHCA hearings repeatedly invoked Hawaiians' political status in contrast to that of both white American citizens and Asian "aliens"—most especially the Japanese, but sometimes Chinese. In relation to citizenship and enfranchisement in the early twentieth century, U.S. territorial policy entailed distinct interlocking conventions that formed a racial triangulation—haole-Native-alien—process of selective assimilation in relation to Hawaiian racialization.

Rehabilitation for racially mixed Asian Hawaiians was unthinkable in terms of the homesteading scheme, whether based on charity or entitlement, because of anti-Asian hostilities which characterized the Japanese and Chinese as a threat to Americanization in the territory. Hawaiians endured policies of assimilation within a historical-legal predicament of forced inclusion within the United States, while Asians were profoundly marked by their exclusion from U.S. citizenship. These different treatments revealed the politics behind the distinct projects of rehabilitation for Kanaka Maoli, on the one hand, and Americanization for Asian peoples on the other, most especially the Japanese.

The disparate treatment of Kānaka Maoli and different Asian groups predated the formal takeover of Hawai'i by the United States. The different experiences of colonialism and immigration, including the global movement of capitalism and imperialism, help to explain the different racialization of Kanaka Maoli—in contrast to that of both the Chinese and Japanese —by white Americans, who had a classic colonial relationship to Kānaka Maoli (Merry 2000). To some extent this difference in treatment is the legacy of the Calvinist missions who saw the Hawaiians as more similar to themselves, despite their views of the "primitives," and therefore more easily assimilable, whereas Asians were firmly regarded as "others" (139). Furthermore, Merry asserts that as sugar workers, migrants from Asian countries "had a typical immigrant relationship to the haole/Hawaiian leadership of the Hawaiian kingdom and later Territory of Hawaii. . . . they remained an alien 'other' while the Native Hawaiians were assimilated into a category of 'us' by the economically and politically dominant whites" (7).

But the haole elite also tended to regard Kanaka Maoli as childlike, benign, irresponsible with money, and friendly, although too sensuous (Merry 2000: 131). As Merry argues, "Whereas the Hawaiians were romanticized and economically marginalized, the immigrant groups from Asia were viewed as a threat by *haole* elites, undesirable as citizens and characterized by morally repugnant habits such as gambling, thievery, and opium smoking, attached to essentialized biological identities. These practices were seen as threatening to the fragile moral capacity of the Native Hawaiians" (ibid.). Merry explains how religion was also a key factor in these projections. That whites viewed Kanaka Maoli as docile and familiar and the Asian groups as "other" was due in part to the fact that Hawaiians had converted to Christianity, which made them seem like subjects of paternal protection and care (128–30). In contrast, the Asian groups came with their own "foreign" religions, and were not the particular focus of Calvinist missionaries. Moreover, they also largely retained their previous religious affiliations.

The on-island movement against citizenship for Chinese immigrants—who constituted the first migrant labor group—was fed by the anti-Chinese organizing in California after the gold rush era. The Californian influence was significant given the west coast's importance for the Hawaiian Islands in terms of contact and trade with the United States. Anti-Chinese sentiment was also fueled by Kanaka Maoli fears that their declining numbers would be overwhelmed by the new immigrants.

The anti-Chinese movement in Hawai'i considered Japanese laborers to be analogical extensions of Chinese "coolies," exemplified by the 1888 organization of the Hawaiian Anti-Asiatic Union that sought to restrict both Chinese and Japanese labor migration (Jung 2006: 79). Yet what set the Japanese apart from other Asian-origin peoples was the Japanese state, which asserted the rights of its citizens abroad, especially to distinguish Japanese laborers from "coolies," and the fact that it was a powerful modernizing state (Jung 2006: 79–80; Okihiro 1991).

The anti-Japanese movement, underway in Hawai'i by the 1880s, was also stoked by parallel American anti-Japanese movements. The anti-Japanese sentiments held by haole characterized the Japanese as an 'alien threat' even as Japanese workers began to make claims in American terms to equal pay for equal work (Okihiro 1991). By the late nineteenth century, the haole elite looked on Asians as plantation laborers who lacked self-restraint and needed (white) authority to control them. Tamura argues that the attitudes toward the Japanese depended on the size of their population, as earlier had been the case with Chinese immigrants. When the Chinese had been proportionately more numerous in Hawai'i in the 1880s, the haole denounced them and praised the Japanese (Tamura 1995: 58). It should be noted that King David Kalākaua first initiated Japanese labor migration to Hawai'i to appease sugar plantation owners. After King Kalākaua's 1881 visit to Japan and two special-envoy missions, led by John M. Kapena in 1882 and Curtis P. Iaukea in 1884, the kingdom legislature allocated $50,000 for Japanese migration (Okihiro 1991: 23). Just over a decade later, these same white elites that praised the Japanese were no longer eager to have them as laborers; once the Japanese became more numerous, they became objects of criticism while the Chinese were praised and their help sought in controlling Issei rebelliousness.

In the 1890s, the pro-U.S. annexation position came to the haole elite as an attempt to resolve their contradictory concerns—needing Japanese labor, worrying about the growing numbers of Japanese, and fearing Japan's imperialist intentions (Jung 2006: 81). For example, immediately prior to U.S. annexation, in an address by the (all-white) Hawaiian Society of the Sons of the American Revolution, on May 22, 1897, President Peter Cushman Jones, then based in Washington, D.C., noted, "We can restrict or exclude Chinese immigration, for we have no treaty with China. But unfortunately, our [U.S.] treaty made with Japan in 1871 contains the 'favored nation' clause, and under its provisions we cannot prevent her people from coming as free immigrants" (Jones 1897: 6). After the 1900 Organic Act, the white American sugar planters of Hawai'i even appealed to Congress for a modification of the Chinese Exclusion Act. They formulated their proposal as a way of destroying the Japanese labor monopoly and saving the territory's economy from what they saw as a Japanese threat (Okihiro 1991: 37).

Moon-Kie Jung argues that while this distinction between Hawaiians and Asian-origin migrants mostly held, particularly in relation to the Chinese, in the late nineteenth century, the "typical immigrant relationship" described by Merry proved to be elusive, especially beyond that period. Jung cautions against overstating the continuities between the racialization of Chinese labor and Japanese labor: "Everyone, including the Japanese themselves, understood the Japanese to be racially different from the Chinese and later, to a considerably greater degree, from Filipinos" (2006: 79). Jung cautions scholars from taking for granted the salience of the panethnic racial categories of "Asian" and "Asian American" in Hawai'i at this time, which can effect "a double conceptual overextension—from the present onto the past and from the metropole onto Hawai'i" and obscure the racialized inequalities and divisions among Hawai'i's Asian-origin workers (56). For example, he argues that the Japanese and Filipinos—despite coming from different prefectures, in the case of Japan, and being of Visayan, Ilicono, and Tagalog backgrounds, in the case of the Philippines—"came to see themselves as Japanese and Filipino 'races'" and did not see themselves, "nor were they seen by others, as together belonging to one Asian 'race'" (ibid.). He argues that haole capitalists conceptualized Japanese, Filipino, and other migrant laborers in racially disparate ways and in so doing set the initial terms of their struggles, where they faced "qualitatively different racisms that articulated with class and nation differently" (61).

Jung's productive critique is based in part on the time period after the passage of the HHCA, where "by the 1920s and 1930s, there was arguably as much difference in racialization between the Japanese and Filipinos as between Hawaiians and 'Asians'" (69). For example, whites saw Filipinos as "un-American," whereas they viewed the Japanese as "anti-American." However, the period most critical to the historical context of the HHCA debates in this case study is from 1900 to 1920.

Questions of citizenship for the different peoples in the territory during the 1920s were a direct consequence of the history of Hawai'i's forced incorporation into the United States from the 1893 overthrow, the 1898 annexation, and the 1900 Organic Act. White American leaders of the 1893 overthrow introduced many restrictive qualifications into the constitution of the Republic of Hawaii. To start, most Hawaiians could not vote in the republic's first election because the new government included property ownership as a requirement for the franchise. This qualification eliminated most Hawaiians since few owned property (Parker 1976: 92). Although leaders of the Republic tried to maintain this voting requirement, after annexation, the U.S. Congress refused to allow so discriminatory a practice. The citizenship clause in the Hawaii Organic Act of 1900 provided that all persons who were subjects under the monarchy, the Republic of Hawaii, and born in the Hawaiian Islands were citizens of the United States (ibid.). Section 4 of the Organic Act states: "All persons who were citizens of the Republic of Hawaii on August twelfth, eighteen hundred and ninety-eight, are hereby declared to be citizens of the United States and citizens of the Territory of Hawaii. And all citizens of the United States resident in the Hawaiian Islands who were resident here on or since August twelfth, eighteen hundred and ninety-eight, and all the citizens of the United States who shall hereafter reside in the Territory of Hawaii for one year shall be citizens of the Territory of Hawaii" (U.S. Congress 1900). As part of this forcible inclusion within the U.S. nation-state, the government unilaterally conferred citizenship on Hawaiian men and women, with Hawaiian men afforded the right to vote, whereas under the Republic of Hawaii, securing that right was determined by one's income (Wright 1972: 22). These newly enfranchised Hawaiian men in the U.S. colony formed a dominant voting block, which the white American economic elite found potentially threatening (Kent 1993). They maintained a majority at the polls until 1924, but they were able to sustain only a brief period of control of the territorial legislature through the Home Rule party, led by the insurrectionary Robert Kalanihiapo Wilcox (Okihiro 1991: 13). While this stipulation of Hawaiian voting allowed for broader inclusion within the colonial political process, it did not positively account for the thousands of Asians who were residing and laboring in Hawai'i at that time.

As Gary Okihiro notes, "Annexation was a mixed blessing for Asians in Hawaii," since it kept the door to Chinese migration closed but opened new possibilities for movement from the territory to the mainland (1991: 36). U.S. laws that denied naturalization to Asian immigrants—who were excluded under the 1870 amended Nationality Act that limited naturalization to free white persons and "aliens of African nativity and persons of African descent" (Ancheta 1998: 23)—thereby disenfranchised the first generation who made up nearly 60 percent of Hawai'i's total population at the time of annexation (Okihiro 1991: 13). The boom in immigration to Hawai'i occurred between 1896 and 1910, with the highest proportion registered in the census of 1900, when 59 percent of the population was recorded as foreign-born (Lind 1980:92).

In 1900 the Asian population—made up of Japanese, Chinese, Korean, Okinawan, and Filipino immigrants—constituted three-quarters of the population over twenty-one years of age, the voting age at that time (Lind 1980: 98). Children born to immigrants in Hawai'i after 1898 were U.S. citizens. But only a very small number were old enough to exercise the rights of citizenship prior to 1920 (most would be of voting age by the early 1930s) (ibid.).[17] And even then, this number only allowed for men's participation.

In 1910, Chinese men made up only 3.9 percent of adult citizens and Japanese men accounted for a mere 0.4 percent (Lind 1980: 100—table 18). Hawaiians, on the other hand, made up 47.5 percent of adult citizens (over the age of twenty-one) by 1910 (100). But by 1920, Japanese constituted 42.7 percent of Hawai'i's population (Tamura 1994: 58). Although Hawai'i's Asian population also included Filipinos, Koreans, and Okinawans, they were not identified as a source of concern at the time in the same way the Japanese were politically targeted, in part due to demographics. In Hawai'i, like the U.S. continent, white Americans perceived the Japanese as a distinct danger as both a source of labor competition and a nationalist threat in the emerging world order (Gulick 1915; Adams 1924).[18]

Eileen Tamura traces these concerns about the Japanese from the political issues of the 1890s to the Americanization movement after World War I that added tensions over religion, the Japanese-language press, Japanese-language schools, and especially dual citizenship resulting from conflicting nationality laws (1995: 580). Japanese who were born in the United States before 1924 were citizens of both the United States and Japan (Tamura 1994: 85). Eventually, in response to requests from Japanese in Hawai'i and the continental United States, Japan revised its nationality laws in 1916 to permit Nisei (except males seventeen to thirty-seven years old, who were subject to military service) to renounce their Japanese citizenship (ibid.).

Because the HHCA originated as a rehabilitation proposal, the early issues with regard to Hawaiians had more to do with how they were faring under Americanization, not whether they were capable of it in terms of national loyalty. While Hawaiians were also nationalistic, they were not perceived as quite the threat the Japanese were. Most Hawaiians still acknowledged the leadership of Queen Lili'uokalani. Perhaps because of this, the army viewed the largely Hawaiian National Guard with suspicion (Linn 1996). But the presence of a Japanese civilian majority, with strong political and cultural ties to its homeland, was seen as more dangerous (155).

Conclusion

The Kanaka Maoli claim to the land was grounded in their indigenous status and was what set them apart from the Japanese and other Asians in Hawai'i. But it was not simply their indigeneity that marked them as distinct; territorial policy makers and U.S. government officials had different understandings of Hawaiians as assimilable and Japanese as "alien" to the project of Americanization. This was mostly due to the view of Japan as a geopolitical predator in the region, the fact that Kānaka Maoli were the largest voting group in the islands at the time, and the struggles between Japanese organized labor on the plantations and the haole, who had economic and political control in Hawai'i through their monopoly of the sugar industry.

This colonial problem worked to structure the framework for discussing Hawaiian rehabilitation and entitlement to the lands in question for homesteading. The contested nature of the 1848 Māhele land division explains why Kalaniana'ole and Wise focused on recovering crown and government lands for homesteading Kānaka Maoli in the 1920s. They asserted that Kanaka Maoli had a right to the lands held by their former sovereign on their behalf. Thus, they argued that all Hawaiians were entitled to these lands, a claim that undergirded their justification for securing lands from the sugar planters and ranchers for the purpose of Hawaiian rehabilitation—as a response to dispossession as well as depopulation, as a form of reparation.

The issues of political organizing, labor, and the specific populations targeted for monitoring were also very important contexts for the debates surrounding the HHCA, especially since the rehabilitation of Kanaka Maoli was problematically linked to white American anti-Asian nativist hostility, especially toward the Japanese. The racial triangulation of white-Hawaiian-Asian was the most salient grouping in Hawai'i at the time, which, in terms of the bluntest racial oppositions, was regarded as haole-Native-alien. Here indigeneity—centered on the colonial experience—was a key factor in the differential racialization, in which comparisons between American Indians and Hawaiians were more apt than between Hawaiians and Asian peoples.

The next chapter details the first hearing on the two territorial proposals for Native rehabilitation and sugar expansion. As we will see in the first debate, the history of the Māhele, Hawaiian depopulation, and the differential racialization of Hawaiians and both Chinese and Japanese were all important determinative factors in how the congressional representatives understood the issues of rehabilitation and Native entitlement. Throughout the legislative process, the category who counted as "native Hawaiian" would be reconfigured in multiple and sometimes contradictory ways in light of these different strands of Hawai'i's history in order to suit the shifting goals of the actors debating the merits of the successive bills.

3   Under the Guise of Hawaiian Rehabilitation

It has been said that there should have been two bills: the one dealing with rehabilitation and the second with other land questions, home rule, increases of salary and so
on. In answer, I say it was impossible to secure action upon two bills. . . . before
the House Committee, the members of our commission were told that in the congested
condition of the House calendar at this time, it was absolutely impossible to consider
two separate measures because it would require two special rules. The sole hope then
was for the Commission and your delegate to get together and make one bill.
—Congressional delegate Prince Jonah Kalaniana'ole Kūhiō, U.S. Delegate's Report,
Hawai'i

IN FEBRUARY 1920, THE TENTH Territorial Legislature of Hawaii (figure 4)
sent a legislative commission to Washington, D.C., to lobby for approval of
two very different resolutions before the House Committee on Territories.
One was Senate Concurrent Resolution 2 (SCR 2), which would provide for
Native rehabilitation. The other was House Concurrent Resolution 28 (HCR
28), which would provide expanded leasing provisions for prime lands for
sugar planters. Congressional delegate Prince Jonah Kūhiō Kalaniana'ole
explained that these two proposals were linked simply for procedural reasons. But the combining of the opposing measures would eventually prove
to be the beginning of the end for the Hawaiian land claims as the basis for
rehabilitation, given the domination of the sugar elite in territorial politics.
The eventual result of the linkage was one bill: House Resolution 12683 (HR
12683). This new draft served to combine both initiatives, as well as several
other smaller proposals that were much less controversial, into one proposal, but it made for a troubling dichotomy of political interests.

One faction of these competing interests in Hawai'i comprised direct
descendants of the first island missionaries who were representatives of the
territorial legislature or legal representatives of the business elite. The territorial legislative commission consisted of Senator Robert Shingle, Representative William T. Rawlins, and Representative Norman Lyman, all known

Figure 4. Tenth Territorial Legislature of Hawaii. HAWAII STATE ARCHIVES.

to be aligned with the Big Five, and Senator John Wise. All the members were appointed by the territorial governor, C. J. McCarthy, who was also part of the commission.[1] They were to assist Kalaniana'ole "in the presentation of any measures formulated in pursuance of the recommendations contained in the resolutions passed by the legislature" (Curry 1920: 1). McCarthy made Senator Wise the head of the team, even though he alone on the commission supported the proposal for Hawaiian rehabilitation. Still, Wise, together with Delegate Kalaniana'ole, was able to set a tone of concern within the hearing by laying out the social conditions of the Hawaiian people that warranted a rehabilitation plan as the solution.

In examining the first hearing before the House Committee on Territories held February 3–10, 1920, during the 66th Congress, second session, this chapter traces the early logic of both Wise and Kalaniana'ole as they aimed to push through their own rehabilitation proposal on behalf of the Hawaiian people. Representative Charles F. Curry of California chaired the committee, which was composed of the following representatives in addition to the delegate from Hawai'i: Edward A. Almon, Alabama; Edward S. Brooks, Pennsylvania; Martin L. Davey, Ohio; Cassius C. Dowell, Iowa; Benjamin G. Humphreys, Mississippi; Albert Johnson, Washington; William C. Lankford, Georgia; James G. Monahan, Wisconsin; James G. Strong, Kansas; and Zebulon Weaver, North Carolina.[2]

First and of primary importance in the debate was an overview of the demographics of Hawai'i's population. Governor McCarthy offered statistics from the last official census of 1910. "At that time the total population was 191,909 of which 29,099 were Hawaiians; part Hawaiians, 12,485; Portuguese, 22,294; Chinese, 21,698; Japanese, 79,663; Spanish, 1,962; Porto Ricans [*sic*], 4,828; other Caucasians, 14,684; Filipinos, 18,196" (U.S. Congress 1920c: 17). These statistics revealed the number of "full-blood Hawaiians" contrasted with the growing number of "part-Hawaiians," a distinction which became a key focus within the debates.

Other issues of concern were the total number of Hawaiians compared to whites and all Asians, and the minority status of whites in relation to all Asians. Of the "part-Hawaiians," in 1910, "Asiatic-Hawaiians" numbered 3,734 (1.9 percent) while "Caucasian-Hawaiians" numbered 8,772. By 1920, the number of the former rose to 6,955 while the latter numbered 11,072 (Lind 1980). As Lind notes, "Beginning with the census of 1920, there is evidence of a distinct increase in the population of Hawaiian ancestry, although this obviously would not be true were it not for the Island practice of classifying all persons with any Hawaiian ancestry as members of that group" (1980: 21). This increase in population statistics among "part-Hawaiians" would eventually become a sticking point in the debates over the rehabilitation proposal. The proposal for rehabilitation, SCR 2, stated that the proposed lands "be leased to persons of whole or part Hawaiian ancestry" (U.S. Congress 1920c: 188). In the early stages of the debate on the proposal, there was not even a discussion of blood quantum, let alone its use as a criterion for inclusion. This was the case because the Hawaiian elites who mobilized around the rehabilitation proposal justified it through an argument that Hawaiians were entitled to the lands which would be used for homesteading. Using a framework of social justice and legal claims, there was no need to distinguish among Hawaiians when it came to discussing eligibility because all were entitled. However, subsequent debates focused on various criteria to determine who would count as "native Hawaiian." By examining the different interests at work in this early stage of the hearings, I explore the logic behind the specific forms of Hawaiian racialization that made the final outcome of the HHCA possible.

In order to gain the attention of the congressmen, both Wise and Kalaniana'ole had to provide an overview of Hawaiian demographics in relation to the history of dispossession via both the Māhele of 1848 and the U.S.-backed overthrow, without letting the desires of the sugar interests overshadow their own concerns and legislative goals. Both of them took part in characterizing the Kanaka Maoli situation in relation to anti-Asian movements that were currently thriving in the islands as well as the United States, especially in California, where Chairman Curry actively campaigned against the Japanese.

In addition to the history of the Māhele and the situation of Kanaka Maoli in comparison to Chinese and Japanese, I examine two other key issues that emerged in the early stage of these debates. The first was the question of constitutionality and whether the Congress had the right to provide allotment lands for Hawaiians as per the proposal without violating the equal protection clause of the U.S. constitution. This question was grappled with in relation to the second key factor in the debates—the comparison between Kanaka Maoli and American Indians vis-à-vis colonial history and land rights. As we will see in chapter 6, both the issues of constitutionality regarding the HHCA and the question of including Hawaiians within U.S. governmental policy on American Indians persist today in the urgent politics of the sovereignty struggle.

Two Competing Resolutions

True to the ideals underlying his territorial proposal in Senate Concurrent Resolution 2 (SCR 2), which outlined a plan for Hawaiian rehabilitation, Senator Wise underscored the dire condition of Hawaiians and advocated aiding Hawaiian recovery via homesteading provisions and privileges. SCR 2 requested that Congress amend the Organic Act to provide part of the public lands in Hawai'i as allotments for settlement by associations and "persons of whole or part Hawaiian ancestry."

Senator Wise pushed for SCR 2 while Representatives Shingle, Rawlins, and Lyman along with Governor McCarthy all lobbied for House Concurrent Resolution 28 (HCR 28), which would change the land laws in Hawai'i to support the sugar elite. The House resolution was eventually conditioned on making "adequate provision" for the purposes set forth in SCR 2 for the Hawaiian rehabilitation through land leasing. This specific connection to the Hawaiian rehabilitation proposal was referred to later as the "joker" in the bill, since it would serve as a rationale for liberal provisions for the sugar elite who would then provide the funds for carrying out the "rehabilitation scheme" (*Pacific Commercial Advertiser* 1920f).

When the United States unilaterally annexed Hawai'i in 1898, the Congress did not apply extensive homesteading laws such as the federal Homestead Act of 1862 to the territory because it was assumed that the Hawaiian Land Act of 1895 under the Republic of Hawaii (as discussed in chapter 2) gave sufficient prioritization to the settlement of small-scale farmers. The Hawaii Organic Act of 1900 provided that the earlier land law under the Republic of Hawaii would remain intact and dictated the uses of the public lands "ceded" to the United States. But the Organic Act had two restrictions: a five-year limit (reduced from twenty-one years) on agricultural leasing and a maximum limit of one thousand acres allowed for leasing by any corporation. A revision in 1908 of the act changed these terms by redefining the lease terms to fifteen years. But it included a withdrawal clause covering lands needed for homesteading or public purposes (Murakami 1991: 45). While the withdrawal clause disappeared in the 1910 amendments to the act, the thousand-acre limit was still in place and was strongly contested by those who were pro-sugar. House Concurrent Resolution 28 requested that Congress amend the Organic Act to empower Hawai'i's territorial governor to exempt one-fifth of highly cultivated sugar lands under general leasing from the homestead laws and to continue existing leases for the highest bidder (Hasager 1997; Murakami 1991: 45; Vause 1962).

SENATE CONCURRENT RESOLUTION NO. 2
10th Legislature, Territory of Hawaii
WHEREAS the distribution of lands under the Kingdom of Hawaii, whereby the power to alienate the same has resulted in the loss to the Hawaiian people of a large part of their original birthright so that the members of the race now constitute a large part of the floating population crowding into the congested tenement districts of the larger towns and cities of the Territory under conditions which will inevitably result in the extermination of the race; and

WHEREAS members of the Hawaiian race or blood should be encouraged to return to the status of independent and contented tillers of the soil, preserving to posterity the valuable and sturdy traits of the race, peculiarly adapted to the islands comprising the Territory of Hawaii, inhabited and governed by peoples of their race and blood as their birthright for a long period of time prior to annexation with the United States of America; and

WHEREAS there is now available or soon to become available large tracts of public lands under the control of the United States of American from which suitable areas could readily be set aside permanently as government lands subject to long term leases and renewals of leases for the encouragement of associations of colonies of individuals of Hawaiian blood for mutual growth and help to bring a rehabilitation of their race and to furnish an incentive for the preservation of the best characteristics of an independent citizenship of Hawaiian blood; now, therefore, be it

RESOLVED by the Senate of the Legislature of the Territory of Hawaii, the House of Representatives concurring, that the Congress of the United States of America be respectfully petitioned herein to make such amendments to the Organic Act of the Territory of Hawaii, or by other provisions deemed proper in the premises, that from time to time there may be set aside suitable portions of the public lands of the Territory of Hawaii by allotments to or for associations, settlements, or individuals of Hawaiian blood in whole or in part, the fee simple title of such lands to remain in the government, but the use thereof to be available under such restrictions as to improvements, size of lots, occupation and otherwise as may be provided for said purposes by a commission duly authorized or otherwise giving preference rights in such homestead leases for the purposes hereof as may be deemed just and suitable by the Congress assembled; and be it further

RESOLVED that copies of this Resolution be engrossed for presentation by the Delegate of the Territory of Hawaii to the Speaker of the House of Representatives, the President of the Senate, and the President of the United States.

HOUSE CONCURRENT RESOLUTION NO. 28
10th Legislature, Territory of Hawaii
WHEREAS, of highly cultivated public lands of the Territory of Hawaii, which have not yet been disposed of to private ownership, there remain but approximately twenty-six thousand acres; and

WHEREAS, it is deemed necessary and proper that the said remaining areas of public lands be conserved and administered in such a way as to promote the best interests and welfare of the Territory of Hawaii, and the citizens and taxpayers generally; and

WHEREAS, the experiences of the past have demonstrated that the present land laws under which public lands of the Territory are administered are inadequate and are so fixed and unchangeable in character as to prevent the territorial administration from formulating and carrying into effect, a land policy suitable to the particular conditions which exist in this Territory regarding the said public lands, and to meet the varying conditions in the several parts of the Territory; and

WHEREAS, it has been demonstrated by the recent land drawings held in connection with the Waiakea and Papaaloa homesteads, that many homesteaders who became entitled, at said drawings, to take up homesteads on said tracts were and are financially and otherwise unable to undertake the heavy financial and other responsibilities attendants upon the cultivation of said lots; and

WHEREAS, at said drawings there were available for homesteading a total of two hundred sixty-one lots, and there were two thousand nine hundred and five applicants for homesteads who participated in said drawings; and

WHEREAS, but for the inelasticity of the present land laws, a sufficient number of properly qualified, capable and bona fide homesteaders could have been selected from said two thousand nine hundred and five applicants; and

WHEREAS, we believe that the remaining public lands of the Territory should be so administered as to produce the greatest benefit to the greatest number of our citizens, and not for the advantage of a small class; and

WHEREAS, the said remaining public lands can be, through proper legislation, so handled and administered as to relieve in part, the present heavy tax burden and at the same time, to build up an independent body of small farmers in this community; now, therefore, be it

RESOLVED by the House of Representatives. The Senate concurring, that the Congress of the United States of America and it is hereby requested to amend the Organic Act of the Territory of Hawaii substantially in accordance with the proposed Act hereto attached and marked Exhibit "A," *after adequate provisions have been made by Congress aforesaid to accomplish the purpose set forth in Senate Concurrent Resolution No. 2* [emphasis added]

(1) So that when any general lease of highly cultivated public lands shall expire, the Governor and the land commissioner of the Territory of Hawaii, may, in their discretion, withdraw from the operation of the homestead laws of the Territory as now existing, not to exceed one-fifth of the area of lands covered by any such general lease, and to lease the same by sale at public auction, for a term not to exceed fifteen years, upon such terms and conditions as may be advantageous to the Territory of Hawaii; provided, however, that the lower Kekaha cane lands, containing an area of about three thousand acres, and four-fifths (4/5) of the Waimanalo cane lands shall be left out of the provision of this Resolution; and

(2) So that in the case of arid lands which are capable of being converted into agricultural lands by the development of under lying and/or contiguous waters for irrigation purposes, the Governor and the land commissioner, with the approval of the land board may lease such arid lands to any person, firm or corporation upon such terms and conditions as may be of advantage to the Territory of Hawaii, and for a sufficient length of time to induce such person, firm or corporation to invest capital in the development of the said water resources for the irrigation of said land, such lease to be without the withdrawal clause now provided for by law; and

(3) So that when any general lease of agricultural lands is about to expire, or has expired, or when any homestead lots are not taken up, or taken up and abandoned, the land commissioner with the approval of the Governor, may be authorized to enter into a contract with any person, firm, or corporation for the continued cultivation of said agricultural lands, until such time as the same may be opened up and available for homesteading, or until such time as the said homestead lot or lots shall be again occupied by a homesteader or homesteaders, and to require of such homesteaders who thereafter shall occupy said lands, that they reimburse such person, firm, or corporation for the expenditures so made in continuing the cultivation of said lands; and

(4) So that any person, who, or whose husband or wife, shall have previously homesteaded not to exceed ten acres of public land, may be entitled to exercise an additional homestead right; and

(5) So as to authorize and empower the governor, the land commissioners, and the land board of the Territory of Hawaii to exercise the power and right of selection of homesteaders in all cases of applications for homestead land, and the right and authority to pass upon the qualifications and capability of any such applicant as a homesteader of such lands; and

(6) So as to allow any citizen to exercise a preference right who has, or whose predecessors in interest have, continuously resided on, and improved any parcel of public land since January 1, 1909; and

(7) So that the commissioner of public lands may be authorized to lease not to exceed one thousand acres of pasture land without submitting the same to land board for approval; and be it further

RESOLVED that copies of this Resolution and of said exhibit be duly certified and forwarded by the Secretary of the Territory of Hawaii to the President of the Senate and the Speaker of the House of Representatives of the Congress of the United States of America, to the Secretary of the Interior of the United States, and to the Territorial Delegate to Congress.

Anti-Asian Support for Native Rehabilitation

Both Kānaka Maoli—Senator Wise and Delegate Kalaniana'ole—as well as all of the white American participants (from the Congress and the territory) seized upon the prospects of Native rehabilitation as an anti-Asian remedy. This was not entirely new; as early as 1911, Delegate Kalaniana'ole presented his case to Congress on the so-called Asian flooding when Hawaiians protested Asian laborers being hired for public works. More often than not, this concern fed into an anti-Asian politics supported by not only white Americans within the territory but also the Hawaiian political leaders such as the prince who strived to secure Hawaiian votes in the legislature. Regarding the unemployment situation, Delegate Kalaniana'ole often negatively focused on Asians in Hawai'i—shifting the burden of responsibility away from the federal government that failed to enforce hiring guidelines for public contractors working on projects such as military fortifications.

The other representatives' perception of the Japanese threat was always articulated in contrast to their understanding of the goals of Americanization. Representative Curry, chair of the House committee, cited a 1917 article by Judge William W. Morrow of the U.S. Circuit Court of Appeals, which projected that within the next decade the majority of the voting population in Hawai'i would be the adult children of Japanese immigrants. The report by Morrow also speculated that the majority would "naturally tend to the building up of Japanese political ideals in the Territory, unless Hawai'i was Americanized" (U.S. Congress 1920c: 18). Chairman Curry expressed his concerns through three actions. First, he petitioned the Japanese parliament to rescind the Japanese law that allowed dual citizenship for Japanese Americans (20). Second, he developed policy amendments that would authorize the "right of selection" by the land commissioner to discriminate against anyone deemed "unsatisfactory as a homesteader" (21)—there was no law at the time that prohibited "aliens" from owning land outside of government lands. And third, Chairman Curry proposed to institute changes in hiring practices where Japanese were present, especially in jobs produced by government contracts.

Henry J. Lyman, a representative in the territorial legislature of Hawaii, expressed his resentment that the federal government allowed its contractors to hire the Japanese "because they work the cheapest" (U.S. Congress 1920c: 22). He argued that this retarded Americanization because it hindered the well-being of American citizens. And Hawaiian senator Wise also argued that Hawaiians in trade labor "could not compete with the Asiatics" (40). Delegate Kalaniana'ole argued for better employment opportunities, claiming that Hawaiians were being left on the fringes of the job market. He claimed that the situation was largely due to employment practices which tended to be geared toward hiring Asians who were not U.S. citizens because they could be employed for lesser wages. The delegate petitioned Congress to restrict labor on military fortifications to citizens, presumably male (41).[3]

Senator Wise and Delegate Kalaniana'ole also made claims regarding Kānaka Maoli that were distinct from issues facing Asians regarding American citizenship. While asserting their Americanness, they simultaneously claimed that Hawaiians held a distinct position given their prior status under the Hawaiian kingdom. Hawaiians recognized as former citizens of the kingdom, then, were still entitled to the lands in question at this time.

The Māhele and the Question of Entitlement

Senator Wise took up the details of the Māhele land division under the Hawaiian kingdom to argue the issue of entitlement in support of the bill. He noted that Hawaiian commoners received very little land in the Māhele division while King Kamehameha and the other chiefs and *konohiki* secured 1,619,000 acres and 984,000 acres were held for the crown. Senator Wise specified, "The common people, however, received only 28,000 acres and always contended that these Crown lands went to the crown in trust for the common people" (U.S. Congress 1920c: 28). He noted that the king had sold his lands to the missionaries but also maintained: "We do not begrudge the missionaries the taking of these lands. I believe they were entitled to these lands for the services rendered to the Hawaiian people. Some got very small portions. I just wanted to bring this in to show how liberal the Hawaiians were to the foreigners . . . that when the Hawaiians had everything they gave everything, and now that the United States has control of all the government lands, *we come to the United States to-day and expect you to have the same feeling and the same liberality and the same liberal spirit, and return some of these lands to the Hawaiians*" (29; emphasis added). Wise figured land as "payment" to "entitled" missionaries in a gift/reciprocity concept. His culturally specific analysis reasoned that the United States was in the position to give as Hawaiians once "gave" to the United States. He asserted that there was a U.S. takeover—the theft of Hawaiian lands. But the solution he proposed was not the "return of stolen goods." Rather, he considered a return of the land to be comparable to the perceived generosity of Hawaiians historically. His proposal was about "liberal" spirit, much like the notion of Hawaiians' "aloha spirit"—an anticapitalist logic where "if one has, one should give." Even while this "gifting" was inscribed ultimately as a "return" of the land, this stance was never fully resolved in logical, moral, or legal terms during the hearings. Hence, the contradiction remained ever present.

> MR. WISE: *We contend that the crown lands belong to the common people.*
> MR. DOWELL: How would you discriminate between the citizens there?
> MR. STRONG: He would have to have an admixture of Hawaiian blood.
> MR. KALANIANAOLE: Were these crown lands under the monarch open to settlement by citizens?

MR. WISE: No.

MR. KALANIANAOLE: Then these lands were held by the crown in trust for the common people?

MR. WISE: Yes; of the Hawaiian race.

THE CHAIRMAN: There is an equity and justice in saying that these crown lands belonged to the Hawaiian people.

MR. DOWELL: I want to get the information.

MR. WISE: I believe the Hawaiians should have the first choice.

MR. WISE: There is only a little of this land left.

THE CHAIRMAN: And there are only about 40,000 Hawaiians and part-Hawaiians.

MR. DOWELL: Suppose he discriminates between Hawaiians?

MR. WISE: The reason why this Senate resolution number 2 was introduced was to overcome that difficulty. The Hawaiian people, those of Hawaiian blood, have rights to these crown lands, for the Government of the United States and the Territory have given them these rights. *We feel that we have not got all that is coming to us.* (U.S. Congress 1920c: 32; emphasis added)

After Senator Wise's contention that the crown lands belong to the common people, Dowell asked him to specifically distinguish which people. Senator Strong intervened that the person would have to have "Hawaiian blood," which he did not quantify—meaning he was unconcerned with limiting eligibility *among* Kanaka Maoli at this stage. Delegate Kalaniana'ole asked about the status of the crown lands with regard to settlement by citizens— meaning former citizens of the Hawaiian kingdom. Senator Wise claimed that these lands were not open to settlement, while Delegate Kalaniana'ole asked whether or not the lands were held in trust for the "common people" by the monarch. Senator Wise answered yes, "of Hawaiian race," which suggests that "the common people" was Kalaniana'ole's code for the *maka'āinana*. The chair even admitted that one could then, by extension, consider the crown lands as belonging to the Hawaiian people. But Senator Dowell foresaw the problem in defining who is Hawaiian and distinguishing among Hawaiians. Senator Wise countered his concern by arguing that all Hawaiians, regardless of "degree" of blood, are entitled to the lands, while Delegate Kalaniana'ole appeared to use his position to strategically open up a space for Wise to make these assertions, because Kalaniana'ole already knew the answers to these questions.[4] "My one desire is to point out how these lands, which we are now asking to be set aside for the rehabilitation of the Hawaiian race, in which a one-third interest of the common people had been recognized, but ignored in the division, and which had reverted to the crown, presumably in trust for the people, were taken over by the republic of Hawaii by an article of the constitution of the republic of Hawaii" (Kalaniana'ole 1921: 129). The delegate further argued, "By annexation these lands became a part of the public lands of the United States, and by the provisions of the organic act are under the custody and control of the Territory of Hawaii" (129–39).

In the hearings, the problem of legally defining who is Hawaiian and distinguishing among Hawaiians would be highlighted once those involved in determining the future of Hawai'i's land laws shifted their focus away from the rationale of Hawaiian entitlement. Eventually, discussions as to who would count as Hawaiian for the leasing proposal focused on differences between "full blood Hawaiians" and "part-Hawaiians." But, at this stage, as one can see in the following excerpt, congressional members somewhat unfamiliar with Hawaiians as a people were relatively open to inclusive definitions of who counted as Hawaiian and were not particularly bothered by an inclusive definition of "native Hawaiian." Nonetheless, territorial representatives argued strongly against inclusive definitions, backed by their firsthand knowledge about Hawaiians. Who counted as "native Hawaiian" for whom and why?

MR. DOWELL: One other matter. I notice in the resolution that you provide for those of Hawaiian blood.

MR. WISE: Yes.

MR. DOWELL: How far do you go with that?

MR. WISE: Anybody with Hawaiian blood.

MR. DOWELL: How much do you consider to be within the resolution; what is your plan?

MR. WISE: I contend that *anybody, even to the thirty-second degree should be included.*

MR. DOWELL: And the thirty-second degree—

MR. WISE: If he had Hawaiian blood in him.

MR. DOWELL: Would be entitled to homestead the same as a full-blood Hawaiian?

MR. WISE: Yes, sir.

MR. HUMPHREYS: I do not think that would be a big problem.

MR. DOWELL: How many mixed blood people are there?

MR. WISE: Sixty thousand six hundred and sixty estimated in 1918.

MR. DOWELL: What are there?

MR. WISE: Mostly white.

MR. DOWELL: Mostly Americans?

MR. WISE: Americans, English, Germans, Europeans, and Chinese.

MR. STRONG: Are there very few Japanese?

MR. WISE: Very few.

GOV. MCCARTHY: There are quite a number of Chinese.

MR. DOWELL: About how many?

GOV. MCCARTHY: The Chinese and Hawaiian mixture makes a fine people. (U.S. Congress 1920c: 45; emphasis added)

Senator Dowell raised the question of defining "Hawaiian" in terms of entitlement, and the debate soon attempted to distinguish among racially mixed Hawaiians. Senator Dowell seemed initially concerned about the number of "mixed bloods." But Senator Wise unequivocally answered: "Anybody, even to the thirty-second degree should be included." This marks the first time ever that a specific blood quantum definition was proposed. Yet in an ironic turn, Senator Wise's effort to emphasize the broad-based, inclusive point of entitlement began to circulate as *the proposed definition*. But this new definition of 1/32 seems to have been introduced merely in order to distinguish Hawaiians from non-Hawaiians in the discussion of indigenous social rehabilitation. It had nothing to do with exclusion at that point.

Senator Dowell continued to investigate the nature of Hawaiian entitlement by probing into specific statistics related to various constituencies of racially mixed Hawaiians. The questions initially began with examples of those also of European ancestry, which prompted Senator Dowell to ask about the Japanese in terms of mixture. Governor McCarthy of Hawai'i interrupted that there were a number of Chinese mixed with Hawaiians. When Senator Dowell asked for statistical counts again, McCarthy praised the racially mixed Hawaiians and Chinese, as if to assure others that this was the next-best hybrid besides those of Hawaiian and European ancestry.

Although the issue of entitlement was far from resolved, at many points in the debate participants focused on issues of preservation and perpetuation of the "Hawaiian race." The goal of returning Hawaiians "back to the land" was soon constructed in terms of charity and protection. Chairman Curry put it in these terms: "Governor, here is the proposition. We are talking away from what is before the committee, or what the committee has in its mind, I think. This land is to be homesteaded for the preservation of the Hawaiian race, for the Hawaiian people, the Hawaiian pure blood and to the 32d degree. The only reason for us to enact this legislation is to protect those people and give them an opportunity to perpetuate their race" (U.S. Congress 1920c: 79). Harry Irwin, attorney general of Hawaii, offered his basis for support of the bill in similar terms: "There can be no doubt . . . that *when these Crown lands were ceded to and accepted by the United States, they were ceded and accepted free and clear of any trust* whatever. . . . In my opinion, therefore, this proposed legislation can be sustained, if at all, not upon any theory that the Hawaiian people ever had any *equitable right or title to these lands,* but only upon the theory suggested in the fifth subdivision as hereinabove set forth, namely *for the purpose of rehabilitating a race of people* who, through circumstances, perhaps beyond their control, are in danger of extermination" (162; emphasis added). Irwin argued against supporting the bill because of the legal claims or rights of Hawaiians to the land and instead emphasized the intention to rehabilitate the Hawaiians.

The Question of Constitutionality

There was a question as to whether the HHCA would pass constitutional challenges based on the equal protection clause of the Fourteenth Amendment because it provided exclusively for native Hawaiians. Attorney General Irwin continued to raise the issue even though others had addressed it in earlier debates. "It has been suggested by some and emphatically stated by others, that legislation of this kind may not be constitutionally enacted for the reason as suggested and stated that it would be class legislation, and therefore in violation of the Constitution of the United States. No particular article of the Constitution has been suggested as being prohibitive of this legislation, nor do I know of any such prohibitive provision of the Constitution" (U.S. Congress 1920c: 162). The reintroduction of the goal of rehabilitation, however, prompted the participants to evade the issues of political status and land title altogether—even though they found the idea of rehabilitation clearly problematic as well.

The situation of American Indians became a key factor at this point in the debates. The representatives worked out the issue of class legislation and entitlement through analogies with American Indians at the time:

MR. DOWELL: We were dealing with a tribe, and we gave them those lands by virtue of an agreement that we made with them. It seems to me that the Indian proposition is hardly parallel with the question we have before us.

MR. CHAIRMAN: I think it is, because the Hawaiians were deprived of their lands without any say on their part, either under the kingdom, under the republic, or under the United States Government.

MR. DOWELL: Her equity. That is true.

THE CHAIRMAN: And the Indians were deprived of their lands regardless of their wishes or welfare, except to say, "You move away from here and we'll give you this. You go away from Georgia and Alabama and Mississippi over into Oklahoma and we will give you those lands. We want these ourselves." Of course there is a treaty proposition, although they were forced to sign. When they would not sign, we went to war with them and made them sign.

MR. DOWELL: That is true, but in principle have we not a different proposition because we have no government or tribe or organization to deal with here?

THE CHAIRMAN: We have the law of the land of Hawaii from ancient times right down to the present where the preferences were given to certain classes of people.

MR. WEAVER: Mr. Chairman, you can legislate for a class if you legislate evenly for that class. No citizen of Hawaii has any title vested or otherwise in the public lands. Therefore when you say that you will allow native Hawaiians to enter upon these lands upon certain terms, it does not carry the idea of class legislation. (170)

Here the issue of class legislation emerged as an issue regarding constitutionality. In response to questions of the basis on which one could legislate for Hawaiian people as a class, Curry suggested that the history of prior class distinctions among Hawaiians was sufficient. Hawaiians as a class were distinct from non-Hawaiians.

The key issue became one of deprivation and responsibility, but the focus was not solely on the U.S. government. In this part of the debate, Hawaiian dispossession was a concern in relation to three different governing bodies— three distinctly different systems: the constitutional monarchy under the Hawaiian Kingdom; the Republic of Hawaii led by those who orchestrated the illegal and armed overthrow; and the United States. While little had changed for Hawaiians at large, their deprivation under the monarchy created an opportunity for the U.S. government to elevate itself above the actions of the kingdom—to demonstrate "her equity." Senator Dowell evoked the treaty status of Indians who hold land while the chair contended that many treaties were unilaterally imposed in the first place and the removal of Indians from their lands had been coerced and enforced by threat and warfare. Senator Dowell insisted that in principle the Hawaiian case was fundamentally different from that of Indians because Hawaiians had no government, tribe, or organization.

The chair again turned the focus on the state of the past Hawaiian monarchy—ancient Hawai'i—where inequality and differences in access to resources rested on status based on lineage, regarded here as "certain classes of people." Senator Weaver intervened by suggesting that to legislate for Hawaiian land leasing was constitutional if done "evenly," to be contrasted with the unevenness of status under the kingdom. He claimed, "No citizen of Hawaii has any title vested or otherwise in the public lands." It seems that he meant any citizen with the exception of Hawaiians. In summary, Senator Weaver argued: "Therefore when you say that you will allow native Hawaiians to enter upon these lands upon certain terms, it does not carry the idea of class legislation" (170). It is unclear what he was arguing for and why, because he offered no distinction between Hawaiians of different "admixtures." It may be that he understood that no other citizens in Hawai'i, other than Hawaiians, claimed rights to the so-called public lands. Thus, the aiding of Hawaiians in securing leases on these lands would not be considered discriminatory toward other citizens in Hawai'i.

The senators discussed class legislation by talking about the transformed political status of Hawaiians. A key question was whether the United States was under obligation because of prior land dealings and, if so, how to negotiate that responsibility when politically dealing with a distinct class of people that would become racialized through blood quantum. Since Hawaiians counted as U.S. citizens, their position was mediated through and in relation to the "racially unmarked" citizens—white Americans, especially those on the continent—and "raced" noncitizens, particularly those from Asia (170). Whether the responsibility was framed in legal, moral, humanitarian, or reciprocal terms, the question remained: to whom must they be responsible? Who was considered to be in need of help, and was that help a form of entitlement?

As the arguments and justifications shifted away from trust obligation and entitlement concerns, the definition of the group under consideration became more exclusive. In any case, the federal solicitor of the Department of the Interior submitted an opinion which favored the constitutionality of the bill by explaining that the federal government had already established a policy of favoring certain classes of people such as veterans and Indians (130–31). But by the end of this hearing, representatives had found other ways to sidestep the problem of class legislation. They did this not by underscoring the political rights of Hawaiians but by limiting the goals of native rehabilitation within the confines of protectionist welfare frameworks.

"The Kuhio Bill"

Despite objections that the two resolutions were in opposition to each other, Chairman Curry suggested the commission develop a single bill by bringing together HCR 28 and SCR2. He explained that in order to get any proposal from the territory considered by Congress at the time, they would need a special rule from the Rules Committee, and that only one proposal was likely to be given time (4). Curry questioned the governor several times as to why the two bills could not come together. In response, McCarthy repeatedly explained very diplomatically that "Senator Wise's proposition is another thing, and it would be sort of new legislation, we feel that the best way to handle it would be by a separate bill" (110). Wise confirmed this, but Curry persisted, "If they do not conflict, why can you not put them in one bill?" Curry pressured them to consolidate, which led to a backlash back in the islands among the planters who were opposed to rehabilitation.

The combination bill was drafted by Harry Irwin, attorney general of Hawai'i.[5] House Resolution 12683 (HR 12683) became known as the "Kuhio Bill" because it was presented to Congress by Delegate Kalaniana'ole (also known as Prince Kūhiō) on February 21, 1920, during the 66th Congress, second session (HR 12683 had a companion Senate bill, S 3971) (Uyehara

1982: 55 n. 50; Murakami 1991: 46). House Resolution 12683 specified no minimal blood definition of "Hawaiian," but that was about all that was retained from SCR 2.

To the surprise of many, HR 12683 included newly proposed amendments to the 1910 Organic Act. For one, the bill would allow for the public auction of *all* cultivated public lands rather than just one-fifth. Second, it repealed provisions that would have required homesteading on demand of twenty-five persons. Third, it allowed the leases to be executed without any withdrawal clause at all. These changes shocked a number of people because they went far beyond what was called for in the "pro-sugar" HCR 28. Even Secretary of the Interior Frank Lane declared that the Kuhio Bill would "kill homesteading"—not just for Hawaiians but for Hawaiʻi's general population (Vause 1962: iv; Murakami 1991: 46).

Hawaiʻi newspaper coverage described a mass meeting held in ʻAʻala Park in Honolulu in response to news of the combined bill. There, J. F. Raymond—who was seeking nomination as Democratic candidate for delegate to Congress instead—asserted that the rehabilitation amendment "would place Hawaiians in the same category as the American Indians on the government reservations in the mainland, instead of giving them a fighting chance to face the world like other American citizens" (*Pacific Commercial Advertiser* 1920i).

The next day, the *Pacific Commercial Advertiser* warned that if HR 12683 passed, it would permit leases to planters with no withdrawal clause, where the highly cultivated lands could be leased at auction to the highest bidder, with 30 percent of the rental monies derived annually to be funneled into a Hawaiian Loan Fund. The report also noted that this new arrangement would place Kanaka Maoli on second-class "public lands" in the territory, thus even more dependent on the financial advances made to them.

J. H. Raymond, a surgeon and rancher who headed Raymond Ranch, urged that no Hawaiian should "barter his birthrights for a veritable mess of pottage" (Burrows 1920). He warned: "The proposed statute plays directly into the hands of the powerful corporations doing business here—in many cases founded by those who came to Hawaii bearing the banner of the cross upon their shoulders and the message of ʻpeace on earth, good will toward men' in their hearts—and reduces the Hawaiian people to the state of the lowliest blanket Indian, living on the sufferance and bounty of those corporations and of the federal government." In another move, Raymond, along with Lorrin Andrews and Jonah Kumalae, sent a cablegram of protest to Washington. They were angry, for they were certain that Congress would not have taken deliberate action to hand over the best lands to the planters and kill homesteading if the commission had not agreed to link the two territorial resolutions, with HCR 28 revised to be contingent on allowing for SCR 2. As these men pointed out, the newly revised proposal went against the sentiments of the territorial legislature that mandated the commission in the first place. Wise denied any role in the matter, as did everyone else. The protestors surmised that Delegate Kalaniana'ole had acted deliberately with the knowledge and consent of the legislative commission (*Pacific Commercial Advertiser* 1920l). Governor McCarthy pleaded that there was a simple misunderstanding and that he and the rest of the commission were surprised by local opposition (*Pacific Commercial Advertiser* 1920a, 1920b, 1920k).

House Concurrent Resolution 28 was amended so it would be effective only "after adequate provision has been made by Congress to accomplish the purposes set forth in Senate Concurrent Resolution No. 2 herewith adopted." The amendment gave Wise the opportunity to wipe out homestead laws in general and substitute them with his own rehabilitation plan for Kanaka Maoli to be financed by the leasing of all the highly cultivated lands in the territory by the plantations (*Pacific Commercial Advertiser* 1920c). But Wise explained, "I inserted an amendment in there after my resolution had gone through. I realized after my resolution had gone through the legislature and this legislation came up for consideration in the Senate that if I did not put that amendment in, my resolution would be of no effect" (111). However, the point of conflict with those in protest was that Congress was convinced that the leasing of all of Hawai'i's highly cultivated lands would be necessary in order to adequately fund the Hawaiian rehabilitation bill. Thus, the linkage of the two opposing resolutions was not the only problem; beyond that, it looked as if homesteading at large was on the brink of being effectively killed under the guise of Hawaiian rehabilitation.

Conclusion

On April 18, 1920, HR 12683 was recommitted as HR 13500, still framed as a resolution for Hawaiian rehabilitation. But HR 13500 also gave strength to the pro-sugar position. It exempted all sugar cane lands and any other lands under existing contract from the available lands to be set aside for Hawaiian

rehabilitation, while it also insulated the lease lands negotiated under Kalākaua's reign from homesteading for Hawaiians (Murakami 1991: 46–47).
Even worse, HR 13500 designated remote lands with poor soil and with little
water or infrastructure for homesteading by Kanaka Maoli (47). Congress
deferred action on HR 13500 and, accordingly, another hearing was sched-
uled. In the meantime, Senator Wise and the others returned to Hawai'i
where they negotiated several compromises in the territorial legislature,
including the definition of "native Hawaiian."

The Virile, Prolific, and Enterprising

Part-Hawaiians and the Problem with Rehabilitation

> It is true that the aboriginal Hawaiians of the pure blood are dying out; but it is not
> true that the Hawaiian race as defined in this act is dying out. The law would go so
> far as to include within the Hawaiian race Polynesians of as little as one thirty-sec-
> ond aboriginal blood. That race is not dying out, as is shown by the census figures;
> and yet that is the race that is purported to be rehabilitated by this bill.
>
> —A. G. M. Robertson at the HHCA hearings, December 1920

THE TESTIMONY OF A. G. M. ROBERTSON marked a turning point in the HHCA bill's transformation because his statements carried wide authority. As a former court judge in the territory, Robertson offered one of the most probing testimonies in opposition to the bill. During the previous session of the Sixty-Sixth Congress, he had already issued a report of his own that documented objections to the rehabilitation bill (Robertson 1920) even though he neglected to attend any of the hearings held on the matter in Hawai'i (U.S. Congress 1920b: 130–31). In Washington, during the second round of debates on the HHCA proposal, which this time were held before the Senate Committee on Territories during the Sixty-Sixth Congress (third session), Robertson's testimony was particularly instrumental in redefining who counted as Hawaiian.

Robertson and his family had a long political history in Hawai'i. He was born in 1867 to Scottish parents who had migrated to the islands before he was born. His father was a legal advisor to Kamehameha IV and Kameha-meha V and was the judge who ruled in the case of Queen Emma Kameha-meha V in May 1864 (discussed in chapter 2), where the decision determined the creation of the crown lands (Hobbs 1939: 66). After being schooled in Oakland, California, Robertson attended Yale Law School (Gilman 1943: 6). He was at Yale during the 1893 U.S.–backed overthrow of the kingdom but soon returned to Hawai'i with his degree. Once there, he joined the Hono-lulu Rifles—the same militia that formed the basis of the Hawaiian League that forced Kalākaua to sign the "Bayonet Constitution" and later instigated the overthrow. In 1895, Robertson served as staff to Sanford B. Dole, president of the Republic of Hawaii. Robertson also held rank as captain and judge advocate on the Hawaiian military commission for the trial of state prisoners on charges of treason for their attempts to restore the queen to the throne—the very same commission that tried John H. Wise and Jonah Kūhiō Kalaniana'ole and found them guilty of treason. Robertson was also deputy attorney general of the Republic of Hawaii in 1895 and a member of the House of Representatives (of the territory) in 1896, 1898, and 1901. He was admitted to the bar of the Hawai'i Supreme Court and in 1899 to the bar of the U.S. Supreme Court and the U.S. Court of Appeals for the Ninth Circuit. An organizer of the Republican Party in Hawai'i in 1900, he served as a delegate to Republican national conventions in 1904, 1908, and again in 1932. Before becoming a U.S. district judge, he served as a member of the Republican national committee from 1904 to 1910.[1] In 1911, President Taft appointed him to be chief justice of the territory and President Wilson reappointed him in 1916. By 1918, he had entered into private practice.

Here, in December 1920, Robertson testified at the hearings on HR 13500, in his capacity as legal counsel for the Parker Ranch—at over 200,000 acres, the largest cattle ranch under single ownership in the United States (Whitehead 1992: 161).[2] A very different set of actors from the territory participated in this second hearing from those who made up the first commission. There was a cadre of witnesses, many of whom were white American lawyers who represented business strongholds in the islands and had a vested interest in Hawaiian lands. Although the national platform of the Republican Party declared support for the rehabilitation of the Hawaiian people, the Big Five business interests did not support HR 13500 (*Honolulu Star-Bulletin* 1921a: 7). But winning their support was vital to the passage of the HHCA, and, as we will see, it came with a high price. In opposition to the rehabilitation portions of the bill, these territorial lawyers, politicians, and businessmen asserted limited notions of indigeneity in relation to their own assumptions about assimilation, "blood absorption," and Americanization. Along with Robertson, there were George M. McClellan, head of the Honolulu Chamber of Commerce; W. B. Pittman, who represented the Raymond Ranch (and who was brother to Senator Key Pittman of Nevada who took part in the Senate committee at the time) (Kalaniana'ole 1921b, report to the legislature: 8);

Figure 5. Reverend Akaiko Akana and Charles Chillingworth. HAWAII STATE ARCHIVES, MAUDE
JONES COLLECTION.

and B. G. Rivenbaugh, former commissioner of public lands in the territory,
who served as the delegate's secretary. Other than Delegate Kalaniana'ole,
there was one other Hawaiian participant, since Wise did not take part
in this round—the Reverend Akaiko Akana of the Kawaiaha'o Church (figure 5), the first Christian church in Hawai'i, which was built between 1836
and 1842.

Senator Harry S. New of Indiana chaired the committee, which was
composed of eleven senators: George P. McLean, Connecticut; Wesley L.
Jones, Washington; Warren G. Harding, Ohio; Frederick Hale, Maine; William E. Borah, Idaho; Reed Smoot, Utah; Key Pittman, Nevada; Robert L.
Owen, Oklahoma; James D. Phelan, California; John Nugent, Idaho; and
George Chamberlain, Oregon (U.S. Congress 1920b: 2).[3] The majority of the
senators were from western states and differed a great deal from representatives from the previous hearing who were largely from the south—both
regions are known for distinctly different historical treatment of American
Indians.

This chapter takes up the second round of debate on House Resolution
13500 (a revision of HR 12683) before the Senate Committee on Territo-

ries in December 1920. HR 13500 became known as the "Kuhio Bill" because the attorney general had drafted it with Delegate Kūhiō Kalaniana'ole. HR 13500 exempted all sugar lands already cultivated from the definition of "available lands" meant to be set aside for homesteading once the leases expired (Murakami 1991: 46–47; Hasager 1997: 171–72). It explicitly designated arid and poor lands for Hawaiians and deleted provisions in the earlier draft that would have freed up additional lands as needed for homesteading (Murakami 1991: 47). The lease periods envisioned were shortened to 99 years from 999 years, and rather than have Congress decide whether to lease or homestead the cane lands, the territorial government was authorized to manage the public lands (Murakami 1991: 47; McGregor 1990: 21). It was in this version of the bill that the one-thirty-second blood quantum definition for "native Hawaiian" first appeared. After the last round of debates, the House Committee on the Territories added the clause extending the benefits of the bill to those of one-thirty-second degree Hawaiian blood as first suggested by Hawai'i's Senator Wise (*Honolulu Star-Bulletin* 1921a: 7).

Participants hotly debated the notion of who "really" counted as Kanaka Maoli for the purposes of rehabilitation and therefore land leasing. The territorial witnesses focused on differences *among* Hawaiian people by blood quantum in order to challenge the one-thirty-second blood criterion embedded in the new draft. In doing so, they reframed the entire issue of defining Hawaiian identity by questioning who exactly was considered to be *in need* of rehabilitation. Moreover, they eventually went so far as to insist that the criterion defining Hawaiian should be "full-blood." In promoting such a criterion, they focused on repopulation as the key form of rehabilitation, which served to remove the focus from Hawaiian entitlements to the land in question. As such, the basis for changing the criterion that would define Hawaiian identity shifted from indigeneity to a category that was specifically racialized.

As the debates progressed, several major issues emerged as key interconnected problems. First was the prominence of racial mixing in Hawai'i that was changing notions of who would count as Hawaiian. Second, there was the possibility of selective assimilation of white-mixed "part-Hawaiians" over those who were Asian-mixed. And third, there was the strong push by prominent sugar and ranching interests in the formulation of the bills to limit the number of Hawaiians who would be eligible for rehabilitation and, in turn, limit the amount of lands allotted to Kanaka Maoli. As I argue in this chapter, this last factor—haole corporate interests—serves as an explanation for the changing rationale for rehabilitation and the push to displace the question of Hawaiians' entitlement to the land.

Dividing Hawaiians

By issuing charges of reverse discrimination, Robertson racialized the debates with a new intensity and in ways that framed concerns for Hawaiians as being against white Americans in the territory. By foregrounding controversial issues of both taxation and antiwhite racial discrimination, he called the proposal's constitutionality into question. Robertson opposed any tax funding from the territory going toward administering the HHCA because it would be money coming "out of the pocket of white taxpayers . . . and handed over to or . . . used for the benefit of the Hawaiian population—as we find it in the stated bill here—of one-thirty-second Polynesian blood" (U.S. Congress 1920b: 10). Robertson argued that the bill "cleave[d]" the island community in two, "separating the whites from Hawaiians and Part-Hawaiians, taxing one for the benefit of the other, discriminating against the one and favoring the other according to the color of his skin and the kind of blood that God has put in his veins" (14). He positioned himself as anti-discriminatory and focused on the distinction made between whites and Hawaiians as the main cleavage produced by the bill, and not the division he himself promoted between Kanaka Maoli in order to undermine the bill overall. Evoking an abstract logic of citizenship and equal rights, he framed the debate as though whites and Hawaiians were on equal footing, while excluding Asians and other peoples in Hawai'i from his analysis.

Delegate Kalaniana'ole questioned Robertson, remarking on the racial terms he employed. The delegate questioned the terms of whiteness embedded in Robertson's usage of "American." He asserted, "By the statement he has been making he is trying to lead you to believe that he is representing the white people. In Hawaii we do not know of such a thing as the white people. All we know is, we are all Americans. My belief is that the majority of the so-called white people are back [sic] of this bill" (U.S. Congress 1920b: 73). In claiming an American identity for all in the colonial territory, Kalaniana'ole seemed to be claiming an alignment of interests with Robertson. These parts of the debate reveal uneasiness on the part of the Hawaiian men about white men distinguishing themselves from Kānaka Maoli rather than seeing themselves together as "Americans." Later, Kalaniana'ole and Akana worked to disrupt the conflation of "American" with a white racial category —as though to mark the whiteness of "American" for the purpose of their own inclusion as Hawaiians who had claim to it as well—even while they also maintained that Hawaiians needed special attention because of the bleak future of Hawaiians "as a race."

Robertson focused discussion on which Hawaiians were "really" in need by translating issues of entitlement into a welfare discourse. Here, he identified the target population in specifically racialized and gendered ways defined by class and attached to blood notions of (in)compentency. Whereas in the beginning of the debates Robertson merely questioned the dividing line between whites and Hawaiians, he then shifted his focus to the specific division between "Hawaiians" (unmarked as unmixed) and "part-Hawaiians." Indeed, he argued that such a distinction had to be sustained when discussing Kanaka Maoli people at all. Robertson next proceeded to separate Hawaiians into two different race groups, the "pure" and the "part," focusing on rehabilitation in the strictest of terms: to save those who were dying out.

Robertson provided statistics to show that "part-Hawaiians" were a race different from "pure Hawaiians." The project of tending to Hawaiians' needs was reduced to the goal of stopping depopulation. Indeed, the 1919 census reported that the number of "pure Hawaiians" plummeted to 22,500 from 142,650 in 1826, while the "part-Hawaiian" population grew from 2,487 in 1872 to about 16,660 in 1919 (Murakami 1991: 44). But Robertson argued that since part-Hawaiians were increasing in numbers, there might be no justification for the entire bill. Robertson asserted, "The part-Hawaiian race must be differentiated from the Hawaiians of the pure blood, and the fact that they are not differentiated in this bill is one of my objections to it, and I believe one of the weaknesses of the bill" (U.S. Congress 1920b: 15). He claimed that the proposal would not make much positive difference to Kanaka Maoli while it would adversely affect white people in Hawai'i.

Robertson went on to make other sorts of distinctions between pure Hawaiians and part-Hawaiians: "The part Hawaiians, the part Caucasian, the part Chinese, and part Portuguese are a virile, prolific, and enterprising lot of people. They have large families and they raise them—they bring them up. These part Hawaiians have had the advantage, since annexation especially, of the American viewpoint and the advantage of a pretty good public school system, and they are an educated people. They are not in the same class with the pure bloods" (U.S. Congress 1920b: 15). Robertson focused on education and the holding of an American viewpoint as indices of assimilation. In each example, he offered no clear description of the other parts of the "admixture" of the various mixed-race figures he summoned, leaving one to wonder what the other racial makeup was of the part-Hawaiians or the part-Caucasians or the part-Chinese. Robertson raised issues of access to class mobility and privilege for mixed-race Hawaiians. The criterion he used to characterize the part-Hawaiians as "American" was based on a classic white Protestant work ethic that stressed competence: virile, prolific, and enterprising. With regard to their growth as a people who were not dying out, the increased reproduction among part-Hawaiians was not only marked as laborious (in the commercialist terms of market labor) but was also masculinized, with a focus on Kanaka Maoli men taking an active role in biological reproduction to strengthen their community. In this common sense, authentic aboriginal Hawaiians were the only ones in need, and thus in the class of pure bloods marked as passive, and therefore feminized as incompetent.

Ultimately, though, Robertson argued that even unmixed Hawaiians were probably beyond the rehabilitation proposed by the bill. For example, discussing full-bloods, he suggested, "The one kind of people do need something in the way of rehabilitation. Whether it can be accomplished by legislation or not is another thing. I think that the remedy is psychological rather than legislative" (U.S. Congress 1920b: 15). Decontextualized from American colonial history, Robertson's strategy for rehabilitating Kanaka Maoli did not account for material disparity or dispossession. Though he did concede that there was need among these Hawaiians, he suggested that their needs might be better met with individual, self-remedial solutions—not by any sort of state action.

Moreover, he adamantly opposed any measure that included "part Hawaiian people . . . [who] cannot be said to need any rehabilitation, and they are not properly put in the same class with the aboriginals in any statute on the subject" (U.S. Congress 1920b: 15). The part-Hawaiians were not considered to be indigent by Robertson: "They are not the proper objects of public charity. The taxpayers cannot, as I look at it, be legally taxed for their subsistence, because they are not in the class that need, that require, that are entitled to, any assistance. They are able to stand on their own feet" (ibid.). Here, it is clear that he is marking the competence of part-Hawaiians. But his analysis implied that the response to the presumed incompetence and indigence of the full-blood "aboriginals" was charity, and he rejected state-enacted welfare measures. His line of argument was dependent upon the position that Hawaiian land entitlement was a nonissue.

Robertson directly pointed to one Hawaiian witness who had offered testimony at the hearing—the Reverend Akaiko Akana of the Kawaiahaʻo Church. Akana was born in 1884 to a Chinese father and a Hawaiian mother. Like Senator Wise and Delegate Kalanianaʻole, he too was educated abroad. Akana studied at the Hartford Theological Seminary in Connecticut, which was known for training many of the early missionaries sent to Hawaiʻi before 1820.[4]

In the debates, Robertson singled out Akana, presenting him as an example of a mixed-race Hawaiian who was not in need of rehabilitation: "Here is the Rev. Akaiko Akana—part Hawaiian and part Chinese, why should I be taxed for his rehabilitation? Yet the bill proposes that" (U.S. Congress 1920b: 15). In a sense, Akana became a Hawaiian straw man in the flesh. Robertson personalized the bill in a way that made the rehabilitation proposal for Hawaiians, defined inclusively, simply absurd. Robertson's rhetorical question as to why he should be taxed for Akana's "rehabilitation" worked to register a dismissal for all part-Hawaiians. If any of the participants, including Akana, had refused to hear the question as only rhetorical and had answered with the affirmative, any thorough answer would have worked to problematize the underlying assumptions of rehabilitation, while also highlighting the unresolved issue of entitlement. Perhaps Akana was not in need of charity but his entitlement to the Hawaiian crown lands was another question entirely. It was the "common sense" of Robertson's questions regarding fair treatment and taxation that kept the issues of indigenous dispossession and the question of Hawaiian sovereignty unrecognized and illegitimate.[5]

Absorption

The debates in the hearings next turned to the question of racial absorption in an effort to discuss the "one-thirty-second" blood rule. Robertson argued that Hawaiian blood "is so readily absorbed" that the line between whites and those who were racially mixed between was arbitrary and absurd. The following excerpt details another stage of the hearings with an exchange between Robertson and Senator George Chamberlain of Oregon.

SENATOR CHAMBERLAIN: Why do you draw the line of those having one thirty-second of the pure blood in them?

MR. ROBERTSON: I think that Senator Wise got that from the grandfather's law.

SENATOR CHAMBERLAIN: You take a man that has one thirty-second of native blood as compared with one who has [one] thirty-third, and you could not distinguish between them to save your life; and yet one comes within this provision and the other does not.

MR. ROBERTSON: The Hawaiian blood is so readily absorbed that a person of one-eighth Hawaiian blood can not be distinguished from a white person, in ninety-nine cases out of one hundred.

SENATOR CHAMBERLAIN: So that it was an arbitrary distinction?

MR. ROBERTSON: So far as I know, absolutely arbitrary. Where it came from I really do not know. (U.S. Congress 1920b: 16)

In an inverted logic, Robertson questioned the bill's definition of "part-Hawaiian" by linking the proposed one-thirty-second classification to the grandfather clause. And while a one-thirty-second definition was not as inclusive as it could have been at the time—to account for all mixed Kanaka Maoli during that period—it would account for five generations of mixing Native with non-Native. What does it mean that Robertson cited what he termed the "grandfather's law," used to exclude African Americans from the franchise, in the context of discussing an inclusive policy for Hawaiians?[6] It is difficult to interpret his citation, but it seems he may have conflated the grandfather clause with the hypodescent rule, as both were used to disenfranchise people of African descent from full citizenship, in order to further argue that the rehabilitation of part-Hawaiians would be discriminatory against whites in the territory.[7] But the confusion did not end there. While the question of arbitrariness was important, it is clear from Senator Chamberlain's point that there was no common understanding of what a one-thirty-second blood criterion to define a person meant. The senator's comparison between one-thirty-second and one-thirty-third—to describe a degree of blood quantum—is revealingly absurd since a one-thirty-third blood quantum definition is mathematically impossible. While he stood uncorrected, the essence of his point was that one-thirty-second is also an arbitrary criterion.

Robertson also revealed his own notions about Hawaiian blood as "readily absorbed" and weak (easily overwhelmed). In his examples of racially indistinguishable mixed-race Hawaiians, he assumed the mix to be Hawaiian and white without explicitly marking it so and focused on phenotypical features. Certainly a person of "one-eighth Hawaiian blood" could be easily distinguished from a person considered white if, for example, they were also Samoan and/or black and/or Japanese. Moreover, a Hawaiian of one-eighth Hawaiian and seven-eighths white blood might indeed be indistinguishable from a white person *to* a white person. However, in a Kanaka Maoli context, a person of even one-thirty-second Hawaiian blood could still be distinguishable—at least to Hawaiians—because recognition is not simply about physical appearance.

Hawaiian society had long been incorporative (Marques 1894), contrary to Robertson's assumption that full-blood Hawaiians would contribute to the diminishing of the Hawaiian people by becoming parents of children who are Hawaiian but mixed-race. Consider the following scenario in the logic of blood quantum. A chiefly Hawaiian woman (who is not mixed and would be considered 4/4 in blood quantum figures) had a daughter by a white man in 1870. In 1888, their daughter (half-Hawaiian) also reproduced with a white man and gave birth to a daughter (one-quarter). That child was not only the granddaughter of a chiefly woman; she was the firstborn grandchild and thus held a special place in the Hawaiian line of descent. In 1906, that granddaughter and her white male partner also had a daughter (one-eighth) who was fourteen years of age at the time of these HHCA debates. How might that "one-eighth blood" great-granddaughter of the nonmixed chiefly woman have been distinguishable from a white person? For one, she would have been connected to a whole line of kin, in relation to whom she would be unambiguously identified. Moreover, her high-ranking lineage alone would make her genealogically distinguished, if not racially distinguishable. But in the dominant racial common sense, racial out-marriage was seen as an index of assimilation *away* from Hawaiianness.

In a contradictory move, Robertson distinguished part-Hawaiians from whites by citing their presence as a majority in electoral politics and institutions. He seemed anxious about Hawaiian control of the legislature, which suggests he was threatened by any legislation that would empower any Hawaiians and thus add to Kanaka Maoli political strength in the face of haole domination. "These part Hawaiians constitute a majority of our legislature and a majority of our officeholders under the Territorial government and under the city and county governments. They dominate the legislature and the electorate" (U.S. Congress 1920b: 16). While it is true that from annexation through at least the early 1920s Hawaiian men held a majority in the territorial legislature, Robertson characterized them as utterly self-serving. He suggested that they would be the beneficiaries of the bill as if they were the only part-Hawaiians (ibid.). And he assumed that they would seize the opportunity for their own benefit by greedily taking up the allotments at the expense of the "other" Hawaiians, most likely their own kin.

In response to Robertson, Senator Smoot of Utah argued that the bill would not discriminate against most non-Hawaiians. Senator Smoot declared, "The beneficiaries under the bill are not only Hawaiians but, as the judge has said, it takes in all who have Hawaiian blood in their veins; but it does not affect anybody on the Hawaiian Islands with the exception of a very few large holders of land that have had the leases at a price that is perfectly unreasonable in many, many cases" (U.S. Congress 1920b: 16). Senator Smoot cut to the core of the issue—that the bill looked ready to empower landholders. He then clarified what he really considered to be the issue: "Now the question is as to whether that provision as to one thirty-second Hawaiian blood is right or not, and on that I believe that the judge has some complaint, and perhaps justly so, although I am not prepared now to say even that; but what we are trying to do is, we are trying to say that *these lands that were the King's lands ought to have originally gone to these people that were under, that were subjects of, that King*" (16–17; emphasis added). In this remarkable intervention, the senator refocused attention on the larger problem at hand: indigenous dispossession and the subsequent moral and legal obligation to Kanaka Maoli. He evidenced ambivalence on the question of blood quantum criterion but nonetheless held a position that was friendly to Hawaiian rights to the land. Hence, if one maintained that the lands should have originally gone to Kanaka Maoli as citizens of the kingdom and their descendants, the idea of rehabilitation would become secondary to that of repayment or replacement. Unfortunately, Smoot mostly retreated from the debate, which quickly shifted.

The question of who would constitute the beneficiary class took priority.

The debate again turned to the issue of birthrates and population revival. A short excerpt about full-blood Hawaiians is instructive:

SENATOR CHAMBERLAIN: Is it not more properly to be said that they are being absorbed rather than dying out?

MR. ROBERTSON: Well, that would be one way of describing it, I should say. For instance, a full-blood Hawaiian woman, say, marries a Part-Hawaiian husband. Of course, their children then are immediately classed as Part-Hawaiians; and in that way the mother's blood is absorbed in the mixed blood of the father, and goes on to the next generation. They are being absorbed in that sense, Senator. (U.S. Congress 1920b: 17)

Robertson's comment raises many questions. It should be obvious that the mother's and father's blood would never be "mixed" with each other's, so *who* could be absorbed into what here? What gendered aspects of community formation and incorporation of otherness are effaced by his assertions? Although white American norms are patrilineal, there is no reason for Robertson to assume that the children would be classified like the father and not the mother, especially given the fact that Hawaiian kinship is matrilocal —where male spouses and children typically reside with or near the women's families—and they were talking about people based in the islands. Here race, gender, and class inform Robertson's fantastic trajectories of so-called racial absorption, where Hawaiian women (unmarked as unmixed) may have found part-Hawaiian men to be their ticket to upward mobility. What was the connection between assimilation and reproduction? Robertson's ideas about racial absorption not only reveal something about how gender structured the processes of Hawaiian racialization; they also speak to the ways in which the sociology of miscegenation was popularized at the time.

As Robertson signaled, it was often the case that full-blood Hawaiian women intermarried with mixed-blood Hawaiians or out-married altogether. Yet Robertson's notions of absorption seemed to invert the more common results from these unions. As will be discussed more fully in the next section, it was customary for part-Hawaiians to affiliate within Hawaiian communities by marrying other Hawaiians, mixed or not. It is also unclear that children from such unions would automatically be regarded as part-Hawaiian.

Robertson's role in this part of the second hearing was an important turning point in the debates. First, he focused on the issue of discrimination against non-Hawaiians. Then he concentrated on discrimination *among* Hawaiians if the rehabilitation legislation passed, by presuming that part-Hawaiians would crush those Hawaiians deemed incompetent. More than any other participant in the hearing, Robertson set the terms of interrogation of the legislative proposal by arguing against the empowerment of any part-Hawaiians.

In the next stage of the hearings, more attention was given to the various kinds of part-Hawaiians and corresponding ideas about such different mixes as they related to different Asians—specifically Chinese and Japanese.

Popular Understandings of Racial Mixing and Assimilation

During the 1920s, popular notions of racial mixing and assimilation were influenced by the scientific studies of the day. For example, in the Hawai'i case, Hawaiian-Chinese mixing was mentioned as a promising example of the best "cross" (Dunn 1928). The most common cross-racial pairings in Hawai'i after European contact were between Hawaiian women and white men (Glick 1970: 280). But after an almost exclusively male group of Chinese arrived in Hawai'i in 1870, Hawaiian women also partnered and reproduced with Chinese men. Writing in 1920, MacCaughey asserted, "At present over half the Chinese men marry Chinese women, while most Chinese women marry Chinese men. A large percentage of the Chinese men marry Hawaiian or part-Hawaiian women. Very few Chinese women marry Hawaiian or part-Hawaiian men. Only one Chinese man has married an American woman; a few Chinese women have been married by American men [. . . .] The most significant feature is the large number of mixed marriages, in which the Chinese, Hawaiian, and Caucasian strains intermingle" (1920: 492). W. A. Kinney—cofounder of the McBryde Sugar Company—also registered his views on the matter of race mixing. Kinney was someone with cultural and political capital in Hawai'i at the time. He had been a key member of the Hawaiian League and therefore a supporter of U.S. annexation (Dougherty 1992: 160). Later, he politically aligned himself with Kalaniana'ole. Regarding Kanaka Maoli and Chinese mixing, Kinney suggested, "There are quite a number of Hawaiian-Chinese crosses from male Chinese and female Hawaiian marriages, but there the contact stops. Most all of these crosses follow the condition and point of view of the mother, and their status under the law is that of Hawaiians. They are American in their education, ideas, language, customs, etc." (Kinney 1927: 194).

Kinney further argued, "The Hawaiian, though friendly to all races, is distinctly American today. He has no other affiliations or inclinations. He has nowhere else to turn; Hawaiian women have inter-married with the Chinese more than any other Asiatic race in Hawaii, and the latter race has had much to do in more ways than one, with the demoralization of the Hawaiian, but no one can claim that the Chinese have at all assimilated the Hawaiian, or have influenced his point of view" (1927: 194). But Kinney did not see this mixing in positive terms. He negatively characterized the Chinese at every turn and blamed them for many Hawaiian social problems.

> The major proportion of Chinese coolies in Hawaii remain single and have brought on that immigration a historical blot of infamous debauchery of native girls little more than children in the tea and cake houses established in the vicinity of the Chinese coolie camps ostensibly run as small restaurants and stores and in truth as dens of infamy catering to the penchant for undeveloped girls peculiar to the unmarried section of this immigration. Sterility of many Hawaiian females attributed to this debauchery in their extreme youth but coming as a by-product of the sugar business conducted on Asiatic lines, the real and only remedy of cutting off this immigration did not appeal even to the religious element of the exploiters. Other reasons for the decline in the native population were more convenient to urge and less self-accusing. (194–95)

Here, Kinney blames the Chinese for the downfall of Kanaka Maoli and even suggests that Chinese men and Hawaiian women were to blame for Native depopulation. Unfortunately, his characterization was not uncommon at the time when the mixing between the two garnered many cultural speculations and explanations.

The Reverend Albert W. Palmer—another key figure in Hawai'i—also commented on the nature of the racial mixing taking place at the time. He served at the Congregationalist Central Union Church in Honolulu, which was a house of worship for many of Hawai'i's haole elite (Tamura 1994: 39). Palmer wrote about Kanaka Maoli in benign terms: "It is also a very fortunate thing that Hawaii's basic race is neither Caucasian, Negro nor Mongolian but the kind-hearted, tolerant, loveable Polynesian whose most characteristic contribution to present-day Hawaii is the spirit of 'aloha'" (Palmer 1924: 73). Palmer also assessed these matches in terms of their eugenic potential: "These interracial combinations have been remarkably successful and, although the pure-blooded Hawaiians are slowly decreasing (the rate of decrease was reduced last decade, however, to 8 percent, from 12 percent the decade before) the part-Hawaiians are rapidly increasing and are characterized in general by a hopeful combination of Chinese or Caucasian energy and ability with Hawaiian beauty and aloha" (ibid.).

As was common at the time, Riley H. Allen—editor of the *Honolulu Star-Bulletin*—also found the racial mixing to be full of romantic (and eugenic) potential. He described Hawai'i as "once a lonely and lovely archipelago inhabited by the brown Polynesians, serenely primitive in its native life, [which] is to-day the world's greatest experiment station of race-mixtures. Here Orient and Occident meet; here North America and Siberia and Antipodes touch; here a current of Latin blood crosses a current of Teuton; Anglo-Saxon and Asiatic, Malay and Micronesian, Slav and Scandinavian, mingle and influence each other" (Allen 1921: 618). But within this "experiment station," Allen noted that Japanese and Koreans were considered the "least fusible," whereas others "intermarry freely with the Polynesian stocks and with each other. . . . and the marriage with Polynesians is fruitful of good results" (619). Here racial mixing is seen as an index of adaptation and improvement, where certain mixes are glorified, exoticized, and compatible with assimilation into the American project.

Interracial reproduction, then, became an indicator for assimilation in both negative and positive senses. Feeding into the myth of the vanishing Hawaiian, interracial relations were used against Kanaka Maoli assertions of indigeneity because they were said to work against indigenous cultural distinctiveness, a distinctiveness inherently tied to claims of sovereignty. By contrast, the Japanese were charged with being incapable of assimilation because their interracial mingling was limited compared to that of the Chinese. MacCaughey, who wrote during the same year as the HHCA debates, noted that "in general, Japanese marry only Japanese; they show remarkable racial aloofness, more so, as a race, than any other in Hawaii" (1920: 492). He found that

All Korean women have married only Koreans. The Korean men have married not only Koreans but also women of Hawaiian and part-Hawaiian blood. . . . The Japanese and Koreans contrast strongly with the Chinese in race mixtures, the former groups evincing strong clannishness in marital selections; the latter groups freely breeding "out."

In general Asiatics in Hawaii breed more freely with Caucasian stock that they do among themselves. . . . Most Hawaiian men marry Hawaiians. Hawaiian women marry freely outside their own race. Notable among the racial preferences of Hawaiian men are their marriages with Caucasian-Hawaiians, Chinese-Hawaiians, and Portuguese. (493)

The number of non-mixed Hawaiian men who married women of other races was less than 20 percent of all marriages during the early years of the territory, but the number of Hawaiian women—mixed and unmixed—who married non-Hawaiians ranged from 40 percent in 1910 to 85 percent in 1960 (Wright 1972: 282).

The issues of birthrate and community formation were important for the ways processes of identity and identification were formulated, assessed, and projected within the HHCA debates. In the following excerpt, "admixture" returned to mark the moment when the inclusive blood quantum criterion was called into question specifically by the offering of an alternative definition. The discussion took place among Senator Key Pittman of Nevada (the brother of W. B. Pittman), along with Senator George Chamberlain of Oregon, Senator John Nugent of Idaho, and, again, Robertson.

SENATOR PITTMAN: Judge, is there any intermixture over there between the Japanese and the Hawaiian people?

MR. ROBERTSON: There is some; not a great deal. I happen to have a client who owns land, too, whose mother was a full-blooded Hawaiian and whose father was a full-blooded Japanese. But there are not a great many part-Hawaiians and part-Japanese. There are a great many part-Chinese and part-Hawaiians; and authorities on the subject say that they make the best cross of any.

SENATOR CHAMBERLAIN: What was the name of that very wealthy family over there with a Chinese father and a native mother?

MR. ROBERTSON: Ah Fong.

SENATOR CHAMBERLAIN: They were half bloods?

MR. ROBERTSON: Yes. One of them married an admiral in the United States Navy. And that is not the only family of great wealth of mixed blood in the islands who are beneficiaries under this act.

SENATOR CHAMBERLAIN: Would that family come under the benefits of the act now before the committee?

MR. ROBERTSON: Yes; and there are a number of other families in the same class. Take the Si Brown family there; the two sons are pretty nearly millionaires in their own rights. They are 50 per cent Hawaiian and Anglo-Saxon, and yet they could take up land under this act as it stands, although white men who have not got a square inch of land would be debarred.

SENATOR CHAMBERLAIN: Could the bill be drawn so as to permit only the aborigines of the full-blood, and that is the full extent to which it should go.

MR. ROBERTSON: Very easily. An amendment here would limit the operation of this bill to the Hawaiians of the full blood, and that is the full extent to which it should go.

SENATOR CHAMBERLAIN: That would be called a decreasing race?

MR. ROBERTSON: That would be a decreasing race.

SENATOR NUGENT: Are there not a considerable number of part Hawaiians who are also in destitute circumstances?

MR. ROBERTSON: I do not think so. You see, Senator, the situation is this, that nobody is indigent out there by reason of the lack of opportunity to work. (U.S. Congress 1920b: 22–23)

Senator Pittman's question about Japanese intermixture with Kanaka Maoli reveals his concerns about Japanese Americanization, with their proximity to Hawaiians seen as an index of political, cultural, and bodily assimilation. Robertson suggested that even in the rare example of Hawaiian and Japanese intermixture, those particular part-Hawaiians held land. Robertson evoked authorities on Hawaiian-Chinese mixes making "the best cross of any." It seems from Senator Chamberlain's question that he was aware of the "Ah Fongs" beforehand.

Known in Hawai'i as "C. Afong," Chun Fong was a prominent Chinese merchant who was active in the social and political life of Hawai'i even during the time of the kingdom. In 1856, he headed up a group of Chinese merchants of Honolulu and Lahaina to give a grand ball honoring Kamehameha IV and Queen Emma Rooke. In 1879 Afong was appointed a member of King Kalākaua's privy council, "but he resigned shortly after this appointment in order to serve as the Chinese (Imperial) Government's Commercial Agent in Hawaii" (Lowe 1972: 24).

Robertson's evocation of Afong's children, because of their father's status in Hawai'i, worked to trivialize and dismiss the social position of all "part-Hawaiians." Hence, the discussion regarding who would constitute "native Hawaiian" within the HHCA became personalized. The Afong family seems to have been mentioned only in order to discount the rehabilitation proposal as a whole.

Robertson's contribution highlighted examples of mixed-race Hawaiians in order to stir anxieties that the bill would benefit the richer mixed-race individuals—those he glossed as the specific beneficiaries in the bill. Robertson mentioned these examples as if they were normative, thus casting doubt on the need for any Hawaiian rehabilitation. He did this by bringing his "local knowledge" to bear on proceedings, using his authoritative status as a judge from the territory. Robertson also used a 50-percent example, the Si Brown family, to demonstrate that part-Hawaiians as a whole did not need any rehabilitation efforts offered in their direction. And in reply, Senator Chamberlain suggested—for the first part of the hearings—raising the criterion to "full-blood." Even if Robertson had affirmatively answered Senator Nugent's question about indigent part-Hawaiians, it would not necessarily have mattered because Robertson emphasized their qualities of industriousness and Hawai'i's climate of opportunity.

Chamberlain specifically suggested drafting the bill to define Hawaiian as "full blood" in response to Robertson's extraordinary examples of wealthy Hawaiian families. Even the focus on need was lost to the issue of population count among "full-bloods." Although Robertson offered no evidence as to whether or not there were part-Hawaiians who were indigent, the rest of the discussions followed as though their well-being was a given and the issue of part-Hawaiians hardly returned to the picture. Robertson's narrow notion of rehabilitation became the standard within the rest of the debates. And his logic was based on the issue of individual competence, since—he asserted—no one was indigent in Hawai'i because of a lack of opportunity.

The Focus on "Full Bloods"

Thanks to Robertson, changing the definition of "native Hawaiian" to include only "full-bloods" became a priority through the end of this particular hearing. Once participants shifted away from an entitlement framework for rehabilitation, in terms of Hawaiians' right to the lands in question, the blood racialization of Hawaiians was able to take hold because they were then basing eligibility for the proposal on a welfare framework and under-standing of who was most deserving. In turn, different constructions of Hawaiianness corresponded to the shift away from recognition of indige-nous entitlement toward the privileging of white property interests in the lands. Specifically, this rehabilitation plan was eventually justified as a form of government charity rather than Hawaiians' right to the land.

George M. McClellan—who represented the Honolulu Chamber of Commerce—argued that "the only possible defense of this bill would be to strike out its application to all part Hawaiians and limit it strictly to those of pure Hawaiian blood" (U.S. Congress 1920b: 88). He went so far as to argue in an explicitly colonialist logic of reverse racism: "There are grave reasons why Congress should provide for the rehabilitation of the Caucasian race in Hawaii. The country is deeply interested in the maintaining of a real Ameri-can community in the Hawaiian Islands. They are interested in that because the maintenance of an American population is absolutely essential to the holding of Hawaii as a strategic military and naval base. Without a popula-tion which is reasonably American, it will be impossible to maintain Hawaii as a real American outpost" (ibid.). Here, it is clear that McClellan was highlighting the threat to whites if Hawaiians were empowered in any way connected to land rights. Moreover, in his commitment to keeping the United States in power, he was invested in holding Hawai'i as a colonial territory—where only whites could maintain it as truly American. Here, the explicit link between the maintenance of whiteness and U.S. imperialism was used to justify the colonial dispossession of Kanaka Maoli land. Mc-Clellan's priority was clearly the project of white Americanization in the Hawaiian Islands at the expense of the land claims of Hawaiians. He went even further by declaring, "It may be summed up by saying that this is the first time in all the history of the United States that any legislation ever came before Congress and was seriously considered which gave rights to a dark race above and against the rights of the white race" (112). Here, the issue of racism is clear, with white entitlement at the center of McClellan's commit-ment, and no concessions whatsoever to the project of Hawaiian rehabilita-tion, let alone Hawaiian sovereignty.

Next, Senator Pittman explicitly proposed to amend the section to re-define who would count as "native Hawaiian" in the same terms that Mc-Clellan proposed. He clarified:

In other words, that this shall apply only to Hawaiians who are of the full blood; and that will rehabilitate only very few of them, because there are only about 22,000 full-blooded Hawaiians, and there can be only two or three hundred homesteads. I do not believe the Delegate will object to that, that it be confined to the full blood instead of the half blood, because he knows and *everybody knows that any part Hawaiian is capable of taking care of himself* and does not need any rehabilitation. (U.S. Congress 1920b: 123–24; emphasis added)

Here, the focus on issues of competence tied to notions of blood quantum was key. Senator Pittman acknowledged that the homesteads planned for allotment might not be sufficient to provide leasing for all "full blood" Hawaiians. How the 22,000 of them, not to mention thousands more part-Hawaiians, could be returned productively to 200,000 acres of the least valuable lands of the territory was a question left undiscussed (Hasager 1997: 188 n. 10).

Mixed Hawaiians were discussed as if they were untouched by the histories of dispossession. By 1919, only 6.23 percent of the property in Hawai'i was held by Hawaiians, and even then, for the most part by wealthy Hawaiians who descended from chiefs totaling approximately one thousand wealthy Hawaiians (Hawaiian Homes Commission 1922: 12). Haole participants assessed the economic status of Hawaiians by citing references to bank deposits and ownership of real and personal property as well as information relating to occupational status. As Yamamura notes, there was a decline "of the Hawaiian index from 169 in professional pursuits in 1890 to 62.5 in 1940 and the Part-Hawaiian index of 371.4 in 1890 to 166 in 1940" (1949: 252). Historically, Hawaiians—both mixed and not—were displaced by new immigrant groups.

In one sharp turn, the debates shifted from a one-thirty-second definition of "native Hawaiian" to "full blood." Robertson eschewed even a one-half definition, in his claim that "any part Hawaiian is capable of taking care of himself." When asked if he was in favor of Senator Pittman's proposal, Delegate Kalaniana'ole took the position that he was there by territorial mandate and not his own agenda. He replied, "No; I am opposed to it, because I am here to carry out the wishes of the legislature and not my own" (U.S. Congress 1920b: 124). The delegate stated his opposition to all the amendments at that time, until he had obtained authorization from the legislature of Hawaii (128). When asked by Senator Pittman if he would rather not see the bill define Hawaiians as full-blooded, Kalaniana'ole simply stated that he "would like to see everybody get the benefit of it in Hawaii. For years past and up to the present time, the Hawaiians have never received any benefits" (128). Again, here they all conceived of rehabilitation in terms of benefits, not clear entitlements. Senator Smoot's query about Hawaiian land rights was quickly evaded. Yet Delegate Kalaniana'ole's push for "everybody" (read: all Hawaiians) suggests his lingering dedication to reparations and entitlement, which entailed an inclusive framework for qualifying Kānaka Maoli in relation to land access. But, as we will see, the territorial legislature would have little sympathy for this way of thinking.

Conclusion

By refocusing attention on Hawaiian welfare and entitlement, territorial advocates who opposed the empowerment of Natives more generally were able to press for their desired limitations on the entire leasing proposal. Those who stood in conflict to Hawaiian homesteading seized the ill-defined concept of rehabilitation while sidestepping the issue of Hawaiian legal rights to the land. Further, the initially inconsistent formulations of rehabilitation allowed for complete redefinitions of the project for the pro-sugar faction. By effacing entitlement, territorial witnesses who participated in the hearings before the Committee on Territories were able to maintain welfare-focused discourses that constructed Hawaiians as a beneficiary class of U.S. citizens with special needs.

Linked to this shift was the question of "admixed" Kānaka Maoli and whether or not they were absorbed into the non-Hawaiian communities. The white Americans from Hawai'i, along with a few congressional representatives, rigidly objectified "full-blooded" or, alternately, "pure" Hawaiians, whose authenticity they saw as predicated on the presumed characteristic of "incompetence" and their incapacity for progress to full U.S. citizenship. On the other hand, these same participants saw "part-Hawaiians" as endowed with upright competency and therefore thought there was no need for them to access land through a governmental policy like the HHCA. Those who worked to justify the exclusion of part-Hawaiians from the allotment plan detailed what they saw as extreme ambitiousness among them—figured as a potential threat to both whites and "pure Hawaiians."

Their racial logic defining Hawaiians was instrumental to the reformulation of who counted as Hawaiian for the purposes of the HHCA. Indeed, their reasoning accounts for the final, decisive shift to a more exclusive rule of one-half blood quantum.

The concept of rehabilitation had been appropriated by the haole elite. The dual claim of U.S. legal and moral responsibility was transformed by an increasing emphasis on moral responsibility through concentration on the poor conditions of Kānaka Maoli.[8] Hawaiian racial definitions constructed the boundary of indigenous inclusion and exclusion, a process structured through the racial triangulation of white-Hawaiian-Asian as haole-Native-alien. Through this matrix, notions of rehabilitation were recoded in ways that worked to further dispossess Kanaka Maoli, even while their rehabilitation remained a stated priority of the legislators.

HR 13500 passed the House on May 22, 1920, but the Senate failed to act on the measure. The bill was then removed from the Senate calendar so that particular measures the senators had found unacceptable could be amended, but it is unclear as to why the bill was stalled. Clearly, the U.S. Senate was influenced by McClellan from the Honolulu Chamber of Commerce. Kalaniana'ole offered one reason the following year in a letter to Governor Charles J. McCarthy (dated March 7, 1921), where he discussed another letter from a Mr. Horner (an agricultural expert in the territory tied to the plantations) to the governor. Apparently, in Horner's letter of February 14, 1921, he referred to a "Fairchild Bill" along the same lines as HR 13500. Kalaniana'ole mentioned being informed by reliable sources that Horner's letter

> caused Senator Poindexter to use "Senatorial Courtesy" to defer any action on the bill by the Senate Committee; that Senator Poindexter, knowing Horner as well as he did, really believed that the Legislative Commission and I were insincere in our efforts to secure the passage of this bill and that our efforts were bent solely in an endeavor to rehabilitate a "few sugar corporations" and "Hawaiian politicians"; that Senator Poindexter after receiving the letter, personally used his "influence" to convince the senator that they were not sincere and, as a result, that they refused to take any action on the bill. (Kalaniana'ole 1921a, letter to McCarthy)

Horner's message would have carried weight. Further, Kalaniana'ole noted that Horner's name was signed to a cable protest as reported in a January 31,

1921 newspaper article that protested the bill on three key grounds. The first was the charge that the bill brought up, for the first time in Hawai'i, "the question of race distinction." This was patently false since race distinctions were made culturally, socially, politically, economically, and linguistically in Hawai'i prior to this proposal—namely, in the Bayonet Constitution of 1887 as a result of white American domination. The second issue raised by Horner was that the bill created an "unjust discrimination against other loyal American citizens." Third, he claimed that it would not rehabilitate the Hawaiian people but instead would create unwarranted and arbitrary power in the commission provided by the bill and would deplete the revenues of the territory as well as increase taxation (Kalaniana'ole 1921a, letter to McCarthy).

At this point, though, the bill was stalled and did not return to the Sixty-Sixth Congress. Vause notes that members of the Senate laid blame for the failure of HR 13500 on Kalaniana'ole, insisting that if he had made the appropriate amendments and resubmitted the bill, it would have passed (1962: 83–84). They complained that he kept the bill out until it was too late for consideration because the Senate was so close to the end of the session that the committee would not be called on again, and a request to the Rules Committee would be needed to report a bill to the floor (Vause 1962: 42). In the meantime, the issue returned to the territory, where Kalaniana'ole would urge the legislature to amend various parts of the bill. In Hawai'i, two new measures would pass that would prove to be drastic compromises that forfeited Kanaka Maoli rehabilitation interests, not to mention land claims. Since these changes in the proposal threatened to severely damage the pro-Hawaiian portions of the bill, a fierce struggle over the entire legislation ensued in the islands.

Limiting Hawaiians, Limiting the Bill
Rehabilitation Recoded

> The one thing I am anxious not to do is give the highly cultivated cane lands to
> Hawaiians, as Senator Pittman, for instance, favored. If we do, they will fail sure.
> As the governor told you long ago, we believe the temptation for them to sit on
> the lanai [veranda] and watch some Japanese do the work would be too great. The
> only way for rehabilitation to benefit the Hawaiian is through his own efforts—hard,
> honest work.
>
> —John H. Wise, quoted in *Honolulu Star-Bulletin*, April 12, 1921

IN HIS APPEAL TO THE SENATE OF the Territory, Senator John H. Wise
characterized Kanaka Maoli very differently than he did in his entreaties to
congressional committee members in earlier hearings. This time, his words
of caution were an attempt to persuade his fellow territorial senators to pass
his proposed Senate Concurrent Resolution 6 (SCR 6), a calculated measure
that was designed to win the support of planter interests and authorize
Hawai'i's governor to extend their leases until such time as Congress acted to
accept or reject the rehabilitation bill. (McGregor 1990: 27). In turn, revenues from the cultivation of these plantations would furnish the government with money to put rehabilitation into effect.

Wise's new territorial measure marked a significant shift from his position that all Hawaiians held claim to crown lands and that rehabilitation was
linked to an entitlement that predated the U.S. takeover of Hawai'i. In a
move that would appeal to those skeptical of Kanaka Maoli entitlements, he
linked the right of rehabilitation to industry—"won efforts" such as "hard,
honest work." Also, he suggested that Kanaka Maoli would probably not
work the land, and that the Japanese would be all too willing to work in the
face of Hawaiian laziness. Although the Japanese were not charged with
outcompeting Kanaka Maoli this time, Wise employed a racial logic similar
to his earlier position that they worked harder than Hawaiians.

This chapter examines the process by which the HHCA bill was revamped in Hawai'i after it was denied passage in the U.S. Senate. The failure of HR 13500 resuscitated the question of opening cultivated lands for Hawaiian homesteading in the bill, because only a small amount of poor-quality land was identified for Kanaka Maoli leasing while the Big Five insisted on holding onto the prime land. The Big Five needed to be swayed for the bill to pass. During 1920 an election campaign was underway in the territory, in which the Republican Party had not endorsed the rehabilitation legislation due to a lack of support from the Big Five (McGregor 1990: 24). As Vause notes, "It was generally known that the sugar corporations were far better represented in Congress than the territory itself" (1962: 94). The changes to the legislation occurred both formally before the territorial legislature and informally among dominant political leaders, and entailed Hawaiian elites' complicity in negotiating with plantation interests whose plans for corporate expansion were at odds with rehabilitative homesteading for Kanaka Maoli.

In the first part of the chapter, I examine some key pieces of private correspondence between territorial witnesses, Delegate Kalaniana'ole, and selected senators from the Committee on Territories. Then, I explore Kalaniana'ole's delegate report to the territorial government of Hawai'i that addressed the rehabilitation bill and his account of barriers to its passage in the Senate. Finally, I track a series of private negotiations between Senator Wise, Kalaniana'ole, and several territorial senators aligned with the Big Five in Hawai'i and their efforts to drastically change the measure in order to secure the support of the Big Five. These covert discussions led to two new territorial resolutions, discussed below, that would limit the formal changes to the HHCA proposal that would eventually be presented in Washington. Because the Big Five operated as an oligarchy in the territory, Wise and Kalaniana'ole needed to gain their cooperation in order to have any provisions for Hawaiian land leasing, especially given the fact that the homesteading program would limit sugar cultivation directly tied to the business interests of the corporations.

In the second part of this chapter, I examine the last hearing on the proposal for the HHCA, when key players traveled from Hawai'i to Congress in order to explain the dramatic revisions of the homesteading proposal that took place back in the territory. There were two contradictory notions about Hawaiian race mixing that alternately prevailed in this final stage of the debates. On the one hand, there was the view that part-Hawaiians were a threat to whiteness, and on the other, that part-Hawaiians were "to all intents and purposes" white people. This two-pronged paradox hinged on the assumption that "part-Hawaiians" meant mixed with Asians in one moment and with white Americans in the next—without fully accounting for the different kinds of part-Hawaiians in the first place.

Longhand Lobbying

Shortly after the committee debates ended in December 1920, A. G. M. Robertson contacted Senator Reed Smoot of Utah in order to reach him before the Committee on the Territories was to meet the next day. He wrote, "I am opposed upon principle to all that part of the bill (HR 13500) which relates to the disposition of the public lands of Hawaii" (Robertson 1921, letter to Smoot). Robertson urged the committee to report against the bill but also noted that if they were to favor it, they should amend it in accordance to the revisions previously proposed by W. B. Pittman and George M. McClellan: "The privileges conferred by the bill, clearly, should be *limited to Hawaiians of the pure blood* who alone arquire [*sic*], deserve, or are entitled in the slightest degree to rehabilitation at the expense of the tax payers of the Territory" (emphasis added). Robertson also suggested two other amendments regarding the sizes of land parcels and the selling of lands to corporations. In relation to his own specific interests in protecting the Parker Ranch, he cited a report by the commander of the Hawaiian Department, U.S. Army, to the secretary of war. The report suggested that products of the ranch were "extremely valuable to the Army in time of Peace. Assuming control of the Hawaiian Islands in time of war its military value will be greatly increased. . . . The passage of the Hawaiian Rehabilitation Bill in its present form will no doubt most seriously cripple the Parker Ranch as a military adjunct" (Robertson 1921, letter to Smoot: 1–2). Here, the interests Robertson had expressed earlier came more sharply into focus. His opposition to the entire bill, like McClellan's, was explicitly tied to U.S. control in the islands, which would be maintained as an "American outpost." Robertson repeated his contention that "from a national standpoint it would seem highly desirable that the Parker Ranch should not be broken up in the manner proposed by the bill under consideration." Thus, if the bill should be supported at all, it "should be amended by eliminating from its operating

[the] lands now held by the Parker Ranch" and mentioned in "lines 15 to 20 (inclusive) on page 4 of the bill" (Robertson 1921, letter to Smoot: 2). Not surprisingly, Robertson was utterly committed to protecting the interests of his client.

McClellan also submitted his own proposed amendments to HR 13500 in a letter to Kalaniana'ole, in which he credited his suggestions to members of the Senate Committee on Territories. He wanted titles I and II to be stricken from the bill because members did not intend to support any formation of a land base for the use of Hawaiian homesteading, even as an experiment. Moreover, he stated, "If, however, your Committee should decide to retain those portions of the Bill in some form, the following amendments are designed to correct some defects of the Bill and to make the proposed experiment more practical." His corrective was to define "native Hawaiian" as any "citizen of the Territory being of the *Polynesian race and of the full blood*" (McClellan 1921, Suggested Amendments: 2; emphasis added).

W. B. Pittman, attorney for the Raymond Ranch, also wrote a letter on that same day, January 10, 1921, to Senator Smoot. Pittman argued that even considering the poor quality of the lands proposed for homesteading, those who needed them the least were most likely to secure them. He noted, "The lands to be set aside by the bill for the purpose of rehabilitating the Hawaiians are barren and untillable, and cannot possibly be worked profitably, and no Hawaiian, regardless of his agricultural ability, can even make a bare living upon any of these lands" (Pittman 1921b, letter to Smoot: 1). Pittman also contended, "All of the lands which are capable of being cultivated at a profit would necessarily go to citizens of means, and would not, in any way benefit those who really need homes" (ibid.). His concession to any Hawaiian need was limited: "A few Hawaiians of pure blood who might be entitled to governmental assistance would not in any manner be benefited by the passage of the present bill, because all of the lands would be taken up by the part-Hawaiians who do not need any rehabilitating and are amply able to take care of themselves, as they are intelligent, industrious and prolific" (2). Here the presupposition was that "full bloods" were not intelligent, industrious, or prolific, and so were in need of protectionist measures with the government as the paternal caregiver.

Like Robertson, Pittman also cited the letter by the commander of the Hawaiian Department of the U.S. Army with regard to Parker Ranch. Pittman maintained that the present homestead laws were "adequate for the protection of all of our citizens, including Hawaiians" and objected to the passage of any bill (Pittman 1921b, letter to Smoot: 1). He offered his arguments nonetheless, even noting, "I do not wish to be understood as withdrawing my objections to the passage of any rehabilitation bill, as I firmly believe that the present land laws are sufficient. . . . I also firmly believe that it discriminates against citizens of non-Hawaiian blood upon the race line" (2). In a separate list of proposed amendments, Pittman repeated McClellan's suggestion to define "native Hawaiian" as "any citizen of the Territory being of the Polynesian race and of the full blood" (Pittman 1921a, Amendments). The fixation on "full bloods" reemerged to limit Kanaka Maoli eligibility, but it did nothing to address his claim that the proposal was discriminatory against non-Hawaiians. Limiting the proposal to unmixed Hawaiians did not resolve this issue.

On February 6, 1921, Senator Harry S. New—chair of the Senate Committee on the Territories—reported that the committee had been "unable to agree with the house bill proposing distribution of public lands to Hawaiians of full or part blood" (*Pacific Commercial Advertiser* 1921f). Later, Senator New wrote a letter to Kalanianaʻole, dated February 23, 1921, stating that he had requested several times that Senator Pittman, Senator Jones of Washington, and Senator McLean of Connecticut submit to him a statement of their principal objections so that Senator New might show them to Delegate Kalanianaʻole before the territorial legislature would meet. However, according to Senator New, those senators never replied. Subsequently, he offered his own objections. While Senator New supported the fundamental principles of the bill, he doubted "the constitutionality of the measure on the ground that it taxes one element of the population of the Island for the exclusive benefit of another." In addition, New objected to extending to "those of one thirty-second Hawaiian blood the benefits of this Act" because it seemed "that when this is done it loses its claim to being an Act designed for rehabilitation of the Hawaiian people." He saw the more inclusive definition as contradictory to the goals of rehabilitation. Hence, he urged that "it should be *limited to full-blooded Hawaiians*" (emphasis added). Senator New also noted the limits of a proposal that would only provide for three hundred families in that it would not "go far enough to accomplish much in the direction of race rehabilitation." He suggested that as "an experiment it might prove a success but as a measure for national relief it cannot accomplish much" (New 1921, letter to Kalaniana'ole). Clearly the concept of Native rehabilitation was still in the senator's line of thinking.

The Delegate's Report

On April 11, 1921, Delegate Kalaniana'ole reported the results of his work on the "so-called Rehabilitation Bill" at the congressional level (Kalaniana'ole 1921b). He addressed the president, the speaker, senators, and representatives of the legislature of Hawai'i, soliciting advice as to what should be done to revive the bill in the coming session of the new Congress. The reasons he offered here as to why the bill stalled differed markedly from those in his letter to Governor McCarthy (discussed in chapter 4). Previously he had explained that the primary reason for the bill's failure to proceed was a letter from an agricultural expert, Horner, to Senator Poindexter urging the senator to use his "senatorial courtesy" to defer any action on the bill because they both believed that the territorial commission and the delegate "were insincere in their efforts to secure passage of the bill and that what efforts they did have were in order to 'rehabilitate a few sugar corporations' and 'Hawaiian politicians'" (Kalaniana'ole 1921a). But in his report to the Hawai'i legislature, Delegate Kalaniana'ole summarized the matter very differently. "Though the Bill itself died with the passing of the last Congress on March 4, I am able to state to you that many of its provisions met no opposition and that the much discussed sections opening the way for the Hawaiians to return to the land were looked upon favorably by the members of both Houses of Congress. . . . Yes, the Bill is dead; but it failed at the last moment in the Senate owing to the congestions of business at the short session of Congress" (Kalaniana'ole 1921b: 1). He construed the outcome as if the matter were solely a procedural problem rather than the obvious conundrum of trying to appeal to the Big Five. In his report, Delegate Kalaniana'ole specified: "Under the special rule, the bill passed the House. It went to the Senate Committee on Territories, whence it was reported out to the senate and went onto the Senate calendar. On account of the congestion in the business of the senate last summer—you may remember that the debates over the German Peace Treaty and the League of Nations occupied the Senate almost exclusively at that time—it was then recommitted to the Committee on Territories, so that an opportunity to hear the opponents of the measure could be given" (6–7). Kalaniana'ole's assessment did not address substantive issues even though he proceeded to make explicit requests of the legislature to give their input on potential amendments, including a more exclusive shift in the blood quantum rule. Since there were very few people directly involved, Kalaniana'ole could have pushed further in a way that would benefit more Hawaiians. But it is clear that he needed to appeal to the Big Five. He explained, "We could not 'give the Hawaiians sugar lands' because the national Congress desired that the highly developed lands be withheld from homesteading. The whole idea and purpose of the Committee was to lease the richer sugar lands, using a portion of the income to carry out the rehabilitation scheme, the balance to be used by the Territory for the benefit of all the people" (4–5). He wrote further that there were specific attempts to solicit advice from the opposition:

> After these final hearings were closed, the Chairman of the Committee, Senator New of Indiana, was very desirous that the Committee take action one way or another. A meeting for this purpose was called. Prior to this meeting, Chairman New had written to all the members inviting the Senators who wanted to amend the bill asking them to attend the meeting and offer the amendments. Only four Senators attended this last meeting—Senators New, Smoot, Jones, and McClain [sic].[1] Senator Smoot moved to report the bill favorably to the Senate. Senators Jones and McClain objected to voting and were then asked by Chairman New if they had any amendments to offer or had any other reason for not voting. Both stated that they knew nothing about the measure and hence were not prepared to vote on it or offer amendment. (6–7)

Senators Jones and McLean objected to meeting and admitted they were unprepared. As discussed above, Senator New's opposition was clearly delineated in his letter to Delegate Kalaniana'ole.

Kalaniana'ole also spoke to the definition of "native Hawaiian" and how it might be best revised in order to move forward. He suggested, "I think a number of the Senators believe that the blood fraction giving the right to share the privileges of the act should be altered. I should say that these Senators believe that the *special rights* should be accorded only to persons of *one-half, one-fourth* or *at most one-eighth Hawaiian blood*" (1921b: 11; emphasis added). It is unclear how Delegate Kalaniana'ole determined that blood quantum was the problem since he did not identify any particular senators who made it an issue. Kalaniana'ole's report to the legislature and the debate transcripts only reveal Senator New's explicit opposition, and it is unclear whether any debate took place. Hence, the delegate was likely making blood quantum an issue here in order to warn the territorial legislators that they would eventually need to revise the definition for "native Hawaiian"—a move he would orchestrate in order to appease the Big Five without informing the representatives on-island.

Calculated Compromises

It may not be a coincidence that the day after Delegate Kalaniana'ole's address to the legislature, Senator Wise introduced Senate Concurrent Resolution 6 (SCR 6) in the territory. His proposal was calculated to win the support of planter interests (McGregor 1990: 27). Before proposing the resolution, Wise met with Governor McCarthy, Attorney General Harry Irwin, and senators Harry Baldwin and Harold Rice (Vause 1962: 85). Senator Baldwin and Senator Rice were both well known as strong supporters of sugar and ranching interests. SCR 6 would authorize Hawai'i's governor to extend sugar leases to the planters until such time as Congress acted to accept or reject the rehabilitation bill. Specifically, Senator Wise suggested that the highly developed sugar lands in Waimanalo, on the island of O'ahu, and Kekaha, on the island of Kaua'i, be withdrawn from the lands identified for homesteading. In turn, he suggested that revenues from cultivation on these lands would furnish the government with money to put rehabilitation into effect. He argued that if the Hawaiian part of the proposal were to fail there would be no funds "and without money the rehabilitation law, even if enacted by Congress, would be a dead letter" (*Honolulu Star-Bulletin* 1921a: 7).

Wise did not maintain any bottom line on redefining the blood quantum, and thus on limiting the number of Hawaiians eligible for rehabilitation. He informed the legislature, "The degree of Hawaiian blood required is not a matter that gives us any worry. We are willing it should be one-eighth; one-fourth or even one half" (*Honolulu Star-Bulletin* 1921a: 7). Furthermore, the senator disclaimed any part in the making of the one-thirty-second blood proposal: "The clause extending the benefits of the bill to those of one-thirty-second degree Hawaiian blood *was not of our making*; the house committee on territories wrote that into the bill" (ibid.; emphasis added). His declaration is curious given that he was the first to propose the one-thirty-second definition in an earlier attempt to push for a more inclusive blood rule. I argue that Senator Wise's priority was to distance himself from any particular stance that would slow down the process of securing territorial approval for the amendments critical to the passage of the bill in the U.S. Senate, which entailed the local backing of haole business brokers in the territory. Wise made the compromise with the planting and ranching opposition in order to guard against further failure of the bill to pass the territorial legislature and Congress (Vause 1962: 91).

When Senator Wise proposed SCR 6, Senator Russell contested the resolution by citing Delegate Kalaniana'ole's address from the previous day. Senator Russell argued, "To get anything through Congress, all our needs must be embodied in one bill, and the thought occurs to me that if this resolution passes, either it must give way to some rehabilitation bill or, if it passes Congress, that it necessarily will block the passage of any rehabilitation measure that might be offered" (*Honolulu Star-Bulletin* 1921a). In what seems like a shortsighted attempt to move the proposal along, Wise insisted on a separation of the issues for expediency. Regarding SCR 6, he replied, "The resolution now before us, if accompanied later by another resolution and a form of rehabilitation bill to be submitted to Congress, will obtain action more quickly than any other way. The two can be embodied in one bill for introduction at Washington" (1).

Senate Concurrent Resolution 6 passed the legislature on that same day, April 13, 1921. The *Star-Bulletin* called it a tactical action by which Wise proved his loyalty to the Rice and Baldwin faction of the territorial senate that was aligned with the Big Five (Vause 1962: 86). The very next day, a meeting was held in the governor's office to discuss new amendments to HR 13500, which would address the congressional concerns outlined by Delegate Kalaniana'ole in his report to the legislature (McGregor 1990: 27). Besides Governor McCarthy and the delegate, territorial legislators Senator Wise, Senator Charles Rice, Senator Harold Rice, Senator Harry Baldwin, and Senator Charles Chillingworth all participated in these private negotiations (McGregor 1990: 27; Vause 1962: 85–87). A second meeting with the same participants—along with key members of the House—was called later that day at Delegate Kalaniana'ole's home. There, both groups finalized the compromises that would be incorporated into proposed amendments (ibid.). It was at these two meetings that the compromise on the blood quantum definition—of one-half for "native Hawaiian"—was decided.

There were four major issues that had to be resolved before the Big Five and Congress would support the Hawaiian Homes Commission Act. These contentious points of negotiation included: (1) the degree of blood quantum defining Kanaka Maoli eligibility; (2) limits on the size of homestead lots; (3) reducing the rehabilitation plan to an experiment for a trial period of five years on the island of Moloka'i; and (4) the deletion of a section from the Organic Act that prohibited corporations from holding or acquiring real estate of over one thousand acres (McGregor 1990: 27; Vause 1962: 87).

Just four days after the territorial senate voted for SCR 6, Senator Wise introduced another proposal—SCR 8, which incorporated the changes negotiated in the private meetings (McGregor 1990: 27).[2] SCR 8 passed with ease in the Senate, but in the House it was denounced as a sellout because it would give only the poorest of the public lands to Hawaiians for homesteading (*Honolulu Advertiser* 1921h; McGregor 1990: 29). Opponents there tried to table the measure but failed. For two days, the territorial legislature debated issues raised in SCR 8. Addressing the House, Governor McCarthy spoke in favor of the measure: "If the native Hawaiian would get out and work, and make a good living for himself and his family, by the sweat of his brow, the race would flourish. That is what the rehabilitation project aims at—not sitting on the fence and playing the ukulele" (*Honolulu Star-Bulletin* 1921c). Here, McCarthy evoked the stereotyped Hawaiian—lazy, passive, and amused. His statement resonates with Senator Wise's presentation, where he envisioned Hawaiians resting on the *lānai* watching others labor away. The governor supported the measure purely on racist grounds and thus advocated for a "pure blood" definition of "native Hawaiian" (ibid.).

The Hawai'i territorial senate had already approved a one-half definition of "native Hawaiian." But this was not automatically accepted in the House. As mentioned in the previous chapter, the majority of territorial representatives in the House were Hawaiian men, many of whom were part-Hawaiian. The minutes of the committee proceedings reported that a blood quantum definition of one-half for SCR 8 was discussed before passage (Territory of Hawaii 1921a). In that committee, territorial house representative J. A. Hoopale of Kalāheo, Kaua'i, representing the sixth territorial district, offered an amendment "striking out the word 'one-half' in the first line of the paragraph (7), subdivision (a) of said section, and inserting in lieu thereof the word 'one eighth' " (1488). This is the only evidence of any direct policy challenges to the change in the blood quantum definition. Representative Paschoal "moved that amendment be tabled," and, without any recorded discussion, his suggestion was seconded by Representative Kawaha and carried; the section passed without amendment (1488). The *Honolulu Advertiser* reported that the Judiciary Committee championed the new measure found within the concurrent resolution to include "one-eighths." The revision was credited to Representative Goodness of the House and stated, "As to provide and allow those persons of not less than one-eighth Hawaiian blood be given preference in the matter of homesteading government lands (*Honolulu Advertiser* 1921a).

Although the House representatives accepted the one-half rule, they worked out other compromises that had to be negotiated in the committee of the whole. scr 8 included three major changes. First, it proposed to make homesteading for Hawaiians a five-year experiment. Second, it repealed the last amendment standing in the way of full sugar development, the provision that no one corporation could hold more than a thousand acres. Third, it redefined the blood quantum legally defining "native Hawaiian" from one-thirty-second (1/32) to one-half (1/2). As the *Honolulu Advertiser* reported, Governor McCarthy, in urging the House vote, "opposed the idea of making the act operative in favor of those having less than one-half Hawaiian blood and was gratified that an amendment extending it to all, who could prove as much as an eighth of Hawaiian blood [was changed]. The purpose was to save the race that formerly owned the land. He cited statistics to show that part Hawaiians were increasing while there was a steady decrease among the full blood members of the race" (*Honolulu Advertiser* 1921e: 10). Here, statistics showing that part-Hawaiians were increasing in number were used against a more inclusive policy, yet the very same argument—that the Hawaiian population could increase even when racially mixed—contradicted the blood logics insisting that "real" Hawaiians were only decreasing. Also notably, Hawaiians of one-half blood are no longer figured as part-Hawaiians; they instead become a stand-in for the full-blood Hawaiians.

The house amendments to scr 8 also called for having three instead of two members of the Hawaiian Homes Commission be "native Hawaiian," for allowing additional lands on the island of Hawai'i to be included in the rehabilitation project, and for including those lands with parts of the island of Molokai as the first tracts to be opened for the project. These concessions were approved and upon recommendation of the committee of the whole and by a vote of 21 to 6, the House of Representatives adopted the amendments (*Honolulu Advertiser* 1921e: 10; *Honolulu Star-Bulletin* 1921b).

Coverage of the vote focused on the contentious nature of the proposal. The *Honolulu Star-Bulletin* reported, "The final action by the house came after one of the stiffest fights that has occurred on the floor of the lower chamber in many years. The opposition all but tore the rehabilitation project to pieces, and on a number of occasions characterized it as an outright attempt to kill homesteading within the territory" (1921b). In addition, A. G. M. Robertson continued to weigh in—this time through an opinion editorial published in the *Honolulu Advertiser* on May 3, 1921. Robertson reminded the public that even Senator New agreed with him that the rehabilitation scheme should be limited to "the full blood" (1921m: 8). He also noted, "It should be remembered that the original bill sailed through the House of Representatives under false colors, but went upon the rocks in the Senate when the facts were exposed. The revised bill seems to have been framed in a little caucus. . . . No public hearing upon the measure was given by the legislature, as in other important matters. The assertions made that the revised bill has met the objections raised against the original measure are not corrected" (ibid.).

I have pointed to the ways in which blood quantum was the pivot point for the homesteading proposal as a whole. Kalaniana'ole had manipulated blood quantum as an issue, as if to prepare the territorial legislature for what was to come from his anticipated negotiations with Rice and Baldwin. Wise, who had previously taken a strong stand in support of an inclusive definition for "native Hawaiian," completely changed his position when he told the legislature that "the degree of Hawaiian blood is not a matter that gives us any worry" (*Honolulu Star-Bulletin* 1921a: 7). Their compromises along these lines entailed a reframing of the proposal as a whole and the rationale for it, not surprising since both Wise and Kalaniana'ole participated in private negotiations in order to win the support of the Big Five. After prevailing in the territorial struggle, the Big Five finally agreed to support the passage of the Hawaiian Homes Commission Act. But even though they managed to get their concessions passed in the territorial legislature, they would have to justify these changes to the senators and representatives back in Washington.

Rehabilitation Recoded

On May 10, 1921, key members traveled from Hawai'i to Congress in order to explain the dramatic revisions of the homesteading proposal that took place in the territory (*Honolulu Advertiser* 1921j, 1921k). These were the same players who had negotiated the compromise in the first place. From the territorial government there were Senator Charles A. Rice, now chair of the Hawai'i legislative committee; Senator Charles Chillingworth, president of the territorial senate; Senator Harold W. Rice; and Senator John H. Wise. Then there were those who monitored land in Hawai'i from their own positions: W. T. Rawlins, former territorial commissioner of the public lands; Sidney Ballou, attorney for the Hawaiian Sugar Planters' Association; W. W. Goodale, manager of Wailua Agricultural Company; and George M. McClellan. In addition, Harry Irwin, attorney general; John R. Desha; and W. R. Farrington, governor designate, attended (U.S. Congress 1921b: 3).[3] Judge F. M. Hatch is mentioned in the newspaper coverage, but there is no record of him taking part in the hearings (*Honolulu Advertiser* 1921j).

Again Representative Charles F. Curry of California chaired the House Committee on Territories, which met on June 9–10, 1921. Representatives who were present at these hearings included Edward B. Almon, Alabama; Edward S. Brooks, Pennsylvania; George P. Codd, Michigan; Cassius C. Dowell, Iowa; Patrick H. Drewry, Virginia; William J. Driver, Arkansas; Albert Johnson, Washington; J. Kūhiō Kalaniana'ole, Hawai'i; Charles L. Knight, Ohio; William C. Lankford, Georgia; Louis T. McFadden, Pennsylvania; Joseph McLaughlin, Pennsylvania; Allen F. Moore, Illinois; James G. Strong, Kansas; Dan A. Sutherland, Alaska; and Zebulon Weaver, North Carolina.[4]

In outlining the changes to the homesteading proposal, W. R. Farrington —governor-designate of the Territory of Hawaii—submitted a supplemental statement which spoke to the multifaceted aims of the bill. He declared: "The purpose of this measure is to preserve the present income bearing public lands from reckless dissipation through alienation to possible speculators, using income to assist in financing an experiment in homesteading which at once satisfies the American principle of land settlement by homebuilders, and gives appropriate recognition to the people of Hawaiian blood" (U.S. Congress 1921b: 57). Farrington explicitly emphasized that the compromise would prevent the break-up of cultivated sugar lands while giving "appropriate recognition to people of Hawaiian blood" through an Americanizing land settlement plan.

George M. McClellan grasped for an explanation that would discount the prospect of inclusiveness in definitions of "native Hawaiian." His entreaty to members of the House committee conflated whiteness with American citizenship: "Here is a Hawaiian intermarried with a Chinese, so that man of half Chinese blood and half Hawaiian blood is given special privileges which are denied to a full-blooded American. We do not object to that, as far as the Hawaiian part of it is concerned, but in doing that we are extending special privileges to people of Chinese blood, which does not to me seem desirable" (U.S. Congress 1921b: 142–43). Here, he equated "full-blooded American" with white U.S. citizen and explicitly named the inclusion of Asians, in this case Chinese, within racially mixed definitions of "native Hawaiian" as a threat to whiteness and its stronghold over the territory. Here "Chinese blood" among "part-Hawaiians" was used to discount Kanaka Maoli indigeneity. Representing the Parker Ranch, in place of A. G. M. Robertson this time, McClellan was part of the last commission from Hawai'i to pitch the HHCA proposal in Washington. On the table was HR 7257 (a revised version of HR 13500 that reflected the territorial amendments), the last draft of the bill, at a hearing before the House Committee on Territories during the Sixty-Seventh Congress, first session, on June 9 and 10, 1921.

The Hawai'i commission had to explain the major shift in the proposed blood quantum. As per resolution SCR 8, the last bill defined "native Hawaiian" as "any descendent *of not less than one-half part of the blood of the races inhabiting the Hawaiian Islands previous to 1778*" (U.S. Congress 1921b: 5). Attorney General Irwin spoke to this particular revision amended in the territorial legislature, noting that it was changed in order to do away with opposition against the bill from the previous hearing: "It was said by the opponents of the bill that a person of one thirty-second Hawaiian blood was *to all intents and purposes a white person;* that as a matter of fact you could not tell the difference between a person having one-thirty-second part of Hawaiian blood and a white person" (15; emphasis added).[5] Again, the example presupposed "intents and purposes" attached to racial distinction and phenotype. Had the example been a mixed-Chinese person with one-thirty-second Kanaka Maoli ancestry, this would not have been asserted. Delegate Kalaniana'ole discussed the compromise by explaining the limitation of the beneficiaries under the act. He reported, "Opposition to the last bill was as to the degree of Hawaiian blood of those whom it would benefit. Another reason for opposing the bill was that it was thought that the Hawaiians should not have the right to homestead any land they wished to homestead" (69). The delegate explained to the House Representatives what had happened during the last hearing before the U.S. Senate committee when they questioned the one-thirty-second definition for "native Hawaiian." Senator Wise also discussed the shift within the blood quantum criterion: "Some people objected to that because it was hard to distinguish between one-thirty-second Hawaiian and wanted one-half part-Hawaiian. Of course I do not agree with that part of the amendment, but still, *in order to put the thing through, I had to agree to it*" (79; emphasis added). Senator Wise did not offer any specific details of the negotiations that took place in Hawai'i. Moreover, he presented his role as if he had simply resigned to the demands of "some people" to "put the thing through." Even so, the exclusively limited definition of "native Hawaiian" was not yet a given.

In response to the explanations about the blood quantum shift, Representative Strong of Kansas suggested re-envisioning a more inclusive criterion. In the following excerpt he, Representative Driver of Arkansas, Representative Almon of Alabama, and Chairman Curry of California addressed Senator Wise with regard to the one-thirty-second definition. Delegate Kalaniana'ole also took part:

MR. STRONG: Well, if this committee should restore that part of the bill permitting Hawaiians of one thirty-second blood participation, what would be the result?

MR. WISE: Why, I think the Hawaiians, so far as the Hawaiians are concerned, they would bless you.

MR. STRONG: Well, I want to be blessed.

THE CHAIRMAN: Do the Hawaiians themselves consider it to be a good scheme to limit it to full-bloods, or half-bloods?

MR. WISE: Yes; a large part seem to agree to that.

MR. DRIVER: The legislature is composed of how many Hawaiians, and how many of the Caucasian race?

MR. WISE: In the senate?

MR. DRIVER: Yes.

MR. WISE: About six Hawaiians.

MR. DRIVER: About how many others?

THE CHAIRMAN: Nine.

MR. WISE: Nine others.

MR. DRIVER: How about the house?

MR. WISE: In the house the majority consists of Hawaiians.

THE CHAIRMAN: Well, it seems that the Hawaiians are in favor of having this limitation?

MR. WISE: Yes; they are.

THE CHAIRMAN: To the full-bloods, and half-bloods.

MR. WISE: Half-blood Hawaiians.

MR. STRONG: You think that that would be the most satisfactory?

THE CHAIRMAN: To them?

MR. WISE: To them.

THE CHAIRMAN: Yes, to them.

MR. WISE: Well, that would be hard to answer.

MR. ALMON: They have answered that under the settlement of this compromise?

MR. WISE: They have authorized the backing up of the bill as it is, and I have no right to ask for any limits or any deviation.

MR. KALANIANAʻOLE: That agreement was put into the bill because of the suggestion of Senator New. That was put in by the legislature to meet the objection. I called on the legislature to ratify just what the Senate wanted, so that we would have easy going in the Senate.

MR. STRONG: What is the objection?

MR. WISE: According to his remarks, he thought it was unconstitutional, but I cannot see where he can reconcile his statement by the remarks that one-half would make it unconstitutional.

MR. STRONG: I agree with you.

MR. WISE: But, as I said, we came over here as beggars, and so we took what we could get. I was told a long time ago that one of your proverbs was never to look a gift horse in the mouth, we took what we could get.

MR. STRONG: No, I think you have great rights. (U.S. Congress 1921b: 79–80)

Here, representatives Strong and Almon seem sincerely concerned and even puzzled by the reasoning being offered. But we must consider how both men represented states that bordered Indian Territory, which may well have made them more familiar with blood quantum politics in relation to American Indian land allotment. In any case, they pointed out the contradictions within charges of constitutionality. Despite their support, Senator Wise was unwilling to seize the moment as a possible opportunity to revise the definition of "native Hawaiian." Here it appears that Delegate Kalanianaʻole may have interrupted Senator Wise in order to effectively reroute the entire discussion. The delegate attributed the blood quantum change to the fact that the representatives from Hawaiʻi were simply responding to Senator New's suggestion to limit the definition of "native Hawaiian."

It would seem that Delegate Kalanianaʻole did more than just facilitate the compromise that shifted the blood quantum criterion defining "native Hawaiian"; he was instrumental to the change. Representative Strong continued to express his concerns until the very end of the debates as to whether the one-half definition was suitable and desired among Hawaiian people. When Senator Wise said that the Hawaiian people would "bless" Strong if the most inclusive blood quantum definition of "native Hawaiian" persisted, he problematized the one-half criterion. Yet Wise did not seize that moment as an opportunity to overturn the decision made in the territorial legislature —he conceded that the one-half definition was agreeable. Even worse, he attempted to make it seem as if he were merely carrying out the will of the Hawaiian representatives in the House rather than that of the Big Five, where he himself played an integral role in striking the deal to appease those with strong ties to the sugar industry.

Reproducing "Part-Hawaiians"

The one-half definition of "native Hawaiian" did not automatically win over those who were opposed to the entire bill, such as McClellan, who was now representing the Parker Ranch (U.S. Congress 1921b: 92). McClellan continued to advocate against the bill by calling into question both its constitutionality and its premise that Hawaiians were under threat of extinction (90). He specifically interrogated the appeals of sentiment for Hawaiians as "a dying race": "Recognizing this as *racial legislation,* it would seem to be the duty of Congress to consider it with reference to, first, the welfare of the

United States, and second, the welfare of Hawaii as a whole. The arguments to Congress for this bill have been lacking in essential frankness and are misleading in the following: First, the claim of a dying race. The bill as drawn represents a group actually increasing in numbers" (87–88; emphasis added). McClellan appealed to the good of the nation-state and of the territory to assess the constitutionality of the bill. He also suggested that even if the bill were to be limited to "full-blood" Hawaiians, he would still find it objectionable because he regarded it as "racial legislation."[6] "Now, I wish to say that the bill as presented here last year on behalf of a dying race was an appeal to the sentiment of this committee, when, in fact, the entire race group represented by that bill, taking both the Hawaiians of the full blood and the part Hawaiians together, were actually increasing in numbers, both in the decade from 1900 to 1910 and the decade from 1910 to 1920. So that it was absolutely misleading to come to this committee and say that that group as represented by this bill were a dying race" (101).

McClellan subscribed to a rigid definition of "native Hawaiian," limiting the identification to those who were dying out, and he continued to question supporting those Hawaiians through homesteading. He also argued that Hawaiians were not meant to farm and that they worked better as mechanics, teachers, bookkeepers, stenographers, and lawyers—"everything but farmers; everything but successful homesteaders" (U.S. Congress 1921b: 119). The exclusion of farming from the roles stated as fit for part-Hawaiians is curious and indicates something unsettling about figuring Hawaiians as keepers or developers of the land. Perhaps this was another way of saying that part-Hawaiians were beyond homesteading.

McClellan continued to push for the most exclusive definition of "native Hawaiian" at "full-blood" (U.S. Congress 1921b: 101). Perhaps more importantly, McClellan also noted that the proposed provisions in the bill were not fit to fully provide for the full-bloods. Still, he continued to dismiss any concerns for part-Hawaiians, advocating against any form of help for any part-Hawaiians "who are increasing in number more rapidly than the Caucasians" (102). He considered reproduction among part-Hawaiians a threat to whiteness in the islands. It was not simply that the part-Hawaiians were reproducing and, by virtue of their growth rate, not figured as the dying Hawaiians; they were also reproducing significantly faster than white people. The haole were already a numerical minority at that time, which had implications for their commitment to Americanizing Hawai'i while threatened by the growing population of Asian peoples who would soon be eligible to vote.

> MR. WISE: The question came up during Mr. McClellan's discussion, "Why rehabilitate the part Hawaiians? Why not restrict this bill to the pure-blood Hawaiians?"
>
> I do not know whether you gentlemen have studied the way of rehabilitating the people, but I have; and there is a professor in Michigan who has been in communication with the secretary of our Hawaiian Society, who believes that the only way to rehabilitate a people is to intermarry the part blood with the full blood. Why? Statistics have shown that the part Hawaiians have increased, and the full blood Hawaiians have decreased. So the best method is to mingle the part Hawaiians, with the full-blood Hawaiians, who have decreased. [Laughter.] *And that is not anything to be laughed at either.*
>
> THE CHAIRMAN: Are you a man of family?
>
> MR. WISE: I have 10 children.
>
> THE CHAIRMAN: Then you have done your share of rehabilitating. [Laughter].
>
> MR. WISE: And I am part-Hawaiian; and I believe that the only salvation of our people is to intermarry the part Hawaiians with the full-blood Hawaiians. . . . And if the Hawaiians have a moral right, an equitable right, to these lands, I can not see, gentlemen, why the part Hawaiians, the three-quarters blood, the one-quarter blood, or the two-sixteenths blood, should be cut out and only the people of the full blood or the half blood get the benefit of it; I can not see why. (140; emphasis added)

Clearly, Wise was torn over the issue. On the one hand he had to support the 50-percent compromise, and yet from this passage it is obvious that his heart simply was not in it. In response to the chairman, Wise insisted that what he offered as a solution was not a laughing matter. It seems their laughter was a response to his use of "rehabilitating" as a euphemism for reproductive sexual activity. What did the focus on Wise's bodily practices signify for notions of Hawaiian sexuality and masculinity? Here we should note that Wise referred to himself as "part-Hawaiian" and discussed his own experience of partnering with another Hawaiian as a response to the need for rehabilitation among Kanaka Maoli. He further suggested that the woman to whom he was married was a "full blood Hawaiian." In turn, Chairman Curry regarded Wise as a competent, actively rehabilitating Hawaiian man. Here, Wise's sense of rehabilitating Hawaiians and the nature of indigenous reabsorption were quite different than those proposed by Robertson in the last set of hearings. More importantly, the senator argued for a generative form of rehabilitation that resisted the easy readings of assimilation; Wise specifically advocated for forms of intermarriage that would increase the number of Hawaiians who would then be able to claim more Hawaiian blood quantum.

Wise not only complicated the notion of "part-Hawaiian" as an inclusive definition; he specifically called on a broader framework of reparations and entitlement to substantiate the Hawaiian claim by pointing out that if they were abiding by a "moral claim" and Hawaiians' "equitable right" to the lands, then to cut out Kānaka Maoli with less blood quantum would be indefensible.

These final debates ended with Delegate Kalaniana'ole simply summarizing that the bill under consideration had been reported to the Hawai'i legislature and "in their deliberations inserted a clause that it was nothing but just that part Hawaiians should be included" (U.S. Congress 1921b: 143). In other words, the delegate reiterated territorial legislative support for the bill before the committee at that moment. In doing so, he preempted further questions—whether by McClellan on one side or Strong on the other—about changing the blood quantum compromise. He did this by asserting that as long as some part-Hawaiians were included, the bill had full support in the islands. Thus, in the end, the U.S. Congress deferred not only to the territorial legislature but to the Big Five.

In that same week, on June 20, 1921, Kalaniana'ole introduced the redrafted bill HR 7257 to the House. Furthermore, Senator Harry S. New of Indiana had introduced an identical companion bill—S 1881—in the Senate on May 25, 1921. With the passage of those two bills, the Hawaiian Homes Commission Act was signed into U.S. federal law on July 9, 1921. In the final version, the section on "Hawaiian rehabilitation" was relegated to an explicitly minor role in this omnibus bill while the colonial form of land expropriation won out. Large corporations were then free to control the bidding at public auctions of leases to the 26,000 acres of highly cultivated "public land" without threat of withdrawal for any homesteads, and without the 1,000-acre limit that had been imposed in the 1900 Organic Act (Murakami 1991: 47). Thus, the major impetus behind the HHCA was revealed—to amend the Organic Act land laws by repealing homesteading for the general public under the pretext of rehabilitating Hawaiians.

At the time of its passage, the HHCA had no statement of purpose. Even though it was initially meant to promote native welfare by providing homesteads and financial aid, the rehabilitation section was ultimately relegated to a minor role in an omnibus bill that secured congressional approval to restructure Hawai'i's land laws. The business elite's successful push for provisions to be added to the HHCA neutralized the potential of the act to empower Hawaiians. These provisions guaranteed the continuation of public land leasing for sugar and ranching interests who won out. That the act was a win for them is made even more clear from the composition of the first Hawaiian Homes Commission appointed in 1921. The executive secretary of the commission was George Cooke, a millionaire rancher of Molokai who was also a former territorial senator and Republican leader (*Honolulu Advertiser* 1921b). Also on the commission were Delegate Kalaniana'ole, who passed away the following year, the Reverend Akana, and Rudolph M. Duncan, roadmaster of the Honolulu Rapid Transit Company (ibid.; Hawaiian Homes Commission 1922: 4).

Conclusion

What began as a well-intentioned plan for rehabilitation became problematically tied to welfare notions that constructed Hawaiians as a beneficiary class using blood criterion as a measure of social competency. Hawaiians of 50-percent or more blood quantum were said to be incompetent and therefore eligible for land leasing under the Hawaiian Homes Commission Act but could not gain fee simple title to the lands designated for Hawaiian homesteading. Conversely, Hawaiians who were less than 50-percent were regarded as fully competent and therefore not in need of any land-leasing assistance since it was assumed that they could effectively compete in the free-market economy and secure their own property, and Asian blood among racially mixed Hawaiians was evoked to discount Hawaiian indigeneity. It was within this operational logic that identity was determined "in the blood." As the bill was progressively transformed, the project became little more than a rationale for changing Hawai'i's land laws to empower the sugar plantations and ranches, a change which destroyed homesteading in the broadest sense for all people in Hawai'i. All along, the planters wanted one particular section of the Organic Act eliminated—that upon expiration of a lease, land would be withdrawn and opened to homesteading (Wright 1972: 32).

Although the act was seen as helping a declining race, it was sharply limited in its potential for rehabilitating Hawaiians. Moreover, by advancing sugar and ranching interests, it adversely impacted small farmers at large. Accounting for the breakdown of the act's original rehabilitative intentions, Ulla Hasager argues that its outcome was a "tripartite form of political cooperation" among the federal and territorial bodies as well as the local ruling business elite (1997: 170–71). While the stated goal of those in support of the HHCA was to increase the Hawaiian population, the act made no provision for any increases in that population in terms of the potential for increased availability of lands for leasing. As it was, only 10 percent of the acres set aside were usable for agriculture and pastoral purposes, and only two percent of that could be could be developed at a reasonable cost (Kent 1993: 76).

The compromise of redefining "native Hawaiian" by a one-half blood quantum criterion—rather than accepting a more inclusive one-thirty-second definition or a hyperexclusive "full-blood" definition—seems to have been a last-ditch effort to contain the bill's impact on the part of its opponents and a desperate attempt, by its supporters, to salvage *some* legislative action. A political compromise, it fully satisfied no one. It is thus ironic that this congressional definition of "native Hawaiian" has had such a lasting impact on Hawaiians, through its continued reification and status as quasi "common sense." There was no acknowledgment by the dominant players that part-Hawaiians who could not meet the 50-percent rule were dispossessed by the land-law transformation. The logic by which their exclusion was figured was that of their American equality, their competency as citizens.

The 50-percent rule both reduced the demands of rehabilitation and limited the number of Kānaka Maoli who could access homesteading lands. Moreover, the blood racialization of Kanaka Maoli, through this legal construction of "native Hawaiian," was the means by which the elites in Hawai'i, both Hawaiian and haole, effaced Hawaiian entitlement to the land. Both Delegate Kalaniana'ole and Senator Wise worked with dominant white leaders in the islands and aligned themselves with their Americanizing agenda. The eventual revision of an inclusive definition necessitated more than just a downsizing of the land base and the number of people who would have access to it; this modification required redefining the relationship of the people to the particular lands in question. The move away from the recognition of Hawaiians' land entitlement corresponds to an emergent welfare approach to the question of Native rehabilitation, and hence to a racialized beneficiary definition based on a blood criterion. That is, Hawaiian blood quantum racialization occurred at precisely the moment when Hawaiian sovereignty claims were disregarded.

Notions of Hawaiian blood properties, processes of absorption in relation to mixed-race Hawaiians, and native assimilation were instrumental to the reformulation of Hawaiians for the purposes of the HHCA. The rationale cut two ways: opponents of the bill used these notions as much as supporters did arguing that some Kānaka Maoli, particularly those who met the one-thirty-second definition of "native Hawaiian," would resent being the objects of charity. Thus, within the debates, a legal construction of part-Hawaiians emerged where Hawaiians who were not full-blood were considered to be beyond the need of rehabilitation. The haole saw part-Hawaiians as a threat to "real Hawaiians" precisely because they represented and produced (in Donna Haraway's terms) "categorical ambiguity and troubling mobility." The arguments against inclusive definitions of Hawaiian identity reveal concern about white property interests and uneasiness about empowering Hawaiians who were also of Asian descent. Ultimately, Hawaiians who did not meet the vagaries of the 50-percent blood quantum rule were deemed ineligible for land leasing on the Hawaiian Home Lands territory. Their mixed-race status would work to their disadvantage; their ineligibility was seen as an advantage for "real" Hawaiians, those who met the 50-percent definition. In the end, Hawaiian land claims were marginalized while an exclusive blood criterion was reified. Indeed this restrictive definition of "native Hawaiian" both upheld and subverted the whole edifice of Hawaiian rehabilitation.

A presumption of assimilation—essential to the blood quantum racialization of Hawaiians—was fundamentally linked to legal classification with regard to citizenship, land entitlement, and constructions of American whiteness in Hawai'i. Discursive constructions of Hawaiianness were formed in the shift away from recognizing Hawaiian entitlement to the privileging of white property interests. Alternative justifications for allotting lands for lease to Hawaiians were thus determined through political and economic management by the state. Through this troubling matrix notions of native rehabilitation were recoded to further dispossess Hawaiians. Rehabilitation remained, however, a stated priority—the edifice that upheld the proposal to amend the Organic Act. Those who tightened the definition of "native Hawaiian" in order to limit the numbers eligible for homesteading also actively worked to limit the amount of lands to be set aside for allotment. This link between a restrictive definition of an indigenous people and the land base reserved for their use is a rather obvious example of colonial power. Less obviously, the restriction of identity was accomplished through redefining the relationship of the people to the lands in question.

The welfare discourse of protection and rehabilitation was the means by which a racialization of identity occurred—thus counting Hawaiians only in relation to their welfare needs—as the logic of "pitied, but not entitled" became ever more manifest. The result was to disqualify alternative discourses of native land entitlement. Hawaiian land, configured as limited property, became a criterion of Hawaiian "racial" classification. The blood quantum criterion was intimately tied to struggles over changing the territorial land policy—the same land policy in which the rule originated and within which it persists. Problematic considerations as to what constituted "public" and "Hawaiian" lands became the grounds upon which Hawaiianness was configured and by which Hawaiians were first legally racially defined. Consistent with what Virginia Dominguez found in her study of whiteness in Creole Louisiana, "property is not just a corollary of racial classification; it is also a criterion of it" (1986: 89). Dominguez also argued that "the legal record makes it very clear that definitions of identity are, in fact, chains of propositions leading to *and* reflecting entitlements and disenfranchisements" (57). Definitions of "native Hawaiian" were chains of propositions that led to and reflected entitlements and disenfranchisements.

To properly hold American citizenship, one had to be assimilable (Jacobson 1998; Lopez 1996). Hawaiians were seen as assimilable while Asians were not. In the Hawaiian case, there seems to be an inversion of this determination of competency. Hawaiians of 50-percent or more blood quantum were said to be incompetent and therefore eligible for land leasing under the Hawaiian Homes Commission Act but could not gain fee simple title to the lands designated for Hawaiian homesteading.

These property interests were reflected and reproduced through the local racial triangulation of white-Hawaiian-Asian (or haole-Native-alien). The property functions of whiteness, as trenchantly theorized by Cheryl Harris, were fully operative in the Hawai'i hearings. Harris concludes, "In the realm of *social* relations, racial recognition in the United States is thus an act of race subordination." Extending this point she further asserts, "In the realm of *legal* relations, judicial definition of racial identity based on white supremacy reproduced that race subordination at the institutional level" (1993: 1741). Legislative definitions of Hawaiian racial identity were similarly based on assertions of white supremacy, reproducing native and Asian race subordination at an institutional level. Thus, in the HHCA debates, whiteness was, in Harris's terms, a "racialized privilege" (1741). The conflation of "full blooded American" with "white" dictated who was said to be able, and interested, in maintaining Hawai'i as a "real" American outpost. This was of special concern to those from the territory who represented white American interests in commerce. Indeed, in the hearings, some part-Hawaiians were considered, in Irwin's terms, for "all intents and purposes white." And in those instances, the Asian mix was erased from the equation. Asian-Hawaiian mixing not only revealed racial intermingling; it signaled the blurring of legal subject status: citizen-alien. White exclusion of Asians was also selective—in relation to Hawai'i and Hawaiians. On the one hand, the sugar elite wanted Hawai'i exempted from the Chinese Exclusion Act. Yet they would work to exclude Hawaiians from counting as native if they had "Chinese blood." And too much Chinese "blood" was always a contaminant of whiteness.

As Harris notes, "Whiteness conferred on its owners aspects of citizenship that were all the more valued because they were denied to others"—the right to reputation and use, and of course, the right to exclude (1993: 1744). But, as I argued in the introduction with regard to American Indians, whiteness also carried the power to *selectively* assimilate. Three kinds of natives were discursively produced in the debates: "part-Hawaiians" whom whiteness could selectively assimilate; "full-blooded" Hawaiians who were racialized as incompetent and therefore in need of protection; and Asian "Part-Hawaiians" whom whiteness would not assimilate. White-mixed "part-Hawaiians" who no longer counted as indigenous were afforded the privilege of whiteness. But this privilege was granted within the overall structures of white domination over property—control that ultimately furthered the dispossession of all Hawaiians.

Since 1959 our longtime politicians have miserably failed in their "trust responsibility." If it were not for *Rice v. Cayetano,* there would be no effort for the so-called
"Native Hawaiian Government Reorganization Act of 2005."

Nevertheless, let us look at the facts about S147 (the Akaka Bill). Beginning with
its phony purpose, through the various versions, to its present form, four things
never changed in this scam: Congressional findings that indigenous Hawaiians meet
the criteria for recognition. A new "Native Hawaiian governing entity" with proce-
dures established and approved by our "apologetic" thief. A definition of Native
Hawaiian that has zero blood quantum. And, an authorization that directs the new
"Native Hawaiian governing entity" to settle indigenous Hawaiian land claims.

According to the 2000 U.S. Census, there were 402,000 people in the United
States claiming Native Hawaiian ancestry and of this figure, 142,000 claimed Native
Hawaiian ancestry only.

The number of potential members in the new "Native Hawaiian governing entity"
is now thousands of times greater than the 24,800 indigenous Hawaiians counted
by the state Department of Hawaiian Home Lands and the 20,000 registered indigenous Hawaiians who stand by the "initiative" of their kupuna [elders and ances-
tors] and the "self-determination" for the "reorganization" of indigenous Hawaiians
that began in 1976.

Yet the state Office of Hawaiian Affairs, our longtime politicians and entrenched
colonized Hawaiians endorse the obliteration of indigenous Hawaiians' "self-determination" by the tsunami wave of Hawaiians who have one native ancestor in 500.

—Samuel L. Kealoha Jr., letter to the editor, *Maui News,* April 22, 2005

SAM KEALOHA JR.'S LETTER IS A PRIME example of the history wrought by
the 50-percent blood quantum definition—a legacy that has long divided
the Hawaiian community. The current political predicament is traceable to
the Hawaiian Homes Commission Act, where the blood racialization of
Kanaka Maoli implicates contemporary Hawaiian sovereignty politics. The
HHCA is directly tied to current legislation that proposes to reorganize the

Native Hawaiian government, which would then lay the groundwork to settle all unadjudicated Hawaiian land claims, as well as contain national claims under international law. If passed, this measure—the Native Hawaiian Government Reorganization Act, commonly referred to as "the Akaka bill" since it was authored by Senator Daniel Akaka (D-HI)—aims to federally recognize the Hawaiian people as a Native Governing Entity under U.S. federal policy. Although Kealoha refers to S. 147, which was proposed during the 109th Congress and failed, Senator Akaka reintroduced the same measure in the 110th Congress, where it still awaits a vote on the U.S. Senate floor (as S. 310) as of this writing.

In his letter, Kealoha is critical of the legislation, but in part for reasons having to do with the way "Native Hawaiian" is defined in the legislation and his own commitment to the 50-percent rule. In this chapter I explore how the colonial legacies of blood quantum politics continue to impact contemporary Native Hawaiian struggles for land and recognition.

The definition of "Native Hawaiian" found in this proposal is inclusive of all individuals who are the descendants of those who inhabited the Hawaiian Islands prior to 1778—a definition based on lineal ancestry (using Captain James Cook's arrival as the threshold date) rather than blood quantum, let alone adherence to the 50-percent rule. Kealoha argues that this "zero blood quantum" definition would create a "tsunami wave of Hawaiians who have one native ancestor in 500," even though it would not allow non–Kanaka Maoli to participate in the model of self-governance. Kealoha contrasts the number of people who claimed Hawaiian ancestry, in addition to any other race, in the U.S. census for 2000 with those who claimed only Hawaiian ancestry. Furthermore, he stresses that "the number of potential members in the new native Hawaiian government entity . . . [would be] thousands of times greater than the 24,800 indigenous Hawaiians counted by the state Department of Hawaiian Home Lands [which administers the lands allotted through the Hawaiian Homes Commission Act of 1920] and the 20,000 registered ones." Here, he implies that Kānaka Maoli who do not meet the 50-percent blood quantum rule, and thus are ineligible for Hawaiian Home Lands, are a threat to those who do.

Without mentioning his former role as a trustee of the Office of Hawaiian Affairs (OHA), Kealoha also charges the current trustees and "entrenched colonized Hawaiians" as ready to endorse the "obliteration of indigenous

Hawaiians' 'self-determination' by the tsunami wave" and suggests that those who meet the blood quantum are *the* "indigenous Hawaiians"—the most authentic and entitled vis-à-vis political claims against the U.S. government. Reminiscent of the guiding colonial logic found in the HHCA hearings, Kealoha cites the probable emergence of more "part-Hawaiians" who don't meet the definition of "native Hawaiian" as a problem in order to argue against an inclusive policy for "Native Hawaiian" within the legislation. He simultaneously acknowledges that their addition would increase the Kanaka Maoli population as a whole while contradictorily asserting that the "indigenous Hawaiians" (read: 50-percenters) are the real Hawaiians who are threatened because their numbers are decreasing. Here again, as with the HHCA, those who meet the 50-percent criterion are used as stand-ins for "full bloods" who need protection.

It is absurd to claim that any living Hawaiian can have just "one native ancestor in 500," since a Kanaka Maoli person gains his or her ancestry through the mother or father, which would account for (at least) one Native forebear. We would then need to count at least one parent's Hawaiian ancestry from one or more of his and/or her parents, and so on. It seems Kealoha actually meant to invoke one *unmixed* native ancestor in 500. Even so, his dismissal of the Hawaiians who have "one [unmixed] ancestor in 500," in favor of those who meet the 50-percent blood quantum, neglects Hawaiian genealogical and kinship practices which are typically inclusive and privilege relatedness. One also has to wonder why the prospect of long-lost Hawaiians coming back into the fold threatens Kealoha, since those of Hawaiian ancestry who might ride the "tsunami" would, by definition, be some Hawaiians' *'ohana* (extended family) and so could be potentially reclaimed, accordingly increasing the population number for all Kanaka Maoli. However, the Hawaiian population total is precisely what he seems worried about given his citation of the 2000 U.S. census data, where some Kānaka Maoli claimed more than one race, in the first census where one could claim more than one category under the racial designations portion of the form.

Kealoha's letter suggests that the ruling in *Rice v. Cayetano,* which struck down Hawaiian-only voting in elections for trustees of the Office of Hawaiian Affairs, is what brought about the efforts for Hawaiian federal recognition. The alleged purpose of the legislation is to *protect* Hawaiians, and the ruling has hastened several lawsuits that aim to dismantle all Hawaiian-specific institutions and programs that are state- and federally funded by charging that they are racially discriminatory. The Department of Hawaiian Home Lands (which administers the lands allotted by the HHCA) and the OHA are among the targets. Such lawsuits have led to a rallying cry among Hawaiians who administer these programs in order to mobilize the native Hawaiian leaseholders who are seen as most vulnerable, and thus would be wise to support federal recognition as a protective measure.

Proponents of the Akaka bill argue that federal recognition would shield Hawaiians from these legal challenges that are based on the equal protection clause of the Fourteenth Amendment of the U.S. Constitution. Nonetheless, Kealoha, like many Kānaka Maoli opposed to federal recognition, sees the real purpose as a way to settle Hawaiian land claims. He also refers to the "apologetic thief" as the arbitrator of justice in his coded reference to the U.S. Apology Resolution that was issued to the Hawaiian people during the centennial memorial in 1993 for the overthrow of 1893. It is no surprise that Kealoha refers to the ruling in *Rice* as the "phony purpose" for the proposal; prior to the case, the grassroots Native-initiative Ka Lāhui Hawai'i had long advocated for federal recognition, from its inception in 1987, but Hawai'i's congressional delegates, including Senator Akaka, opposed their proposal for nation-within-a-nation status.

Although Kealoha opposes the proposal for Hawaiian federal recognition on the grounds that it undercuts the Hawaiian right of full self-determination that exceeds this model, his argument is undermined by his attachment to the 50-percent rule as a criterion for those who are part of a collective sovereignty claim. If one accepts blood quantum classifications *at all* in the context of the Hawaiian sovereignty struggle, then one is already relying on a model that is counter to a prosovereignty position. Since the HHCA, blood quantum classifications of Hawaiianness have consistently been used to enact, substantiate, and then disguise the further appropriation of land while they obscure and erase sovereignty claims and conceptions of identity as a relation of genealogy to place. Blood quantum is to allotment as genealogy is to sovereignty. In other words, blood quantum modalities entail allotment in relation to the *individual* whereas genealogy better enables an emphasis on the continuing *collective* political claims of Kanaka Maoli.

Not only has the 50-percent rule, created through the HHCA, left Kanaka Maoli a troubling legacy—one mired in outsiders' divisive perceptions of who counts as a "real" Hawaiian—the criterion has also re-emerged in several important and problematic ways. It was enshrined in the very act that provided for Hawai'i's admission to the union in 1959. Then it was used in the creation of the OHA's legal mandate. The 50-percent rule was likewise a key factor in the ruling in *Rice v. Cayetano*. And, as a result of that ruling, defenders of Hawaiian-specific funding sources and institutions now cite the HHCA as proof that the United States has a trust obligation to the Hawaiian people in general (not simply those who meet the 50-percent criterion). Their claim undergirds the current push for Hawaiian federal recognition.

In this chapter I first provide a status report on the HHCA as a program with continuous problems of mismanagement, as well as the persistent conflicts over the 50-percent rule in relation to the leasing provisions. I study the details of *Rice v. Cayetano* in order to show how the 50-percent blood rule was a central factor in the U.S. Supreme Court majority opinion. It is crucial to explore the implications of the ruling, which has proved to be pivotal for Hawaiian sovereignty politics because it has intensified the sense of urgency among different Kanaka Maoli political groups, as well as the state agencies which oversee federal funding for Native Hawaiians and Hawai'i's congressional delegation to pursue their varying agendas and political visions for resolving the outstanding sovereignty claims. I also offer an account of the campaign for federal recognition, the way that model relies on a limited form of indigenous self-governance, and how the history of the 50-percent rule looms in the background of the proposal. And finally I investigate the implications of the U.S. Apology Resolution and the segment of the Hawaiian sovereignty movement that opposes federal recognition in favor of independence from the United States, and how they tend to questions of inclusion and belonging for a potential citizenry under their envisioned nation-state. I evaluate these different sovereignty projects in light of the lessons learned from the colonial logics and ideologies at play in the HHCA hearings and its final outcome.

Broken Trust

In the decades since the passage of the HHCA, various moderate challenges to the 50-percent rule have been mounted. One was as early as 1953 in a state senate resolution asking Congress to permit children with less than 50-percent Hawaiian blood quantum to inherit Hawaiian Home Lands leases from parents' holdings. The resolution passed 14–1 with only Senator Herbert K.H. Lee voting against it. He asserted that the change would be contrary to the purpose of rehabilitation (*Honolulu Star-Bulletin* 1953). The Hawaiian Civic Club also opposed the measure when it was presented as a bill before the House. In agreement with the club was Charles Chillingworth, a former territorial senator and a member of the legislative committee that traveled to Washington in June 1921 for the last round of hearings on the HHCA. He was still on the political scene, but this time he was chair of the Commerce Committee. Chillingworth asserted that the measure could be "the beginning of the end" of the HHCA if it passed (ibid.).

In 1971, the Department of Hawaiian Home Lands acknowledged publicly that beginning in 1961 it had prioritized leasing awards to full-blood Hawaiians. But in that next decade the practice was thrown out under the department's new rules and regulations. From then on the department maintained that the awards would be based on the date of application. In media coverage, Richard Paglinawan, then the deputy of the department, said that the earlier priority perpetuated "homestead occupancy by generations of full-blooded Hawaiians when they should be rehabilitated for life in the 'broader community'" (Alton 1971). Here we see yet another notion of Hawaiian rehabilitation in which native Hawaiian homesteading was thought to facilitate another form of assimilation.

By the end of the next decade, there was a notable challenge to the 50-percent blood quantum rule but it had little to do with the leasing provisions of the HHCA. The test was directed at and within the Office of Hawaiian Affairs (OHA). Trustees of the OHA who initiated the challenges were advised by the state legislature that any change in the blood quantum rules require putting an option for a state constitutional amendment on the statewide ballot. And so, just ten years after its inception, in 1988 the OHA held a referendum among voters to determine whether there was broad support for changing the definitions of "native Hawaiian" and "Hawaiian" into one single definition, counting all with any Hawaiian ancestry as a single beneficiary class for the OHA trust. Voters agreed, by an overwhelming margin, that there should be an all-inclusive definition of Hawaiian for this purpose since such a change would not affect the leasing of the Hawaiian Home Lands as specified in the HHCA (because it is determined by a congressional act). Even though 83 percent of those who voted favored a broad definition, such a change was not pursued or implemented (Yamaguchi 1989). In 1989, the OHA held yet another referendum on the same question to satisfy the legislature, which had determined that the wording on the first proposal was unclear. In this second vote, the majority of voters again approved of the broadest definition but the legislature held the bills that followed (Glauberman 1989a: 4).

The Department of Hawaiian Home Lands has been plagued with serious charges of mismanagement, misconduct, and breach of trust. In 1991, after an eleven-year investigation, the Hawaii Advisory Committee of the U.S. Commission on Civil Rights issued a report on the mismanagement of the trust by the state. The document, *A Broken Trust,* accounted for seventy years of abuses (Dulles 1991). Among the findings were chronic instances of illegal uses and transfers of land for U.S. military use, public parks, various county facilities, and even leases to private parties for commercial purposes. That same year, the front page of the *Wall Street Journal* printed an exposé by Susan Faludi, "Broken Promise: How Everyone Got Hawaiians' Homelands Except the Hawaiians" (ibid.). Between the time of the passage of the HHCA in 1921 and these two reports in 1991, fewer than 6,000 native Hawaiians received land leases; an estimated 30,000 had died while on the waiting list for the Hawaiian Home Lands and another 22,000 were still waiting (Trask 1994: 74). Following the release of the reports, the Hawai'i state legislature finally allowed Hawaiians the right to sue the state for breaches of the Hawaiian Home Lands trust (Barayuga 1991: 1). While these problems persist, there was one modest gain in the leasing provisions. In 1992, the state of Hawai'i passed statutes allowing native Hawaiian leaseholders to designate their children as successors under the lease if they meet a blood quantum criterion of one-fourth Hawaiian blood. And in 1994, the state extended this provision to permit grandchildren of native Hawaiian leaseholders to become successors if they meet the quarter blood rule (Garcia 1997: A1). Congress did not authorize this amendment to the Hawaiian Homes Commission Act until 1997 (U.S. Congress 1997: 105–16).

But 1995 revealed yet another layer of scandal. The department found that during the territorial period, from 1900 to 1959, the government sold over 13,000 acres of Hawaiian Home Lands that had not been properly identified as part of the land trust. The Department of Hawaiian Home Lands got a settlement from the state instead of pressing a land claim to pursue rightful title (Pang 1995: 1). That same year, the state legislature created a panel to determine compensation owed to Hawaiians for breach of trust. Over 4,700 claims, representing charges by 2,700 claimants, were filed that year. But by October 1999, the panel had issued opinions on only 47 percent of the total number of claims filed, representing 400 claimants (Barayuga 1999:1). The rest of the complaints either did not make it through the administrative process or were dismissed. Of the claims with issued opinions, the legislature acted on only two (ibid.). As a result of such blatant disregard, a class action lawsuit was filed on December 29, 1999, on behalf of the 2,700 claimants, charging the state with breach of trust (Morse 1999).

In addition to the broken trust and mismanagement that have meant that many remain waiting for their leases, it is unclear whether the lands allotted would hold all those on the list now, let alone the 30,000 who died while waiting. While the stated goal of those in support of the HHCA was to increase the Hawaiian population, the act made no provision for any increases in the Native population in terms of the amount of land set aside for leasing. This has led to an exodus of Hawaiians relocating to the U.S. continent (Halualani 2002).

Rice v. Cayetano

On February 23, 2000, the U.S. Supreme Court handed down their ruling in the case of *Rice v. Cayetano* (No. 98–818). The decision held in favor of Harold F. Rice, a fourth-generation resident of Hawai'i, who argued that his having been denied the right to vote in the Office of Hawaiian Affairs trustee elections violated both the Fourteenth and Fifteenth Amendments of the U.S. Constitution. It bears mentioning that Harold F. Rice is a direct descendant of Senator Harold Rice and Senator Charles Rice, both of whom took part in the HHCA hearings as territorial witnesses and who participated in the private negotiations with Governor McCarthy to negotiate the blood quantum criterion from one-eighth to one-half.

Since the OHA's inception in 1978, trustee elections had been limited to residents of Hawai'i defined as "native Hawaiian," with 50-percent or more Hawaiian blood quantum, or "Hawaiian," with any amount less than 50-percent Hawaiian blood quantum. The OHA is governed by a nine-member elected board of trustees and holds title to all real or personal property set aside or conveyed to it as a trust for native Hawaiians. It was established to hold in trust the income and proceeds derived from a pro rata portion of the trust established for lands granted to the state (MacKenzie 1991: 33).

In *Rice,* the Court's majority held that the state's electoral restriction enacted race-based voting qualifications and hence was in violation of the Fifteenth Amendment's guarantee that the right of citizens to vote will not be denied or abridged on account of race, color, or previous condition of servitude.

The central question in the *Rice* case was whether or not the administration of the OHA trust violated the U.S. Constitution. On behalf of the respondent, Benjamin Cayetano, then governor of Hawai'i, the state argued that OHA's limitation on the right to vote was not based upon racial preference but on the unique status of Hawaiian people in light of the state's trust obligations and that the limitation on the right to vote for the OHA trustees was based on a legal classification determined by the beneficiaries of the trust managed by OHA. Importantly, the state submitted that the classification met rational basis review under *Morton v. Mancari* 417 U.S. 535 (1974). *Morton* upheld American Indian preferences as constitutional by establishing a precedent that the Fourteenth Amendment's equal protection guarantees are not infringed by legislation that benefits American Indians due to their political relationship to the United States. The state maintained that the voting classification was *rationally* tied to its fulfillment in upholding a congressional requirement because the United States has a "special relationship" with "Native Hawaiians" which was analogous to the federal government's relationship with American Indian tribes. The state also submitted as evidence the numerous federal acts that had brought American Indians and Native Hawaiians together—over 150 pieces of legislation since 1903 (http ://www.nativehawaiians.com/fed-acts.html; accessed in 2003). But the Court would not entertain the possibility that Kanaka Maoli fall under the ruling in *Morton* because the U.S. federal government does not recognize Kanaka Maoli collectively as a sovereign entity.[1]

The defense of the trust and its beneficiary limitation (and therefore its voter limitation) was based on the nature of the trust relationship between the United States and Hawaiians as traced to the HHCA and its subsequent reification in the Hawai'i State Admission Act. It is important to note that of all the amicus briefs filed on behalf of Governor Cayetano and the state of Hawai'i, all but one relied on the argument that the United States' plenary power over Indians, based on the Supreme Court's interpretation of the commerce clause of the U.S. Constitution, also extends to Hawaiians. Perhaps not surprisingly, the only one that did not make this concession was that submitted by the State Council of Hawaiian Homestead Associations—representing those who happen to have the most immediate investment in the integrity of the HHCA. Their amicus brief cited the early acknowledgment of native entitlement to the Hawaiian crown lands during the HHCA hearings. The other briefs serve as a concession because if Hawaiians are said to fall within the reach of the commerce clause, that means they are subject to congressional plenary power—a doctrine crafted by the Supreme Court's interpretation of the clause used to justify American Indian dispossession as well as American Indian tribal nations as domestic dependent sovereigns (Wilkins 2002).

In defense of Hawaiian-only voting for the OHA trustee elections, the state maintained that it was merely upholding a congressional requirement that Hawai'i carry out the trust while accepting the definition of "native Hawaiian" as per the Hawaiian Homes Commission Act. The act was carried through statehood in 1959 as a formal condition of admission to the union. Section 5(f) of the act details five purposes for the income and proceeds derived from the leases of the crown lands. These include support of public education, the development of farm and home ownership, public improvements, provision of lands for public use, and "the betterment of the conditions of native Hawaiians." Because the act did not determine a formula for the allocation of public land trust income among the five specified purposes, the 1978 constitutional amendment that created the OHA did not define the pro rata share (MacKenzie 1991: 33). However, the Hawai'i state legislature set the share at 20 percent, probably in response to the purpose mandating "the betterment of the conditions of native Hawaiians" (33). (Even so, the state government has not transferred the one-fifth of the revenue from these lands to the OHA for the benefit of Hawaiians who meet the 50-percent rule—further fueling the sovereignty movement.) Also, article 7, section 4 of the Hawai'i state constitution provides that lands ceded to the state of Hawai'i by the federal government at the time of admission to the United States will be "held by the State as a public trust for native Hawaiians and the general public." Although the public trust concept has not been delineated by the courts, the special designation of native Hawaiians as beneficiaries plausibly indicates that Hawaiians are entitled to benefits as Hawaiians over and above any benefit as state citizens (Matsuda 1988a: 139).

While the arguments in *Rice* managed to keep blood quantum at bay in some of its forms, the very question of Hawaiian/non-Hawaiian was framed in terms similar to those made in the Congress during the debates about the HHCA (Kauanui 2005c). That is to say, the distinction between who counts as Hawaiian and who does not was itself vehemently interrogated—not by those presenting the arguments themselves but by the justices of the Court during the presentation of the case.[2] One way blood constructions emerged in that case was when the justices focused on the logic of dilution. They also relied on blood quantification to undermine indigenous conceptualizations of Hawaiianness and belonging, which rely on genealogical connections that privilege kinship and lineal descent by including all those who possess Hawaiian ancestry (ibid.). For example, Justice Scalia focused on blood quantum to challenge the legal definitions of "Native Hawaiian" found in most federal funding legislation for Kanaka Maoli that are most inclusive and include all descendants of the original inhabitants of the Hawaiian Islands prior to 1778. Scalia found these inclusive definitions based on ancestral descent. He impatiently stated, "And you are defining Native Hawaiian now to mean any Hawaiian and . . . So 148 [*sic*] will do it. . . . [even] if you have 195th Hawaiian blood" (U.S. Supreme Court 1999: 54). He invoked these hypothetical figures to suggest that one's ancestry is arbitrary.

The logic of dilution also resurfaced when Justice Breyer attempted to clarify that a more inclusive definition of Hawaiian (other than that based on 50-percent blood quantum) was covered in one way or another by two separate trusts under the OHA. He declared, "That I think is the problem. It seems to me . . . that everyone who has one Hawaiian ancestor at least gets to vote, and more than half of those people are not Native Hawaiians. They just have a distant ancestor" (U.S. Supreme Court 1999: 39). He seemed preoccupied with physical appearance and racial recognizability.

Even after lawyers in the case pointed out to him that U.S. code allows for tribal membership defined in terms of lineal descendancy, Breyer repeatedly evoked the figure of the "remote" aboriginal ancestor to seemingly dismiss native identification based on such inclusive regard for ancestry. He asked, "How do we extend that to people 10 generations later, who had 10 generations ago one Indian ancestor? I mean, that might apply to everybody in the room. We have no idea. . . . You just have one ancestor 10 generations ago" (U.S. Supreme Court 1999: 47–48). Breyer's assumption is that such matters of ancestry are both arbitrary and irrelevant. Also, he refused to take account of the fact that one cannot have an ancestor from ten generations without also having that same line be just one generation away. Not only does it mean the person has an ancestor one generation back; it also means that the person is likely to know the name of some ancestors ten generations prior. Many Kānaka Maoli, if not most, can connect to an *Aliʻi* ancestor *and* trace their moʻokūauhau further back than ten generations, which is precisely what makes many people uneasy about indigeneity since this rootedness throws into question the place of the neocolonial settlers.

In his concurrence with the majority opinion in the case, Breyer specifically targeted Hawaiian ways of accounting for indigenous ancestry as meaningless. He declared: "There must . . . be . . . some limit on what is reasonable, at the least when a State (which is not itself a tribe) creates the definition. And to define that membership in terms of 1 possible ancestor out of 500, thereby creating a vast and unknowable body of potential members—leaving some combination of luck and interest to determine which potential members become actual voters—goes well beyond any reasonable limit." Breyer's limit, like the position expressed in Kealoha's letter to the editor, seems most *unreasonable;* ignoring culturally specific differences regarding kinship, he presumes that genealogy is the arbitrary modality of identity when it is blood quantum that is arbitrary. The majority targeted these expansive practices as meaningless, which played a key role in the Court's decision to allow any and all residents of Hawaiʻi, regardless of ancestry, the right to vote in Office of Hawaiian Affairs trustee elections.

The *Rice* case renewed debate over the difference between "native Hawaiian" and "Hawaiian" and who is entitled to federal recognition, land, and monetary revenues because the 50-percent blood quantum was a major factor in the Court's ruling. The majority of the Court deemed the state obligations to Hawaiians insufficient to convince them of the unique political situation of Kanaka Maoli that justified the exclusive OHA elections process. Favoring Rice, the Supreme Court based its ruling on three major findings.[3] First the majority found that because the OHA trustee elections are administered by the state, and not a separate quasi-sovereign, they are elections to which the Fifteenth Amendment applies (the Court did not rule on the Fourteenth Amendment). Second, they found that the limited voting franchise failed to comply with that amendment. Third, it was clear to the Court that the voting classification was not in line with the classification of the beneficiaries of the programs that OHA administers because, while the bulk of funds appear to be designated for "native Hawaiians" (as per the 50-percent rule), both "native Hawaiians" and "Hawaiians" who reside in the state are allowed to vote in the OHA elections. OHA is restricted to using its public lands trust funds only for the benefit of its beneficiaries who do meet the 50-percent rule. The Constitution does not establish a source of funding for "Hawaiians" who do not meet the 50-percent definition.

The outcome of *Rice v. Cayetano* is predicated upon the politics of race and entitlement described by my account of the HHCA, where the erasure of indigeneity is in keeping with deracination and the alienation of Hawaiians from the land. The blood quantum policies that survive in Hawai'i enable white American economic, political, and social domination that endures through manifestations such as the ruling. That the history of the HHCA legislation emerged in the case shows how blood racialization remains critical to the ongoing issues of citizenship, Hawaiian identity, and sovereignty.

The case opened up the way for a number of suits (*Carroll v. Cayetano, Arakaki v. Lingle*) designed to dismantle all federal and state-supported programs that assist Kanaka Maoli with education, health, and housing funding that had been granted through dozens of congressional legislative acts specifically for Native Hawaiians and in acts where Hawaiians are included as Native Americans. The *Arakaki* case even contests the legal standing of the Hawaiian Home Lands territory and the OHA. In the lawsuit, sixteen Hawaii residents claim the agency and Act violate the equal protection clause of the 14th Amendment and should be dismantled. This case has gone up to the Ninth Circuit Court of Appeals in a decision over whether the plaintiffs have standing as state taxpayers. The judge removed the Hawaiian Homes Commission Act from the case and declared that element of the complaint a political question. In February 2007, the Federal Appeals Court stopped short of dismissing the 2002 lawsuit but overturned its own earlier decision, finding that the plaintiffs lacked legal standing. The court sent the case back to U.S. District Court in Honolulu to determine if any of the plaintiffs are eligible "in any other capacity." On April 16, 2007, Judge Mollway ruled that no plaintiffs have standing. The plaintiffs filed an amended complaint, but the motion was denied, thus putting an end to the lawsuit. Still, disregarding the history of blood identity particular to Hawaiians, the plaintiffs argue that "Hawaiian" should be used to describe all Hawai'i residents.

Federal Recognition

The ruling in the *Rice* case has also hastened the pursuit of U.S. federal recognition among Kanaka Maoli in a campaign led by U.S. senators Daniel K. Akaka and Daniel Inouye of Hawai'i. They argue that it would provide Native Hawaiians with the political status shift, like that of American Indians, that would shield them from constitutional challenges of equal protection. In March 2000, just months after the ruling in *Rice,* Hawai'i's congressional delegation formed the Task Force on Native Hawaiian issues, chaired by Senator Akaka. As its immediate goal, the task force aimed to clarify the political relationship between Hawaiians and the United States through the U.S. Congress.

The legal rationale for the legislative proposal that would change Hawaiians' political status rests on two claims. First, supporters, and the legislation itself, name the history of the U.S.-backed overthrow and the subsequent 1993 apology issued as a joint Senate resolution that calls for reconciliation. Second, advocates point to the HHCA as evidence of an existing trust relationship between the U.S. government and the Hawaiian people, so that federal recognition is understood as an extension of that relationship. Relying on the HHCA as evidence of a political relationship seems problematic given the way the act constructed "native Hawaiians" as a beneficiary class based on the 50-percent definition, which is clearly racial.

Ironically, those residing on the Hawaiian Home Lands—once deemed the most incompetent because of their "fifty-percent" Hawaiian blood quantum—have been cast as bearers of the nation and carriers of the Akaka bill. Yet they are still characterized as vulnerable and needing the Akaka bill for their own "protection" even as they are simultaneously viewed as the least assimilated and therefore the most authentic.

That is not to say that Kanaka Maoli do not or should not have an acknowledged political relationship to the U.S. government. However, the way that Hawaiians' eligibility for federal recognition is currently framed is problematic because it undermines the full sovereignty claim in several ways. First, as a congressional act, the HHCA is not comparable to a treaty between two nations. As discussed in the introduction, the U.S. government signed a series of treaties and conventions with the Hawaiian kingdom, though these have not been acknowledged as a basis for Hawaiian treatment within federal policy. Indeed, the political agreements between the United States and the kingdom were never about cession of land or any form of governance; they were primarily affirming friendship, commerce, navigation rights, access to Pearl Harbor, and streamlining postal exchanges. Thus, the U.S. government has never viewed these treaties in the same way it has those with American Indian tribal nations—primarily because of the kingdom's inclusion in the Family of Nations, and Hawai'i's geographical distance from the continental United States. All of these aspects explain why the kingdom should still be regarded as a foreign nation under the commerce clause of the U.S. Constitution, even though the United States makes a distinction between foreign nations and Indian tribes in order to affirm its own sovereign power over that of tribal nations.

Could the HHCA be construed as a race-based classification as charged in the lawsuits subsequent to the ruling in *Rice?* Given the blood definition of "native Hawaiian" through the 50-percent rule found in the HHCA, the Court would likely find it so. Had the HHCA provided land leasing to *all* Kanaka Maoli, the HHCA would have managed to steer away from the arbitrary race-based classifications produced by the blood quantum definition. In 1920, Delegate Kalaniana'ole arguably foresaw an attack upon the Hawaiian Rehabilitation Bill as an unconstitutional measure and forestalled this by asking the U.S. attorney general for assistance. He was assured that the HHCA would pass the constitutionality test. As discussed in chapter 3, this issue arose during the hearings in the House, but the Committee on Territories had seemed satisfied with the opinions of the attorney general of Hawai'i and the solicitor of the Department of the Interior. Attorney General Irwin believed that although Hawaiians could not claim any land for homesteading under the law, the law did not prohibit the granting of lands for their use. In addition, the federal solicitor submitted an opinion which favored the constitutionality of the bill by explaining that the U.S. government had already established a policy of favoring certain classes of people such as veterans and American Indians (U.S. Congress 1920c: 130–131).

During the 106th Congress, Senator Akaka introduced legislation that would federally recognize Kanaka Maoli. Although the proposal did not pass

and continues to be opposed by U.S. senators reluctant to expand indigenous rights for Hawaiians, the legislation was resubmitted (with a revised
draft each time to make it more palatable to Republican opposition) in the
years that followed its first failure to pass (Kauanui 2005b). Defeat of the
proposal had been managed each time through informal filibusters, with
different senators putting anonymous holds on the bill (Borreca 2007). In
addition, the proposal had been held up numerous times due to various natural disasters and national events (among them Hurricane Katrina, the
confirmation of John Roberts as chief justice of the U.S. Supreme Court, and
the U.S. war on Iraq). Meanwhile the Republicans and Democrats have used
the bill as a political football. For example, Senator Akaka and Senator
Inouye were among only three Democrats in the entire Congress who agreed
to vote for legislation that would open the Arctic National Wildlife Refuge to
oil drilling. They did so in exchange for a promise from Ted Stevens (R-AK)
to support the Akaka bill in return. At the time of this writing, the bill
currently awaits a floor debate in the Senate, since the Senate Committee on
Indian Affairs approved S. 310 on May 10, 2007. The bill (HR 505) also gained
approval in the Natural Resources Committee of the House on May 2, 2007
(Bernardo 2007). Some speculate that the new Democratic majority in the
Congress could allow for passage of the bill. However, the Bush administration strongly opposes the measure, according to an official from the Department of Justice, because it sees the proposal as something divisive along
"racial and ancestral lines" (Camire 2007).

Since the measure was first proposed in 2000, an area of concern for both
Kanaka Maoli proponents and opponents of the bill was the proposed definition of "Native Hawaiians" included in the measure—racial and ancestral
divisions of a different sort from those signaled by the Bush administration.
If the legislation passes, the final definition would serve as a standard in
determining (and limiting) Hawaiian people's political participation. Only
Kānaka Maoli who could meet the standard would be allowed to participate
in the creation of the Hawaiian governing body that would then be recognized by the United States as the Hawaiian nation.

The current Senate bill (S. 310) uses the term "aboriginal, indigenous,
native people," defined as "people whom Congress has recognized as the
original inhabitants of the lands that later became part of the United States
and who exercised sovereignty in the areas that later became part of the

United States" (10–11). Oddly, the proposal also uses the term "indigenous, native people" to mean "the lineal descendants of the aboriginal, indigenous, native people of the United States" (12). Here the term "aboriginal" is dropped to describe contemporary descendants of the original inhabitants of the islands. Last, the measure defines "Native Hawaiian" as

> (i) an individual who is 1 of the indigenous, native people of Hawaii and who is a direct lineal descendant of the aboriginal, indigenous, native people who-
>> (I) resided in the islands that now comprise the State of Hawaii on or before January 1, 1893; and
>> (II) occupied and exercised sovereignty in the Hawaiian archipelago, including the area that now constitutes the State of Hawaii; or
>> (III) an individual who is 1 of the indigenous, native people of Hawaii and who was eligible in 1921 for the programs authorized by the Hawaiian Homes Commission Act (42 Stat. 108, chapter 42) or a direct lineal descendant of that individual. (12–13)

Mention of the HHCA and those who were eligible for the program in 1921 and their descendants seems unnecessary because if it includes those residing in the islands *on or before* January 1, 1893, that would, by definition, *already* include those who were eligible for the HHCA program in 1921 (and their descendants). The author of the bill most likely employed the HHCA in order to assert that there is already a trust relationship between the United States government and the Hawaiian people. While this definition does not work to limit Hawaiian participation, some fear that the ultimate definition could change to the 50-percent rule once the governing documents are submitted to the Department of the Interior for approval. This apprehension is not unfounded.

There is evidence that the Department of the Interior, which would oversee any Hawaiian governing entity created by passage of the proposal for federal recognition, wants to limit the proposal to those who are "native Hawaiian" by the definition of the HHCA. In December 2002, the Senate Committee on Indian Affairs submitted an earlier version of the bill (S. 746) to the Department of the Interior. Officials marked it up substantially, after it circulated through several executive offices and the State Department. In the markup, the Department of the Interior completely deleted the definitions for "aboriginal, indigenous, native people" and "indigenous, native people." Indeed, they removed these words entirely. Moreover, they drastically revised the definition of "Native Hawaiian" to mean "any descendant not less that [*sic*] one-half part of the blood of the peoples [*sic*] inhabiting the Hawaiian Islands previous to 1778" (section 2(3)). They made the 50-percent blood rule the standard, but without any reference to the HHCA. Their adjustment was reflected in the next revised version of the bill (S. 1783), where the term "Native Hawaiian" is defined as "all Native Hawaiian people who were eligible in 1921 for the programs authorized by the Hawaiian Homes Commission Act . . . and their lineal descendants" (section 2[5][A]). Here the specific reference to lineal descendants is limited to those few who derived some benefit from the congressional act.

Even if the definition for all "Native Hawaiians" in the proposal was inclusive by providing for all lineal descendants of Kanaka Maoli ancestry, the federal recognition model of self-determination limits the sovereignty claim to independence from the United States and the restoration of a nation-state of Hawai'i. In addition, the U.S. model is, by definition, only for those who are indigenous. Thus descendants of non-Hawaiians who were citizens of the kingdom and therefore have a rightful place in the citizenry would be excluded.

These independence initiatives have gained momentum in the wake of the *Rice* case, especially since the Supreme Court refused to consider the history of Hawai'i as a nation. Moreover, as mentioned earlier, some Kānaka Maoli have responded to the ruling by seeking federal recognition, which would close down the possibility for Hawai'i's independence. But federal recognition would also set up the process to settle all Hawaiian claims and resolve the issue from the federal end. Although the U.S. senators portray the Akaka bill as a way to "give" Hawaiians their sovereignty, it is most likely that the federally driven push for the bill has to do with compelling Hawaiians to surrender title to 1.8 million acres of land—the government and crown lands of the Hawaiian kingdom that have never been adjudicated, let alone sold or given away. If the bill were to pass, there would finally be a federally recognized Native governing entity that would be empowered by the U.S. government to negotiate a land claims settlement.

Not everyone supporting federal recognition agrees with this assessment. Several are involved in the United Nations Permanent Forum on Indigenous

Issues and are currently mobilizing around the Declaration on the Rights of Indigenous Peoples that was adopted by the United Nations General Assembly in September 2007 because they are specifically concerned with developing international law so that it responds to indigenous peoples. But their work is not centered on the claim of Hawai'i's independence as a nation-state under international law.

In response, those who support the right to independence under international law have galvanized their resistance to the quest for federal recognition because it threatens the claims to independence that exceed U.S. domestic policy and law. This split within the sovereignty movement has been nothing short of an all-out battle among Kānaka Maoli. Moreover, the division is not only about the different models of self-determination, one under U.S. policy for Native Americans and the other under international law, which would provide for restoration of an independent nation-state through U.S. decolonization and/or de-occupation of the Hawaiian Islands; the split is also constituted by the question of indigeneity itself as a basis for the sovereignty claim, and, within the realm of the indigenous claim, the persistent question of who counts as Hawaiian. Regardless of which model of self-governance and sovereign expression, the question remains as to whom to include and exclude.

The U.S. Apology and the Differing Claims to Independence

In Hawai'i today, legal strategies for gaining independence can be divided into two different categories—decolonization and de-occupation. The first takes up the political process of decolonization under UN protocols, while the second utilizes the Law of Nations and The Hague Regulations for the restoration of the Hawaiian Kingdom. Activists involved in either strategy propose a range of governing models, including restoration of a constitutional monarchy, a parliament, or a bicameral legislature. There are a number of organizations and individuals working for the support of Hawai'i's independence: Kekuni Blaisdell with the Pro-Kanaka Maoli Sovereignty Working Group; Bumpy Kanahele with the Nation of Hawai'i; Pōkā Laenui (also known as Hayden Burgess) of the Institute for the Advancement of Hawaiian Affairs; Keanu Sai with the Hawaiian Patriotic League of the Hawaiian Kingdom; and Henry Noa with the Reinstated Kingdom. Besides these developments, there are also several individuals who claim the throne, but it is unclear what role some of these people are taking within any part of the sovereignty movement.

A fundamental building block in the case for full independence is the U.S. Apology Resolution, passed through a Joint Senate Resolution, Public Law 103–150, one hundred years after the U.S.-backed takeover of the kingdom, by which the U.S. government apologized to the Hawaiian people for its complicity in the overthrow in 1893. Significantly, the apology states, "The indigenous Hawaiian people never directly relinquished their claims to their inherent sovereignty as a people or over their national lands to the United States, either through their monarchy or through a plebiscite or referendum" (U.S. Congress 1993b). As then-senator Slade Gorton (R-WA) warned, prior to its passage, "The logical consequence of this resolution would be independence" (U.S. Congress 1993a). Perhaps, then, it should not come as a surprise that the apology includes a disclaimer at its very end, which states, "Nothing in this Joint Resolution is intended to serve as a settlement of any claims against the United States" (section 3). Still, the apology recounts the history of dispossession as a fact according to the U.S. government.

Importantly, the joint resolution defines "Native Hawaiian" as "any individual who is a descendent of the aboriginal people who, prior to 1778, occupied and exercised sovereignty in the area that now constitutes the State of Hawaii" (section 2). This definition can be used as a model for any Hawaiian sovereignty project that is indigenous-specific as a way of thwarting the 50-percent rule enshrined by the HHCA. Because *all* Kanaka Maoli (defined by lineal descent) are referenced in the U.S. Apology, it stands to reason that *all* Kanaka Maoli have a claim to full self-determination to "their inherent sovereignty as a people or over their national lands," a position quite different from Kealoha's, which posits that those who meet the 50-percent blood quantum criterion are *the* "indigenous Hawaiians" with a right to self-determination. At stake besides the right to self-determination under international law are 1.8 million acres of crown and government lands of the Hawaiian Kingdom—the "national lands" referred to in the U.S. Apology. Kanaka Maoli lost these lands and the ability to be self-determining through unilaterally imposed annexation and statehood.

Given that Hawaiian political sovereignty was not lost via conquest, cession, or adjudication, those rights to nation-state status are arguably still in place under international law. Along with the competing interests for control of a future government in Hawai'i, the legal approaches themselves are a source of intense debate. Historically, the United Nations allows colonies the opportunity to freely choose their own political status, as expressed in UN General Assembly resolution 1514: "All peoples have the right to self-determination; by virtue of that right, they freely determine their political status and freely pursue their economic, social, and cultural development." The options for self-determination include integration within the colonizing country, free association with that country, or independence from that country. Hawai'i's eligibility for decolonization calls into question the way the United States acquired Hawai'i and relies on a history of the Hawaiian Islands as an unorganized and unincorporated territory from 1898 to 1900 and as an organized and unincorporated territory from 1900 to 1959 (U.S. Congress 1900).

For some within the independence movement, there are problems with this process with regard to the Hawai'i case. United Nations protocols for decolonization were designed for former colonies that may or may not have indigenous minorities. In cases of their presence, indigenous peoples were rarely regarded as distinct within the process of decolonization itself. Hence, if Hawai'i were reinscribed onto the UN list of non-self-governing territories and the United Nations allowed for a lawful referendum on Hawai'i's status, it is unclear who would get to vote on the self-determination status. Within the current movement, those who support the decolonization process do so by privileging Kanaka Maoli as the "self" in "self-determination." Others see the construction of indigeneity and decolonization as obstacles to independence.

Keanu Sai, a proponent of restoring the kingdom, argues that the UN process of decolonization is fundamentally for peoples who have not yet attained independence. He notes that as a recognized nation-state Hawai'i had already achieved recognition of its independence as of 1842, when the United States and members of the international community also accepted the kingdom's independence through treaty relations. Thus Sai and other supporters of the kingdom distinguish themselves from those promoting a decolonization agenda. Their political project of de-occupation relies not on UN declarations about self-determination but rather on the history of international laws of occupation, drawing on regulations created during the Hague Convention IV of 1907 (article 43). They insist that the kingdom remains a sovereign and independent state and never was a U.S. colony. In other words, because the U.S. Congress unilaterally annexed Hawai'i through its own domestic law, they argue that the kingdom was never really annexed and its territory is merely *occupied* by the United States. Accordingly, they identify as kingdom subjects and demand that the recovery process, as well as all charges against the United States, be guided by The Hague Regulations.[4]

Those putting their energy toward de-occupation contest all reconciliation efforts made by the United States such as the Apology Resolution, which affirms the right of Hawaiians to self-determination as indigenous people within the U.S. domestic sphere. They argue that mobilizing Hawaiians around the term "indigenous peoples" renders Hawaiians a dependent people because, in current conditions, indigenous peoples are not afforded the right to full self-determination under international law (Lâm 1992). However, with the U.N. adoption of the Declaration on the Rights of Indigenous Peoples, this right has been affirmed, albeit in paradoxical ways.[5] Again, de-occupation advocates declare their status as nationals who are *already* independent. They also promote a vision wherein no distinctions are made between Kanaka Maoli subjects of the kingdom and those who are non-Hawaiian. This position has become widespread among those promoting independence via the de-occupation strategy, creating a false binary between what counts as independent or dependent by assuming that the assertion of a Kanaka Maoli identity as indigenous entails a concession of political dependence. But just because provisions for indigenous peoples might not be the most appropriate political strategy at this time for proponents of Hawai'i's independence does not mean that Kanaka Maoli are not an indigenous people.

We can see the tensions between indigenous and nonindigenous claims to Hawaiian sovereignty in another group, formed by Henry Noa, that also promotes restoration of the kingdom but split from Keanu Sai's project. That Kanaka Maoli sovereignty group, claiming to be "The Lawful Hawaiian Government," issued a t-shirt in the late 1990s that asked, "Got Koko?" (as in "Got Blood?"). The lettering is positioned next to a graphic reminiscent of a drop of blood. Instead of being only red, the drop contains the colors blue, red, and white—making up a condensed image of the Hawaiian flag within the outline of the drop. Under the question with its attendant drop, the shirt states the following: *Jus Soli, Jus Sanguinis, Jus Because.* This unabashed declaration of the group's reliance on the laws of "place of birth" and "right of blood" is justified by *"jus because"—just* because—a play on words using Hawaiian Creole English (commonly known as "pidgin" in Hawai'i). Here "The Lawful Hawaiian Government" insists on marking indigenous-specificity by the *koko* (blood) without articulating why. Reluctance to do away with this system persists, even though the kingdom allowed non-Hawaiians to become citizens.

In assessing the pros and cons of each strategy between decolonization and de-occupation under international law, it is difficult to determine how existing approaches for Hawai'i's independence respond to the indigenous-specific history of subjugation under U.S. colonialism *and* U.S. occupation. The question, it seems, is whether indigenous self-determination is compatible with independence models of sovereign expression and whether reconciliation for Kanaka Maoli is a primary concern among those who support a nation-state of Hawai'i, in whatever form. Kanaka Maoli might be the beneficiaries for a reconciliation case, but they are not the only plaintiffs for a restitution case. But just because the kingdom allowed non-Hawaiians to become citizens does not mean that the Hawaiian people are not the ones who bore the brunt of U.S. colonialism exemplified by the imposition of the 50-percent blood quantum rule.

Independence proponents could develop a model that would work for Kanaka Maoli without forfeiting national claims under international law. For example, descendants of non-Hawaiian citizens of the kingdom in 1893 could be protected by the sovereign jurisdiction of the kingdom which in turn can be located under the self-determination right of the Kanaka Maoli people who allowed Hawaiian nationhood to be expressed in the form of a monarchy. Under such an arrangement, there need be no diminution of Hawaiian peoplehood or nationhood. And whether people pursue decolonization or de-occupation, both the overthrow of 1893 and the annexation of 1898 need to be considered when determining voting eligibility for any plebiscite about Hawai'i's political status or the recognition of contemporary kingdom citizens. Logically, the year of choice should be when the aggrieved entity—the Hawaiian kingdom—suffered the wrong needing remedy. As a response to de-occupation activism, those supporting decolonization highlight the fact that international law continues to be based on Western concepts of inherent moral and cultural superiority over indigenous peoples; hence they are not as quick to rely on the laws of occupation which were originally used to justify colonial subjugation in the first place. Clearly the issue of indigeneity and the sovereignty claims for those of Hawaiian "blood" are far from resolved.

As I have argued, blood quantum is a colonial project in the service of land alienation and dispossession. Furthermore, it has dire consequences for political activism because does not allow for the building of Kanaka Maoli political power; it is ultimately about exclusion, while it also reduces Hawaiians to a racial minority rather than an indigenous people with sovereignty claims. On the other hand, Hawaiian kinship and genealogical modes of identification allow for political empowerment in the service of nation building because they are inclusive. Not only is the genealogical approach more far-reaching: it is embedded in indigenous epistemologies that are rooted in the land. As for the question of blood quantum within the broader field of Native studies, critiques of indigenous uses of blood quantum should not simply be dismissed as though they are unrelated to U.S. federal policy, as such policy is premised on indigenous dispossession. Blood quantum is simply an arbitrary and racial attempt at gauging the cultural and political commitments of any one person. In addition, indigeneity can no longer be neglected in relation to the study of racial formations and the legal construction of race. Critical race theorists need to consider how whiteness constitutes a project of disappearance for Native peoples rather than merely signifying privilege. Rather than rely on logics of subordination or discrimination in analyses of the uses of blood quantum classification, we must be mindful of how the racialization of indigenous peoples follows a genocidal logic.

The legacy of the 50-percent rule has divided Kanaka Maoli in more ways than one. First, it has split the Hawaiian population in terms of those now considered "fifty-percenters" and the "less than fifties" (Trask 1996). Second, it has estranged those who affirm the blood quantum criterion and those who are opposed to any form of blood quantum measurement, regardless of how they themselves would be classified within this racial schema. Third, given the HHCA and the 50-percent rule it created as a legal category, the state segregates Kanaka Maoli on the basis of this criterion in its own policies and institutions such as the OHA, even though the OHA requests separate funding for the "less than fifties" from the state legislature in order to circumvent this mandate. In addition, although federal funding earmarked exclusively for Kanaka Maoli, as provided by other acts of U.S. Congress, such as the Native Hawaiian Health Act and the Native Hawaiian Education Act, is not restricted by the 50-percent definition and includes all those Hawaiians by lineal descent, these same sources of funding and the institutions created to administer their attendant programs are now challenged as racially exclusive by non-Hawaiians.

The state defense of this exclusivity, limited to Kanaka Maoli in general, is the implementation of the HHCA at the state level—a justification that is a contradiction in terms given that the HHCA only provided for "native Hawaiians" by the 50-percent definition. Thus, in order to sidestep this inconsistency, which was already identified in the *Rice* case, the state government in Hawai'i (including the legislature, the current governor, and OHA) proposes to have Kanaka Maoli federally recognized as a Native governing entity.

But the paradox for Kanaka Maoli is that the state of Hawai'i, and arguably the U.S. government, has its own investment in seeing this political goal obtained because it would limit Hawaiians' full sovereignty claim and extinguish land title—namely, the kingdom, crown, and government lands—and thus settle the state's ongoing "Hawaiian problem." So, just like the HHCA, the federally driven legislation threatens to amount to yet another land grab in the guise of "protecting Hawaiians." Furthermore, this model of indigenous self-governance under U.S. domestic policy threatens to establish the 50-percent rule in yet another context: the potential Hawaiian nation-within-a-nation.

In the HHCA, rehabilitation remained a stated priority; however it was actually the edifice that upheld the proposal to amend the Organic Act in order to empower the haole elites who wanted more Hawaiian land—in the name of keeping Hawai'i American. Those who tightened the definition of "native Hawaiian" in order to limit the numbers eligible for homesteading also actively worked to limit the amount of lands to be set aside for allotment. In the HHCA, the restriction of identity was accomplished through redefining the relationship of the people to the lands in question. This is precisely what is once again at stake in the contest over federal recognition.

Proponents of the legislation are not simply tightening the definition of Hawaiians who could be part of the "Akaka bill nation"; they are actively restricting the form that nation may take and attempting to accomplish this through redefining the relationship of the people to the lands in question—the kingdom, crown, and government lands—which they have already deemed "public lands."

Just as the U.S. framework does not do justice to the specific Hawaiian sovereignty claims, there is a radical difference between the creation of a beneficiary group (defined by blood notions of "race") and the creation of a sovereign collective (defined by indigenous genealogical practices). Blood quantum classification cannot account for the emphasis on relatedness in genealogical practices—forms of identification that serve to connect people to one another, to place, and to the land. These connections are grounded in sovereignty, self-determination, and citizenship, not racialized beneficiary status. The discourse of "racial equality" continues to be leveled as an attack on Kanaka Maoli claims—those based on collective inheritance and the sovereign claim to full nationhood under international law—as well as the meager U.S. federal funds earmarked for Native Hawaiians. Thus, now more than ever, Kanaka Maoli must insist on our own genealogies and their attendant responsibilities to our land and descendants.

Notes

Introduction: Got Blood?

1. Even the amount of the lands set aside is uncertain; the HHCA "did not specify the boundaries of these lands, but identified them only by place name, with estimates of acreage," and the current inventory of lands is 17,000 acres less than the 203,500 acres said to have been set aside within the HHCA (Murakami 1991: 66).

2. To make matters even more complicated, in addition to the Department of Hawaiian Home Lands, each of the following state offices has its own definition of Native Hawaiian: Department of Education (DOE); Department of Health (DOH); Aids Surveillance Program (ASP); Behavioral Risk Factor Survey (BRFS); Diabetes Control Program (DCP); Health Surveillance Program (HSP); Office of Health Status Monitoring (OHSM); Cardiovascular Disease Prevention and Control Program (formerly the State Hypertension Program); Department of Human Services (DHS); Family and Adult Services Division; Hawaiʻi Housing Authority (HHA); Office of Youth Services (OYS); Department of Labor and Industrial Relations (DLIR); Department of Public Safety (DPS); Department of the Attorney General, Crime Prevention Division; and the Office of Hawaiian Affairs (OHA).

3. According to the Native Hawaiian Data Book of 2004, there are over 34,327 qualified native Hawaiians on the applicant waiting list to receive homestead leases, but since applicants can apply for two types of leases among the residential, agricultural, or pastoral lots, duplicating may occur on the list. The Department of Hawaiian Home Lands estimates the unduplicated statewide total number of applicants at 20,000 (table 6.09, *Department of Hawaiian Home Lands Acreage, Lessees, and Applicants by Islands: 2003 and 2004,* http://www.hawaii .gov/dbedt).

4. Congress authorized this last amendment to the Hawaiian Homes Commission Act in 1997 (U.S. Congress 1997: 105–16).

5. The 1982 provision set by the state needed congressional consent for that legislation because it amended the 50-percent blood criterion included in the Hawaiian Homes Commission Act (See U.S. Congress 1997a).

6. There is a linguistic conundrum due to the fact that blood is often used as a metaphor for ancestry, while blood quantum and genealogy are often thought to

be coterminal. Indeed, the etymological roots of "blood" show its origins in Middle English by 1200, where " 'blood' increasingly connotes lineage, descent, and ancestry in association with royal claims to property and power and presages modern conceptions of race' " (Meyer 1999: 235). In many cultures, blood was viewed as a powerful element—a quintessential substance that transmitted special qualities. Certainly there needs to be research conducted using Hawaiian language sources in order to understand Kanaka Maoli conceptions of blood prior to Western encroachment.

7. To date, there are five key works that address the Hawaiian Homes Commission Act that led to the rule: Vause 1962; Murakami 1991; McGregor 1990; Hasager 1997; and Halualani 2002. While all five offer provocative analyses of the act, none of them offers a sustained examination of the determination of the blood quantum criterion in relation to the key political questions underlying the nature and impulses of the act. For example, Halualani includes a short section on the HHCA, but it is both incomplete and problematic. There is also a slippage with the terminology she uses; e.g., when describing the HHCA and the 50-percent rule, she refers to "Native Hawaiian" instead of "native Hawaiian" (Halualani 2002: xiv), both of which have different legal definitions. The HHCA only refers to "native Hawaiians"—those who meet the 50-percent blood rule. Halualani also asserts that "U.S. federal and local state mandates define Hawaiian identity as derivative of a specific blood amount" and that "Hawaiianness, therefore, has become inexorably bound to 'prehumanity,' 'native,' and 'blood' images because of the historically extensive presence of Western power and U.S. neocolonialism" (xvi). But this equation does not add up; it does not follow that just because the concept of Hawaiian identity was legally based on blood criterion, Hawaiianness is inevitably associated with a notion of "prehumanity." Halualani again argues that Hawaiians were thought of as "prehuman" elsewhere in this context (xxxiv), but the logic is especially curious given the overdetermined discourses of assimilation that operated in the HHCA, which defined Hawaiians by blood in the first place—and did so in the context of a plan to return urbanized twentieth-century Kanaka Maoli "back to the land."

8. Sally Merry points out the parallel intellectual arguments of the time that focused on urban disintegrations and the valorization of rural dwelling found in the Chicago School of urban sociology (Merry, personal communication, email, July 2, 1999). The Chicago School emerged during the 1920s and 1930s with a research focus on the urban environment, especially Chicago itself. Researchers saw the city as their "laboratory," where they sought evidence as to whether urbanization and increasing social mobility were the causes of social problems (Bulmer 1984; Wirth 1991).

9. Gordon's formative work examines how between 1890 and 1935 there were definitive shifts in the meaning of "welfare," which was ultimately coded as a pejora-

tive term (Gordon 1994: 1). Whereas " 'welfare' could accurately refer to all of a government's contributions to its citizens' well-being," the label now connotes ill-being and grudging aid to the poor (1–2).

10. Ishibashi 2004, 10.

11. In 1986, Kānaka Maoli who were not racially mixed were said to number less than 3.8 percent of the Hawaiian population (Blaisdell and Mokuau 1994: 53).

12. The attorneys representing the plaintiff were set to appeal the case to the U.S. Supreme Court, but the trustees of the Kamehameha Schools were finally able to settle the case out of court.

13. Joel Williamson details how an "alliance between black and mulatto Americans in Reconstruction occurred primarily in the lower South rather than in the upper South" (1995: 78–79). In reference to Horace Mann Bond, a black-identified sociologist, Williamson argued, "Insofar as Negroes accepted the blackness of the seemingly pure white speaker—and of others strikingly light—they too accepted the one-drop rule" (109). And "by that time the racial code of the South pervaded the nation, and Negroes as well as whites had come to accept as universal what came to be called the 'one-drop rule' " (1). He argues that by the mid-1920s "nearly all of the pre-1850 mulatto exclusiveness had faded" with the onset of the Harlem Renaissance. Naomi Zack also argues that the Harlem Renaissance "marked an abrupt change in this entire tradition of exclusivity within black culture" (1993: 96). She traces how "visibly mixed-race blacks and visibly white-race blacks threw in their lot with the apparently pure-race blacks" and that they took up this designation on the "premise of democracy among themselves" (96–97). Noting the black pride, culture, and achievement cultivated during this period, Zack argues that while nothing of "substance, of immediate practical value, was lost. . . . what was lost was the concept of mixed race as a theoretical wedge against racism and against the concept of physical race. . . . [and] lost all means of challenging the asymmetrical kinship schema of racial inheritance and the attendant oppressive biracial system" (97). Zack refers to this as a moment of "cultural suicide"—the death of a force capable of defeating American racism—and its persistence as the "intellectual tyranny of the one-drop rule" (103). While seemingly motivated by a keen desire for emancipation, Zack's thesis has unsettling and unsettled implications for indigenous peoples who experience an asymmetrical kinship schema of racial inheritance that fulfills dispossession.

14. Any discussion of blood, inheritance, and race is implicitly also a discussion of sex and reproduction. Attitudes toward interracial sexual relationships depended on the racial groups involved. The process of mixing itself is connected to sexuality and antimiscegenation laws. As Matthew Frye Jacobson argues, "The policing of sexual boundaries—the defense against hybridity—is precisely what keeps a racial group a racial group" (1998: 3). Of course, we need to account for the contrasts between assimilative projects and boundary drawing "antipollu-

tion" approaches to relationships understood as interracial and how they differed historically for American Indian and white mixes versus African American and white ones.

15. Barbara Fields has also underscored the illogical nature of the hypodescent rule with her observation that a white woman may give birth to a black child, but no black woman can give birth to a white child (Fields 1982). See also Hollinger 2003.

16. These characteristics distinctly mark the period of reform that saw American Indians as assimilable. This is not to say that other, powerfully negative images of the native did not also persist—ones that were used earlier to enforce social separation. The period of isolation for Indian policy was prior to the Civil War (Utley 1984).

17. Dippie maps the shift away from the presumption that Indians were doomed to disappear: "Thus while continental expansion made a shambles of the concept of a separate Indian country, the reservation system, rather than a program for Indian assimilation, emerged as the official 'alternative to extinction' " (1982: 75).

18. See Lowe 1996 and Ancheta 1998 for two provocative accounts of "foreign racialization" and "outsider racialization" imposed on Asian Americans through white American nativist anti-immigrant rhetoric and governmental policies. Federal laws such as the Chinese Exclusion Act of 1882 (and the Geary Act of 1892, which extended that exclusion, as well as further legislation in 1902 and 1904), the Immigration Act of 1924, and the McCarran-Walter Act of 1943 contributed to the legacies of discrimination (Lowe 1996; Ancheta 1998).

19. Griffiths argued that blacks were being identified as a competitive threat to "the white man of the South," which marked a "new antagonism to the Negro" (6). "The situation cued by the fact that the Negro is showing ambition, a willingness to work and to save, and a desire to accumulate property, presents unexpected difficulties, because the Negro has not been generally accused of being ambitious, industrious or thrifty" (6). He further argued that "the points of similarity between the case of the Negro in the South . . . and the Japanese in Hawaii . . . are sufficient to be more than passing interest" (7).

20. Besides the examples one can build on from Harris's work, there are other specific cases that reveal a similar process of selective assimilation of Native Americans while excluding blackness. The works of Susan Greenbaum (1991), Helen C. Rountree (1990), and Karen Blu (1980) provide prime historical cases where having black "blood" legally precluded identification as Native.

21. All of the treaties discussed herein can be found online where they are archived at http://www.hawaiiankingdom.org/treaties.shtml.

22. Because Hawai'i was maintained as a territory for nearly six decades before being admitted as a state, there is a constitutionality issue regarding annexation. Concerning the authority to acquire and establish interim governments for "ac-

quired territories," Chief Justice Taney, in *Dred Scott v. John F.A. Sanford* (60 U.S. 393; 1856), stated: "There is certainly no power given by the Constitution to the Federal Government to establish or maintain colonies bordering on the United States or at a distance, to be ruled and governed at its own pleasure; nor to enlarge its territorial limits in any way, except by the admission of new States." Even though Taney noted that "it has been held to authorize the acquisition of territory, not fit for admission at the time, but to be admitted as soon as its population and situation would entitle it to admission," and that the propriety of admitting a new state is made by the discretion of Congress, Hawai'i's annexation seems questionable within the framework of the U.S. Constitution.

1. Racialized Beneficiaries and Genealogical Descendants

1. Faith Gemmil is an activist from the North Slope region of Alaska who has worked to stop oil drilling in the Arctic National Wildlife Refuge (ANWR) in order to protect the Gwich'in customary lands and the caribou that are central to their culture. The connection between the Gwich'in struggle and Kanaka Maoli sovereignty issues goes beyond both being indigenous peoples; there is evidence that the Council for Native Hawaiian Advancement is funded by the Arctic Slope Regional Corporation, which is bankrolling the campaign for Hawaiian federal recognition through the legislative proposal known as the "Akaka bill" (discussed in chapter 6). Senator Daniel Akaka, along with Senator Daniel Inouye—both Democrats from Hawai'i—voted to support the drilling in ANWR in exchange for support from Senator Ted Stevens (the highest-ranking senator at the time, a Republican) for the federal recognition bill (Kelly 2003).

2. Interestingly, when Queen Lili'uokalani translated the Hawaiian language text *He Kumulipo*, she translated "He Kumulipo" as "*The* Kumulipo," not "A Kumulipo." The queen undertook this work while imprisoned in 'Iolani Palace, where the self-appointed authorities of the Republic of Hawaii held her captive for treason after the overthrow of the kingdom, when Kanaka Maoli tried to restore her to the throne. In the introduction to *The Kumulipo: An Hawaiian Creation Myth,* she noted several reasons for the publication of the work, one of which was that "it is the special property of the latest ruling family of the Hawaiian Islands, being nothing less than the genealogy in remote times of the late King Kalakaua,—who had it printed in the original Hawaiian language,—[*sic*] and myself" (1978 [1897]: np).

3. Valeri posits that they were first cousins (1985: 170). However, the same generation used the sibling terms of address, which may be the source of discrepancy between Valeri's reading and Kame'eleihiwa's.

4. Sahlins asserts, "Hawai'i is missing the segmentary polity of descent groups known to cognate Polynesian peoples: organization of the land as a pyramid of embedded lineages, with a corresponding hierarchy of ancestral cults, property

rights, and chiefly titles, all based on genealogical priority within the group of common descent" (1985: 20). Ambilineality lends itself to fixed assets and territories, whereas Hawaiian kinship as bilateral was not fixed in the same way, especially given the redistribution of lands under the Mōʻi. Ambilineal descent groups, ramages, involve the formation of discrete and exclusive units. This works in contrast to bilateral systems because it involves claims to group membership, property, and status through only one parent (albeit with some choice).

5. With regard to tracing ascent, Romanzo Adams noted that "it must be remembered that while a person has only two parents and four grandparents he may have thirty-two ancestors in the remote fifth generation, and he is in poor luck, indeed, if there is not least one of them of whom he may be proud. The old Hawaiians and their modern descendants are like other peoples in that they tend to trace their ancestry back to the progenitor of most glorious memory" (Adams 1937: 100). In the contemporary sovereignty context, one could argue that this works in the opposite direction—where Kanaka Maoli broadly see their *kuleana* (duty and responsibility) to protect Hawaiian lands and sovereignty claims as a result of being *descendants* of a sovereign people.

6. Nearly two decades after Western contact, the Hawaiian monarchy emerged after 1810 with the political ascendancy of Kamehameha and his subjugation of all the islands under his rule. Adrienne L. Kaeppler details the role of genealogy and how material culture, as it was an integral part of social traditions that were transformed, assisted in modifying attitudes that would, she argues, ultimately equate prestige with power during late-eighteenth- and early-nineteenth-century Hawaiʻi (Kaeppler 1985). Kamehameha's dominance effected a transformation in Hawaiian society which spurred a change from the belief that "genealogical prestige gives power and therefore authority" to the principle that "power gives authority and therefore prestige" (Kaeppler 1985: 106). Furthermore, Kaeppler argues that the notion of "power equals authority" was altered to "status equals authority," based on notions of traditional concepts (108). However, Noenoe Silva contests Kaeppler's assessment of Kamehameha and the transformation. Silva argues that "Kamehameha followed the exact pattern set out on the moʻolelo of ʻUmi and Kawelo—that of a junior line ascending to 'kū i ka moku' [assume power over the island] based on religion and power" (Silva, personal correspondence, March 7, 2005).

7. The 1890 census for Hawaiʻi reported 89,990 for all "races," 34,436 of whom were classified as "Hawaiian ('native')" and another 6,186 classified as "part-Hawaiian (half-caste')" (Schmitt 1968: 74). Of course, these figures do not account for the Kanaka Maoli already residing outside the islands by that time, in places such as the west coast of North America.

8. In the contemporary period, there is often conflict within Kanaka Maoli communities when non-Hawaiian *adults* who have been incorporated into Hawaiian

families through *hanai* assert that it makes them Kanaka Maoli rather than simply part of their respective adopted families like any other member—with all the responsibilities, privileges, and challenges that entails. In other words, this is a form of identity appropriation, where some people attempt to access the cultural capital they feel comes with Hawaiian identity and the sovereignty rights attached to it. For a sharp analysis of how these assertions have created the construct of the "Hawaiian at heart," see Hall 2005.

9. Kameʻeleihiwa notes that in terms of the genealogical hierarchies, the object was "to elevate one's *mana* in the eyes of the people and escape the pit of commonality; this was another symbolic *ʻimihaku* (to search for a source of *mana*). There were two ways *mana* could be obtained: through sexual means and through violence" (1992: 46).

10. Silva offers a critical analysis as to how this story has been read as one that "legitimates female subordination to male authority in the Hawaiian religion system," especially in contrast to the Pele stories that assert "an unruly female power" (Silva 2003: 118). For readings of the Hawaiian religious system and the role of men, see Valeri 1985.

11. Census reports in Hawaiʻi date back to 1847 and included the categories "Native" and "Half-caste" (Glick 1970: 278).

12. Kamakau notes that Hawaiians called him "Olohana" (1992 [1961]: 146).

13. Kamakau explains that Isaac Davis, who had also arrived on the same ship—*the Eleanor,* and Young "became favorites ... of Kamehameha and leaders in his wars, and from them are descended chiefs and commoners" (1992 [1961]: 146–147).

14. Like was the editor and Nāwahī was the owner and business manager of the paper. For a rich study of Hawaiian print media during this period, including the newspaper *Ke Aloha Aina,* see Silva 2004.

15. Henry Abelove has suggested that the anxieties produced by the genealogical model may have more to do with ancestry not being seen as arbitrary so much as unknowable or unverifiable in Western epistemologies at the time (personal communication, October 23, 2001).

16. Merry documents debates in the Hawaiian kingdom legislature in the mid- to late nineteenth century concerned with "rich foreigners enticing [Hawaiian women] ... away from their husbands" (2000: 252). Already, the kingdom placed a new emphasis on the nuclear family and the enclosure of women within it (255).

17. I assume some of the members of the Hui were racially mixed from viewing photographs of them, since many are obviously also of European ancestry. John E. Bush and Emma ʻAʻima Nāwahī, along with Robert K. Wilcox, are some well-known leaders of mixed ancestry who were, nonetheless, not suspected of divided loyalties at this time and were generally spoken of as Kānaka Maoli rather than as hapa (Silva, personal communication, April 12, 2006).

2. "Can you wonder that the Hawaiians did not get more?"

1. In 1919, a new arrangement entailed that the purchase of the crop of sugar in Hawai'i that year was to be made by the sugar equalization board, which in turn deposited it with the refiners. The same arrangements were also implemented in Cuba and Puerto Rico for their sugar crops in order for the refiners to refrain from purchasing individually (*Honolulu Star-Bulletin* 1918d).

2. Dillingham was re-elected head of the Chamber of Commerce on January 15, 1919. Born in Hawai'i in 1875, he was educated at the elite Punahou School, the Newton, Massachusetts, high school, and eventually Harvard University. Once back in Hawai'i he served in the military under the Republic of Hawaii after the overthrow. By 1902 he organized the Hawaiian Dredging Company, which handled the opening and development of the harbors of Hilo, Kahului, and Honolulu. As well as being a contractor, he served as director of numerous companies, including various sugar corporations and banks (*Honolulu Star-Bulletin* 1919a).

3. Throughout this volume, I refer to Jonah Kalaniana'ole Kūhiō as Kalaniana'ole, in accordance with conventional U.S. usage. Historically, Hawaiians refer to him as Kūhiō or Prince Kūhiō, in deference to his royal lineage.

4. For details on the trial of the queen regarding the insurrection, see "Trial of a Queen" 1995.

5. William Little Lee wrote all the legal codes as attorney general for the kingdom beginning in 1847 and also drafted the constitution of 1852 (Lâm 1985: 110; Kame'eleihiwa 1992: 298–300; Merry 2000: 5–6).

6. Linnekin points to four statutes enacted in 1850 that, in combination, "made it impossible for commoners to subsist on the land without participating in the market economy, either through produce sales, cash cropping, or wage labor" (1990: 195). One was the Kuleana Act, which allowed commoners the right to be awarded their land in fee simple; the second was a law giving foreigners the right to own land in the kingdom; the third opened three more ports to foreign commerce on Hawai'i Island (which had until that point only been allowed in Lahaina on Maui Island and Honolulu on O'ahu Island); and the fourth abolished payment of taxes in kind, requiring Hawaiians to instead pay land, labor, and poll taxes to the kingdom in cash (195–96). By the mid-1840s, government taxes had to be paid in cash, which forced people in areas remote from foreign commercial activities to shift to port towns to earn the necessary money (Ralston 1984: 31; Linnekin 1990: 195). These changes also led to a different process of class formation (Ralston 1985: 31). Carolyn Ralston explores the shift in commoner Kanaka Maoli lives, noting that between 1778 and 1854, life patterns for the *maka'āinana* changed from those of affluent subsistence farmers who were self-sufficient in terms of nearly all the essentials of life to those of a class of unskilled and predominantly landless peasants who were dependent on their own labor to

supply the food and increasing number of foreign goods required to sustain life (Ralston 1984: 22).

7. The scholar Keanu Sai contests the prevailing scholarship and offers a radically different analysis. Drawing on a report submitted as part of the minister of interior's report to the 1882 kingdom legislature by W. D. Alexander, which was later published as *Brief History of Land Titles* in the Hawaiian Almanac in 1891, Sai argues that Kanaka Maoli tenants received in excess of 180,000 acres (Sai, personal communication, March 28, 2006; Sai 2005). He asserts that the figure of 30,000 acres for the *maka'āinana* lands is accurate only when calculated from the number of Land Commission awards. Purchasers of portions of the government lands were issued royal patent grants, which differed from the royal patents issued upon Land Commission awards, since recipients of these were not required to obtain their award from the commission (Chinen 1958: 27–28). Sai argues that the real dispossession for the *maka'āinana* originated from the Bayonet Constitution—forced on King Kalākaua in 1887—that institutionalized property qualifications for the enfranchisement of citizens (Sai, personal communication, March 28, 2006).

8. In establishing the Territory of Hawaii under the Organic Act of 1900, Congress asserted that the federal government held absolute title to these lands. But the Act of 1900, like the Joint Resolution, allowed the territory administrative control and use of the lands in what was, as Melody Kapilialoha Mackenzie suggests, a special trust under the federal government's proprietorship (1991: 27).

9. The first federal legislation to mention Hawaiians along with American Indians was an appropriations bill in 1906 to fund "ethnological researches among the American Indians and natives of Hawaii under the direction of the Smithsonian Institution" (U.S. Congress 1906a).

10. McGregor does not detail the gender contours of the membership of the organization and it is unclear as to whether or not Hawaiian women joined.

11. Houston Wood analyzes this phenomenon, calling it "the rhetoric of the kama'āina anti-conquest," where Euro-Americans obscured both their origins and the effect of their presence in Hawai'i by asserting innocence while securing hegemony.

12. Prior to the Bayonet Constitution that the haole elite thrust upon King Kalākaua, some kingdom officials considered the Japanese and Kanaka Maoli to be from a "cognate race" and believed that if Japanese settlers were to "amalgamate" with them, they could produce a new and vigorous race (Jung 2006: 81). During his tour of Japan in 1881, Kalākaua even proposed to Emperor Meiji the formation of a "Union and Federation of the Asiatic nations and sovereigns" (Jung 2006: 81). But eventually, Kalākaua distinguished between "Asiatics" and Polynesians when he promoted pan-Polynesian unity through a federation plan with Sāmoa and Tahiti (Osorio 2002).

13. As Indian women were entitled to allotments, there were protective provisions in the act that guarded against land acquisition through interracial marriages. In sec. 182, the "Rights of white men marrying Indian women; tribal property" are defined in the following way: "No white man, not otherwise a member of any tribe of Indians, who may after August 9, 1888, marry an Indian woman, member of any Indian tribe in the United States, or any of its territories except the Five Civilized Tribes in Indian territory, shall by such marriage after August 9, 1888, acquire any right to tribal property, privilege, or interest whatever to which any member of such tribe is entitled" (http://www.law.cornell.edu/uscode/25/181.text.html).

14. Vine Deloria Jr. and Clifford Lytle argue that Senator Dawes, who designated the act, "had almost single-handedly secured passage of the General Allotment Act which was eventually named after him, [and that] federal Indian policy had been made sporadically on the basis of personal belief and philosophy among administrative and legislative members. The belief in private property, deeply held by the reformers of Lake Mohonk, was sufficient to carry the day and get allotment affirmed without much evidence of the effect it would have or was having on Indians themselves" (1984: 42). Deloria and Lytle contrast the allotment period with the reform movement of the 1920s that "began to concentrate on the actual conditions under which Indians then lived and sought some major effort by the federal government to improve the situation" (42). He also points out that the first major report on American Indian conditions was *The Red Man in the United States,* written by G. E. E. Lindquist for the Inter-Church Movement in 1919 (42).

15. Citizenship was conferred upon all allottees under the General Allotment Act and served as proof of one's capability to assimilate and individualize. Hence, citizenship for American Indians was contingent upon abandoning tribal affiliations and acquiring private property. The Indian Citizenship Act of 1924 conferred U.S. citizenship on those who were missed or excluded by the General Allotment Act.

16. Deloria and Lytle note that the Omnibus Act of 1910 "attempted to bring forward and make consistent all the revisions and amendments of the General Allotment Act, which had been made on a piecemeal basis during the thirty-three years since its passage" (1984: 38).

17. For an example of the literature that focused on racial difference and the Americanization of Hawai'i's children, see Allen 1921.

18. For a history of the labor movement in Hawai'i from 1900 to 1940 that includes a treatment of plantation labor and "racial unionism," see Johannessen 1956.

3. Under the Guise of Hawaiian Rehabilitation

1. Governor Charles J. McCarthy had been appointed by Woodrow Wilson and later became head of the Honolulu Chamber of Commerce (Wright 1972: 33).

2. House committee members who were absent from the meeting included rep-

resentatives John M. Baer, North Dakota; Scott Ferris, Oklahoma; George B. Grigsby, Alaska; Louis T. McFadden, Pennsylvania; John R. Ramsey, New Jersey; Nicolas J. Sinnott, Oregon; and John T. Watkins, Louisiana.

3. In House floor debates later that year, Delegate Kalaniana'ole argued that "if Congress makes it mandatory that only citizen labor be employed on Federal work from the Territory, gradually the skilled labor from the mainland will come to the islands, and the Hawaiians and other citizens will return to their former trades from which they were driven by the alien, and thereby make Hawaii an American community" (U.S. Congress 1920b: 7454–55).

4. The following year, while still pushing the HHCA through its passage, Kalaniana'ole wrote an article for the *Mid-Pacific Magazine* in which he asserted, "The lands mentioned in this bill, which are to be set aside and leased for 99 years at a nominal rental to those of Hawaiian blood, are principally crown lands on which the Kalakaua leases made 30 years ago are about to expire. I feel that as the United States came into possession of these lands after they had been confiscated by the successful revolutionist, with the aid of the United States minister, that Congress in its wisdom will recognize our claims" (Kalaniana'ole 1921: 130).

5. Beers suggests that Delegate Kalaniana'ole foresaw an attack upon the Hawaiian Rehabilitation Bill as an unconstitutional measure and forestalled this by asking the U.S. attorney general for assistance and was "assured that the Act would pass the test of constitutionality" (1974: 14).

4. The Virile, Prolific, and Enterprising

1. Perhaps counterintuitively, given his apparent disdain for Kanaka Maoli, in 1907, Robertson married a Hawaiian woman, Ululani McQuaid, who was an opera singer (1943: 6).

2. Palmer Parker was a Massachusetts sailor who jumped ship in Hawai'i in 1809. Eventually, he won the favor of Kamehameha I and married his granddaughter Kipikāne in 1816. In the 1830s, Parker herded and slaughtered cattle for Kamehameha III in the Waimea region on the island of Hawai'i. In 1847, Parker received two acres of land from Kamehameha III. This became the basis for the enormous Parker Ranch, which has been in continuous operation by the same family to the present day (Whitehead 1992: 160–61).

3. These committee members were alternately present during the various days of hearings, December 14, 23, 24.

4. For more information about Akana, see DeFries 1992, an edited collection of Akana's essays, including his 1918 manuscript, "The Sinews for Racial Development," "dedicated to the progress of the Hawaiian young people of the Territory of Hawaii."

5. These were the same "common sense" claims made in the 2000 U.S. Supreme Court ruling in *Rice v. Cayetano* that are discussed in chapter 6.

6. For example, in North Carolina, in order to vote all men were required to pay

poll taxes, and, except for those whose forebears had been eligible to vote prior to January 1, 1867, to pass a literacy test. As Glenda Elizabeth Gilmore details, that amendment would take effect on July 1, 1902, but white men (whose ancestors could have voted) would not have to take the literacy test until 1908 (1996: 120). According to Gilmore, this kind of exemption was known as the "grandfather clause."

7. While the inclusive rule would have excluded Hawaiians with less than one-thirty-second Hawaiian blood quantum, it would not have disenfranchised Hawaiians in the ways that the grandfather clause excluded the majority of black people from exercising the franchise. Moreover, a one-thirty-second definition for "native Hawaiian" would not have been analogous to the one-thirty-second rule that once defined blackness.

8. In a sense, this split parallels the American Indian context as described by David Wilkins, who discusses this divergence as a form of "bifurcation" which classifies the federal government's relationship to tribes as (1) moral obligations and (2) legal obligations (1997: 159). He writes, "The question of the federal government's *moral obligation* to tribes is a recurring one" (158). Or, as Murray L. Wax put it, "When funds are allocated by the federal government, they usually are rationalized on the moral grounds of a neglected and abused class of citizenry, rather than on the grounds of treaty obligation" (1997: 52).

5. Limiting Hawaiians, Limiting the Bill

1. Delegate Kalaniana'ole probably meant to instead refer to Senator McLean since there is no trace of a McClain in the records of the hearings. As discussed above, Senator New's letter to Delegate Kalaniana'ole on February 23, 1921, explained the level of these senators' involvement.

2. This was originally reported in the newspapers as SCR 7, not SCR 8, but the coverage listed the same amendments found in SCR 8 except one (not found in SCR 8) that would have the Secretary of the Interior approve all lands withdrawn for leasing (*Honolulu Advertiser* 1921g).

3. The record does not identify Desha's affiliation nor include a testimonial delivered by him. Also, it is not clear whether the McClellan listed here is the same McClellan, as representative of the Honolulu Chamber of Commerce, who testified in the December 1920 hearings. In this round of debate, he is identified as legal counsel to trustees of the Parker Ranch.

4. The hearing records do not indicate which committee members were present on each day of this particular set of debates in June 1921.

5. I have been unable to locate any transcripts from the territorial sessions that reflect such debate.

6. This question continues to haunt Hawaiians in the twenty-first century. Currently, a series of lawsuits is directed at dismantling Hawaiian programs and

funding, on the basis on charges of unconstitutionality regarding the HHCA. See the discussion in chapter 6.

6. Sovereignty Struggles

1. The Court determined that it would review the legislation in question with a rational basis analysis rather than subject the case to strict scrutiny dictating all other cases understood as race-based.

2. Although the official transcripts available from the case as heard before the Court do not identify which Justice said what, I was present in the courtroom when the case was presented, and am therefore able to attribute each quote to a specific judge.

3. *Rice v. Cayetano, Governor of Hawaii,* 528 U.S. 495 (2000), 146 F3d 1075 reversed. See the syllabus and ruling of the case at http://supct.law.cornell.edu/supct/index.html.

4. For information on this political position, see the Hawaiian Kingdom Web site (http://www.hawaiiankingdom.org).

5. The declaration itself has a central contradiction regarding the right to self-determination. Although Article 3 states that all indigenous peoples have the right to self-determination, Article 46 stipulates that the assertion of this right should not threaten the territorial or political integrity of the existing nation-states that encompass indigenous peoples. For more information, visit http://www.iwgia.org/sw248.asp.

Bibliography

Adams, Romanzo. 1924. *The Japanese in Hawaii: A Statistical Study Bearing on the Future Number and Voting Strength and on the Economic and Social Character of the Hawaiian Japanese.* New York: National Committee on American Japanese Relations.

———. 1929. *Further Developments of Race Contacts in Hawaii.* Honolulu: Institute of Pacific Relations.

———. 1933. *The Peoples of Hawaii.* Honolulu: American Council Institute of Pacific Relations.

———. 1934. "The Unorthodox Race Doctrine of Hawaii." In *Comparative Perspectives on Race Relations,* edited by Melvin M. Tumin, 81–90. Boston: Little, Brown and Company.

———. 1937. *Interracial Marriage in Hawaii: A Study of the Mutually Conditioned Process of Acculturation and Amalgamation.* New York: AMS Press.

Akana, Reverend Akaiko. 1992. "Sinews for Racial Development." In *Light upon the Mist,* edited by Eleanora M. DeFries, 3–54. Kailua-Kona: Mahina Productions.

Alexander, W. D. 1891. "A Brief History of Land Titles in the Hawaiian Kingdom." In *Thrum's Hawaiian Annual,* 105–24.

Allen, Riley H. 1921. "Education and Race Problems in Hawaii." *American Review of Reviews,* December, 613–24.

Alton, Helen. 1971. "Ethnic Priority to Hawaiian Lands May Be Discarded." *Honolulu Star-Bulletin,* September 22, C-7.

Ancheta, Angelo N. 1998. *Race, Rights, and the Asian American Experience.* New Brunswick, N. J.: Rutgers University Press.

Anderson, Atholl. 1991. *Race against Time.* Dunedin: Hocken Library, University of Otago.

Anderson, Ian. 1993. "Re-claiming Tru-ger-nan-ner: De-colonising the Symbol." *Art Monthly Australia,* December, 31–42.

Barayuga, Debra. 1999. "Hawaiians Sue to Preserve Claims." *Honolulu Star-Bulletin,* September 30, 1.

Barker, Joanne Marie. 1995. "Indian Made: Sovereignty, Federal Policy, and the Work of Identification." Qualifying essay, History of Consciousness, University of California, Santa Cruz.

———. 2003. "Indian U.S.A." *Wicazo Sa Review* 18, no. 1 (spring): 25–79.

Barringer, Herbert R. 1994. *Asians and Pacific Islanders in the United States.* New York: Russell Sage Foundation.

Beers, William Henry. 1974. *Prince Jonah Kuhio Kalanianaole.* Honolulu: Hawaii State Library System Centralized Processing Center. Originally published by Hawaii County Library, Hilo, Hawai'i, in 1930.

Ben-zvi, Yael. 2006. "Where Did Red Go? Lewis Henry Morgan's Evolutionary Inheritance and U.S. Racial Imagination." *CR: New Centennial Review* 7, no. 2: 201–29.

Bennett, Judith. 1976. "Immigration, 'Blackbirding,' Labour Recruiting? The Hawaiian Experience, 1877–1887." *Journal of Pacific History* 11: 3–27.

Bernardo, Rosemarie. 2007. "Akaka Bill Gets Support in House." *Honolulu Star-Bulletin,* May 3, 2.

Bindt, Henry M. 1923. "Theory That Hawaiians Are 'Dying Race' Not Borne Out by Actual Conditions Here." *Honolulu Advertiser,* December 30, 8.

Biolsi, Thomas. 1995. "The Birth of the Reservation: Making the Modern Individual among the Lakota." *American Ethnologist* 22, no. 1: 28–53.

Biolsi, Thomas, and Larry J. Zimmerman. 1997. *Indians and Anthropologists: Vine Deloria, Jr. and the Critique of Anthropology.* Tucson: University of Arizona Press.

Bishop, Rev. S. E. 1888. "Why Are the Hawaiians Dying Out? Or, Elements of Disability for Survival among the Hawaiian People." Presentation to the Honolulu Social Science Association.

Black, Henry Campbell. 1990. *Black's Law Dictionary,* 6th ed. St. Paul, Minn.: West Publishing Co.

Blaisdell, Kekuni, and Noreen Mokuau. 1994. "Kānaka Maoli, Indigenous Hawaiians." In *Hawai'i Return to Nationhood,* International Working Group of Indigenous Affairs–Document 75, edited by Ulla Hasager and Jonathan Friedman, 49–67. Copenhagen: IWGIA.

Blu, Karen. 1980. *The Lumbee Problem: The Making of an American Indian People.* Cambridge: Cambridge University Press.

Boris, Eileen. 1995. "The Racialized Gendered State: Constructions of Citizenship in the United States." *Social Politics* 2: 160–80.

Borreca, Richard. 2007. "Akaka Bill's Necessity Stressed." *Honolulu Star-Bulletin,* May 15, 3.

Brah, Avtar. 1996. *Cartographies of Diaspora: Contesting Identities.* London: Routledge.

Bulmer, Martin. 1984. *The Chicago School of Sociology: Institutionalization, Diversity, and the Rise of Sociological Research.* Chicago: University of Chicago Press.

Burrows, Dudley. 1920. "Raymond Ready to Spend Last Cent in Fight on Land Bill." *Pacific Commercial Advertiser,* March 28, 1.

Burrows, Edwin G. 1947. *Hawaiian Americans: An Account of the Mingling of Japanese, Chinese, Polynesian, and American Cultures.* New Haven, Conn.: Yale University Press.

Camire, Dennis. 2007. "Akaka Bill Strongly Opposed." *Honolulu Advertiser,* May 4, 23.

Carriaga, Roman R. 1936. "The Filipinos in Hawaii: A Survey of Their Economic and Social Conditions." Unpublished thesis, University of Hawai'i.

Chinen, Jon J. 1994 [1958]. *The Great Mahele: Hawaii's Land Division of 1848*. Honolulu: University of Hawai'i Press.

Churchill, Ward, and Glenn T. Morris. 1992. "Key Indian Laws and Cases." In *The State of Native America: Genocide, Colonization, and Resistance*, edited by M. Annette Jaimes, 13–21. Boston: South End Press.

Clifford, James. 1992. "Traveling Cultures." In *Cultural Studies*, edited by Lawrence Grossberg, Cary Nelson, and Paula A. Treichler, 96–112. New York: Routledge.

Coffman, Tom. 2003. *Nation Within: The Story of America's Annexation of the Nation of Hawaii*. Kenmore, Wash.: Epicenter Press.

Coman, Katharine. 1978. *The History of Contract Labor in the Hawaiian Islands*. New York: Arno Press.

Conroy, Francis Hilary. 1949. "The Japanese Expansion into Hawaii, 1868–1898." Ph.D. dissertation, University of California.

Curry, Charles F. "Rehabilitation of Native Hawaiians." Report to accompany H.R. 13500. Chairman Curry of the Committee on Territories, Report No. 839. House. 66th Cong., 2d sess., April 15, 1–12.

Davenport, William. 1994. *Pi'o: An Enquiry into the Marriage of Brothers and Sisters and Other Close Relatives in Old Hawaii*. Lanham, Md.: University Press of America.

Davis, F. James. 1991. *Who Is Black? One Nation's Definition*. University Park: Pennsylvania State University Press.

DeFries, Eleanora M. 1992. "Akaiko Akana, 1884–1933." In *Light upon the Mist: A Reflection of Wisdom for the Future Generations of Native Hawaiians*. Kailua-Kona: Mahina Productions.

Deloria, Vine Jr., and Clifford Lytle. 1984. *The Nations Within: The Past and Future of American Indian Sovereignty*. New York: Pantheon.

Dippie, Brian W. 1982. *The Vanishing American: White Attitudes and U.S. Indian Policy*. Lawrence: University Press of Kansas.

Dominguez, Virginia. 1986. *White by Definition: Social Classification in Creole Louisiana*. New Brunswick, N.J.: Rutgers University Press.

Dougherty, Michael. 1992. *To Steal a Kingdom: Probing Hawaiian History*. Waimānalo, Hawai'i: Island Press.

Dulles, John F. II. 1991. *A Broken Trust: The Hawaiian Homelands Program: Seventy Years of Failure of the Federal and State Governments to Protect the Civil Rights of Native Hawaiians*. Los Angeles: Hawai'i Advisory Committee to the United States Commission on Civil Rights, Western Regional Division.

Dunn, Leslie C. 1928. *An Anthropometric Study of Hawaiians of Pure and Mixed-Blood*. Cambridge, Mass.: Papers of the Peabody Museum of American Archaeology and Ethnology, Harvard University.

Du Puy, William Atherton. 1932. *Hawaii and Its Race Problem*. Washington D.C.: United States Government Printing Office.

Dutton, Clarence E. 1884. *The Hawaiian Islands and People: A Lecture Delivered at the*

U.S. National Museum: Under the Auspices of the Smithsonian Institution and the Anthropological and Biological Societies of Washington. Washington, D.C.: Judd and Detweiler, Printers.

Espiritu, Yen Le. 1995. *Filipino American Lives.* Philadelphia: Temple University Press.

Faludi, Susan. 1991. "Broken Promise: How Everyone Got Hawaiians' Homelands Except the Hawaiians." *Wall Street Journal,* September 9, 1.

Federal-State Task Force on the Hawaiian Homes Commission Act. 1983. *Report to the United States Secretary of the Interior and the Governor of the State of Hawai'i.* Honolulu: United States Department of the Interior.

Fields, Barbara J. 1982. "Ideology and Race in American History." In *Religion, Race and Reconstruction: Essays in Honor of C. Vann Woodward,* edited by J. Morgan Kousser and James M. McPherson, 143–77. Oxford: Oxford University Press.

Foster, Frank Harty. 1965. *Maori Patients in Public Hospitals.* Department of Health Special Report Series, no. 25. Wellington, New Zealand: R.E. Owen, Government Printer.

Fuchs, Lawrence H. 1961. *Hawaii Pono: A Social History.* San Diego: Harcourt Brace Jovanovich.

Garcia, Joseph. 1997. "U.S. House Gives Hawaiian Rights to Grandchildren." *Honolulu Advertiser,* March 12, A1, B4.

Garroutte, Eva Marie. 2003. *Real Indians: Identity and the Survival of Native America.* Berkeley: University of California Press.

Gilman, Laselle. 1943. "Fifty Years in Law: A.G.M. Robertson 50 Years a Lawyer." *Honolulu Advertiser,* July 14, 1, 6.

Gilmore, Glenda Elizabeth. 1996. *Gender and Jim Crow: Women and the Politics of White Supremacy in North Carolina, 1896–1920.* Chapel Hill: University of North Carolina Press.

Glauberman, Stu. 1989a. "New OHA 'Quantum' Vote Planned." *Honolulu Advertiser,* November 21, A4.

———. 1989b. "Vote Favors Single Definition of 'Hawaiian.'" *Honolulu Advertiser,* January 21, A3.

Glick, Clarence E. 1970. "Interracial Marriage and Admixture in Hawaii." *Social Biology* 15, no. 4: 278–91.

Gordon, Charles. 1945. "The Racial Barrier to American Citizenship." *University of Pennsylvania Law Review* 93, no. 3: 237–58.

Gordon, Linda. 1994. *Pitied But Not Entitled: Single Mothers and the History of Welfare, 1890–1935.* New York: Free Press.

Greenbaum, Susan. 1991. "What's in a Label? Identity Problems of Southern Indian Tribes." *Journal of Ethnic Studies* 19, no. 2: 107–26.

Griffiths, A. F. 1915. "More Race Questions." Presentation to the Social Science Association, March 1.

Grimshaw, Patricia. 1989. *Paths of Duty: American Missionary Wives in Nineteenth Century Hawaii.* Honolulu: University of Hawai'i Press.

Gulick, Sidney L. 1915. "Hawaii's American-Japanese Problem: A Description of the Conditions, a Statement of the Problems and Suggestions for Their Solution." *Honolulu Star-Bulletin,* n.p.

———. 1916. *America and the Orient: Outlines of a Constructive Policy.* New York: Missionary Movement of the United States and Canada.

———. 1918. *American Democracy and Asiatic Citizenship.* New York: Charles Scribner's Sons.

———. 1937. *Mixing the Races In Hawaii: A Study of the Coming Neo-Hawaiian American Race.* Honolulu: Hawaiian Board Book Rooms.

Hall, Lisa Kahaleole. 2005. " 'Hawaiian at Heart' and Other Fictions." *The Contemporary Pacific* 17, no. 2 (fall): 404–13.

Halualani, Rona Tamiko. 2002. *In the Name of Hawaiians: Native Identities and Cultural Politics.* Minneapolis: University of Minnesota Press.

Handy, E. S. Craighill, and Mary Wiggen Pukui. 1935. *Ohana, the Dispersed Community of Kanaka.* Honolulu: Institute of Pacific Relations.

———. 1972. *The Polynesian Family System in Ka-'u, Hawaii.* Rutland, Vt.: Charles E. Tuttle Company.

Haraway, Donna. 1993. "Teddy Bear Patriarchy: Taxidermy in the Garden of Eden, New York City, 1908–1936." In *Cultures under United States Imperialism,* edited by Amy Kaplan and Donald E. Pease, 237–91. Durham, N.C.: Duke University Press.

———. 1997. *Modest_Witness@second_Millennium. FemaleMan©_Meets_OncoMous TM.* New York: Routledge.

Harris, Cheryl L. 1993. "Whiteness as Property." *Harvard Law Review* 106: 1709–91.

Harris, Marvin. 1964. *Patterns of Race in the Americas.* New York: W. W. Norton.

Hasager, Ulla. 1997. "Localizing the American Dream: Constructing Hawaiian Homelands." In *Siting Culture: The Shifting Anthropological Object,* edited by Karen Fog Olwig and Kirstin Hastrup, 165–92. New York: Routledge.

Hasager, Ulla, and Jonathan Friedman. 1994. *Hawai'i Return to Nationhood.* Copenhagen: International Working Group for Indigenous Affairs, Document no. 75.

Hatch, F. M. 1906. "Conditions in Hawaii." In *Proceedings of the Annual Meeting of the Lake Mohonk Conference,* 83–88. New York: Lake Mohonk Conference.

Hau'ofa, Epeli. 1995. "Our Sea of Islands." In *Asia/Pacific as Space of Cultural Production,* edited by Rob Wilson and Arif Dirlik, 86–98. Durham, N.C.: Duke University Press.

Hawaiian Homes Commission. 1922. "Rehabilitation in Hawaii." *Bulletin of the Hawaiian Homes Commission,* no. 2 (December): 1–27.

Hing, Bill Ong. 1993. *Making and Remaking Asian America through Immigration Policy, 1850–1990.* Stanford, Calif.: Stanford University Press.

Hobbs, Jean. 1935. *Hawaii: A Pageant of the Soil*. Stanford, Calif.: Stanford University Press.

Hollinger, David A. 2003. "Amalgamation and Hypodescent: The Question of Ethnoracial Mixture in History of the United States." *American Historical Review* (December): 1363–90.

Honolulu Advertiser. 1920. "Protest against Land Measure Is Laid on M'Clellan." June 23, 1.

———. 1921a. "Back-to-Soil Policy Given New Impetus." April 14, 1.

———. 1921b. "Cooke Certain as Secretary of the Homes Commission." September 15, 1–2.

———. 1921c. "Delegate and Wife Receive High Honors." April 25, 1, 4.

———. 1921d. "Hawaii Land, Labor Bills Meet Favor." June 16, 1.

———. 1921e. "Homes Bill Amendments Are Offered." April 23, 1–2.

———. 1921f. "Negro Radicals Are Blamed in Tulsa Riot by Own Race." June 4, 1.

———. 1921g. "New Plan for 'Homes' Bill Is Submitted." April 17, 1.

———. 1921h. "Organic Act Amendments Pass Senate." April 19, 1–2.

———. 1921i. "Rehabilitation Commission." May 2, editorial page.

———. 1921j. "Rehabilitation Commission Is to Depart May 10." May 6, 1.

———. 1921k. "Rehabilitation Mission Leaves for Coast Today." May 10, 1.

———. 1921l. "Rehabilitation Scheme before House Friday." April 21, 1.

———. 1921m. "The Revised Rehabilitation Bill." May 3, editorial page.

———. 1921n. "Robert W. Shingle Will Be Endorsed for Governor Today." April 21, 1.

———. 1953. "Civic Club Fights Change in HHC Racial Provisions." April 17, 13.

Honolulu Star-Bulletin. 1918a. "Kekaha Buys Kauai Lease for $200,000." December 6, 1.

———. 1918b. "Land Question Is Bound to Be Injected into '19 Legislature." December 7, 2.

———. 1918c. "Problems of Waiakea Are Threshed Out." December 6, 1.

———. 1918d. "Sugar Board to Buy All Island Crop." December 3, 1.

———. 1918e. "Will Homestead Kekaha Acreage When Lease Ends." December 7, 4.

———. 1919a. "Dillingham, Head of Business Men, to Be Reelected." January 15, 2.

———. 1919b. "Hawaiians to Control Work on Local Docks." April 4, 1–2.

———. 1919c. "Helping the Homesteader." February 8, 6.

———. 1919d. "Homesteaders Seek Purchase Waiakea Mill." April 12, 1.

———. 1919e. "Japanese Make Petitions for Naturalization." January 13, 1.

———. 1919f. "Kuhio Told That C. of C. Will Not Surrender Rights at Washington." June 19, 7.

———. 1919g. "Seek to Keep Filipinos from Hawaiian Isles." March 31, 6.

———. 1919h. "Waiakea Mill Is Scored by Homesteader." April 14, 1.

———. 1921a. "Caution Urged by Senator in Land Proposal." April 12, 1, 7.

———. 1921b. "Rehabilitation Measure Passes House By 21 to 6 after Bitter Opposition." April 23, 1.

——. 1921c. "Rehabilitation Should Be Limited to Hawaiians of Pure Blood, Says Governor." April 23, 1.

——. 1937a. "John H. Wise." August 13, editorial page.

——. 1937b. "John Wise, Sr. Dies; Services at 2 Saturday." August 12, 1, 5.

——. 1953. "Senate Okays Hawaii Blood Homes Ruling." April 16, 6.

——. 1995. "Vanishing Hawaiians." April, n.d., n.p.

Hooper, Anthony, and Judith Huntsman. 1985. *Transformations of Polynesian Culture.* Auckland, New Zealand: Polynesian Society.

Howard, Alan. 1990. "Cultural Paradigms, History, and the Search for Identity in Oceania." In *Cultural Identity and Ethnicity in the Pacific,* edited by Jocelyn Linnekin and Lin Poyer, 259–80. Honolulu: University of Hawai'i Press.

Hoxie, Frederick E. 2001. *A Final Promise: The Campaign to Assimilate the Indians, 1880–1920.* Lincoln: University of Nebraska Press.

Ishibashi, Koren. 2004. "Hawaiian Population Update." *Policy Analysis & System Evaluation (PASE) Report.* Honolulu: Kamehameha Schools.

Jacobson, Matthew Frye. 1998. *Whiteness of a Different Color: European Immigrants and the Alchemy of Race.* Cambridge, Mass.: Harvard University Press.

Jaimes, M. Annette. 1992. "Federal Indian Identification Policy: A Usurpation of Indigenous Sovereignty in North America." In *The State of Native America: Genocide, Colonization, and Resistance,* edited by M. Annette Jaimes, 123–38. Boston: South End Press.

Johannessen, Edward. 1956. *The Hawaiian Labor Movement: A Brief History.* Boston: Bruce Humphries.

Jones, Peter Cushman. 1897. *An Address by the Hawaiian Society of the Sons of the American Revolution.* Honolulu: Hawaiian Society.

Jung, Moon-Kie. 2006. *Reworking Race: The Making of Hawaii's Interracial Labor Movement.* New York: Columbia University Press.

Kaeppler, Adrienne L. 1982. "Genealogy and Disrespect: A Study of Symbolism in Hawaiian Images." *Res* 3 (spring): 82–107.

——. 1985. "Hawaiian Art and Society: Traditions and Transformations." In *Transformations of Polynesian Culture,* edited by Antony Hooper and Judith Huntsman, 105–31. Auckland, New Zealand: Polynesian Society.

——. 1988. "Hawaiian Tattoo: A Conjunction of Genealogy and Aesthetics." In *Marks of Civilization: Artistic Transformations of the Human Body,* edited by Arnold Rubin, 157–70. Los Angeles: University of California, Museum of Cultural History.

Kalanianaole, Prince J. K. 1921. "The Story of the Hawaiians." *Mid-Pacific Magazine* 11, no. 2: 117–31.

Kamakau, Joseph. 1921. "Hawaiian Advice to Hawaiians." *Honolulu Advertiser,* June 14, 3.

Kamakau, Samuel Manaiakalani. 1991 [1964]. *Ka Po'e Kahiko: The People of Old.* Honolulu: Bishop Museum Press.

——. 1992 [1961]. *Ruling Chiefs of Hawaii*. Revised edition. Honolulu: Kamehameha Schools Press.

Kameʻeleihiwa, Lilikalā. 1991. *Wāhine Kapu: Divine Hawaiian Women*. Honolulu: ʻAi Pōhaku Press.

——. 1992. *Native Land and Foreign Desires*. Honolulu: Bishop Museum Press.

Kanaʻiaupuni, Shawn Malia, and Carolyn A. Liebler. 2005. "Pondering Poi Dog: Place and Racial Identification of Multiracial Native Hawaiians." *Ethnic and Racial Studies* 28, no. 4 (July): 687–721.

Kanaʻiaupuni, Shawn Malia, and Nolan Malone. 2004. *Got Koko? Hawaiian Racial Identification and Multiracial Diversity*. Population Association of America. Honolulu: Kamehameha Schools.

"Kanaka Nian, In re." 1892. *Reports of Cases Determined in the Supreme Court of the Territory of Utah from the January Term, 1889, to the June Term, 1890*. John M. Zane, Reporter. Vol. 6: 259–63. Chicago: Callaghan and Co.

Kaplan, Amy, and Donald E. Pease, eds. 1993. *Cultures of United States Imperialism*. Durham, N.C.: Duke University Press.

Kauanui, J. Kēhaulani. 1998. "Off-Island Hawaiians 'Making' Ourselves at 'Home': A [Gendered] Contradiction in Terms?" *Women's Studies International Forum* 21, no. 6: 681–93.

——. 2005a. "The Multiplicity of Hawaiian Sovereignty Claims and the Struggle for Meaningful Autonomy." *Comparative American Studies* 3, no. 3: 283–99.

——. 2005b. "Precarious Positions: Native Hawaiians and U.S. Federal Recognition." *Contemporary Pacific* 17, no. 1: 1–27.

——. 2007. "Diaspora, De-racination and 'Off-Island' Hawaiians." *The Contemporary Pacific* 19, no. 1: 137–60.

Kelly, Anne Keala. 2003. "The Alaska-Hawaiʻi Connection: How Inupiat, Gwich'in, and Native Hawaiian Power Bases Impact both ANWR and Native Hawaiian Federal Recognition." *Native Americas Hemispheric Journal of Indigenous Issues* 20, no. 3: 26–35.

Kelly, Marion. 1980. "Land Tenure in Hawaiʻi." *Amerasia Journal* 7, 57–73.

Kent, Noel. 1993. *Hawaiʻi: Islands under the Influence*, 2nd ed. Honolulu: University of Hawaiʻi Press.

Kim, Claire Jean. 1999. "The Racial Triangulation of Asian Americans." *Politics and Society* 27, no. 1 (March): 105–38.

Kinney, W. A. 1927. *Hawaii's Capacity for Self-Government All but Self-Destroyed*. Salt Lake City: Frank L. Jensen.

Konvitz, Milton. 1946. *The Alien and the Asiatic in American Law*. Ithaca, N.Y.: Cornell University Press.

Lâm, Maivân Clech. 1985. "The Imposition of Anglo-American Land Tenure Law on Hawaiians." *Journal of Legal Pluralism* 23: 103–28.

——. 1989. "The Kuleana Act Revisited: The Survival of Traditional Hawaiian Commoner Rights in Land." *Washington Law Review* 64, no. 2: 233–88.

———. 1992. *At the Edge of the State: Indigenous Peoples and Self-Determination.* Boston: Brill Academic Publishing.

LaVelle, John P. 1999. "The General Allotment Act 'Eligibility' Hoax: Distortions of Law, Policy, and History in Derogation of Indian Tribes." *Wacazo Sa Review* 14, no. 1 (spring): 251–302.

Like, Edward L. and E. A. Nawahi. 1897. "The Leaders Belong to the People and the People Belong to the Leaders." *Ke Aloha Aina,* October 23, 4–5. Reprinted and translated by Keao Kamalani and Noelani Arista in *'Ōiwi: A Native Hawaiian Journal* (1998): 88–99.

Liliuokalani. 1964 [1898]. *Hawaii's Story by Hawaii's Queen.* Rutland, Vt.: Charles E. Tuttle Co.

Liliuokalani of Hawai'i. 1997 [1987]. *The Kumulipo: An Hawaiian Creation Myth.* Honolulu: Pueo Press.

Lind, Andrew W. 1955. *Hawaii's People.* Honolulu: University of Hawai'i Press.

———. 1978. *Hawaii's Japanese: An Experiment in Democracy.* New York: Arno Press.

———. 1980. *Hawaii's People.* Honolulu: University of Hawai'i Press.

Linn, Brian McAllister. 1996. "The Long Twilight of the Frontier Army." *Western Historical Quarterly* 27: 141–67.

Linnekin, Jocelyn. 1990. *Sacred Queens and Women of Consequence: Rank, Gender, and Colonialism in the Hawaiian Islands.* Ann Arbor: University of Michigan Press.

Linnekin, Jocelyn, and Lin Poyer, eds. 1990. *Cultural Identity and Ethnicity in the Pacific.* Honolulu: University of Hawai'i Press.

Liptak, Adam. 2003. "Private School under Fire for Race-Based Admissions." *Seattle Times,* June 29. http://seattletimes.nwsource.com.

Lopez, Ian F. Haney. 1996. *White by Law: The Legal Construction of Race.* New York: New York University Press.

Lowe, C. H. 1972. *The Chinese in Hawaii: A Bibliographic Survey.* Taipei: China Print.

Lowe, Lisa. 1996. *Immigrant Acts: On Asian American Cultural Politics.* Durham, N.C.: Duke University Press.

Lydecker, Robert C. 1918. *Roster, Legislatures of Hawaii, 1841–1918: Constitutions of Monarchy and Republic, Speeches of Sovereigns and Presidents.* Honolulu: Hawaiian Gazette Co.

MacCaughey, V. 1920. "Race Mixture in Hawaii." *American Journal of Physical Anthropology* 3, no. 4: 492–93.

MacKenzie, Melody Kapilialoha, ed. 1991. *Native Hawaiian Rights Handbook.* Honolulu: Native Hawaiian Legal Corporation and the Office of Hawaiian Affairs.

Malo, David. 1951. [1838]. *Hawaiian Antiquities (Moolelo Hawaii).* Translated by Nathaniel B. Emerson. Honolulu: Bishop Museum Press.

Malone, Nolan J. 2005. "Laupa'i Kanaka: Native Hawaiian Population Forecasts for 2000 to 2050." *Policy Analysis & System Evaluation (PASE) Report.* Honolulu: Kamehameha Schools.

Marques, A. 1894. "The Population of Hawaii: Is the Hawaiian a Doomed Race? Present and Future Prospects." *Journal of the Polynesian Society* 2: 253–70.

Matsuda, Mari. 1988a. "Law and Culture in the District Court of Honolulu." *American Journal of Legal History* 32: 16–41.

———. 1988b. "Native Custom and Official Law in Hawaii." *Law and Anthropology* 3: 135–46.

Matsumoto, Valerie J., and Blake Allmendinger, eds. 1999. *Over the Edge: Remapping the American West.* Berkeley: University of California Press.

McClain, Charles, ed. 1994. *Asian Indians, Filipinos, and Other Asian Communities and the Law.* New York: Garland.

McGregor, Davianna Pōmaikaʻi. 1990. "ʻĀina Hoʻopulapula: Hawaiian Homesteading." *Hawaiian Journal of History* 4: 1–38.

Merry, Sally. 2000. *Colonizing Hawaii: The Cultural Power of Law.* Princeton, N.J.: Princeton University Press.

———. 2003. "Christian Conversion and 'Racial' Labor Capacities: Constructing Racialized Identities in Hawaiʻi." In *Globalization under Construction: Governmentality, Law, and Identity,* edited by Richard Warren Perry and Bill Maurer, 203–38. Minneapolis: University of Minnesota Press.

Meyer, Melissa L. 1999. "American Indian Blood Quantum Requirements: Blood Is Thicker Than Family." In *Over the Edge: Remapping the American West,* edited by Valerie J. Matsumoto and Blake Allmendinger, 231–52. Berkeley: University of California Press.

Morse, Harold. 1999. "Home Lands Lawsuit to be Filed Today, Could Total $100 Million." *Honolulu Star-Bulletin,* December 29, 1.

Murakami, Alan. 1991. "The Hawaiian Homes Commission Act." In *Native Hawaiian Rights Handbook,* edited by Melody MacKenzie, 43–76. Honolulu: Native Hawaiian Legal Corporation and the Office of Hawaiian Affairs.

Nose, Roberta. 1967. "Robert W. Wilcox, Hawaii's First Delegate to Congress." *Hawaii Historical Review* 2, no. 6: 436–55.

Noyes, Martha H. 2003. *Then There Were None.* Honolulu: Bess Press.

Okihiro, Gary Y. 1991. *Cane Fires: The Anti-Japanese Movement in Hawaii, 1865–1945.* Philadelphia: Temple University Press.

———. 1994. *Margins and Mainstreams: Asians in American History and Culture.* Seattle: University of Washington Press.

Omandam, Pat. 1998. "1998 UN Report: Annexation Could Be Declared Invalid." *Honolulu Star-Bulletin,* August 11, 1.

Omi, Michael, and Howard Winant. 1994. *Racial Formation in the United States.* New York: Routledge.

Osorio, Jonathan Kay Kamakawiwoʻole. 2002. *Dismembering Lāhui: A History of the Hawaiian Nation to 1887.* Honolulu: University of Hawaiʻi Press.

Pacific Commercial Advertiser. 1910. "People Hawaii with Filipinos." November 15, 6.

——. 1920a. "Blame for Land Leasing Action Is Sidestepped by Commission." April 1, 1.

——. 1920b. "Commission Preparing Official Statement in Answer to Criticisms." March 31, 1.

——. 1920c. "The Commission's Report." April 1, 4. Morning ed.

——.1920d. "Congressional Party Due to Arrive July 9." June 22, 1.

——.1920e. "Congress to Act on Hawaii Bills Prior to Recess." May 13, 1.

——. 1920f. "Homesteading Is Doomed if Bill Passes Congress." March 11, 1.

——. 1920g. "Irwin Called on to Referee New Citizenship Case." June 23, 1, 4.

——. 1920h. "Kuhio and Wise Will Represent Republicans of Isles at Chicago." June 1, 1.

——. 1920i. "Rehabilitation Bill Is Received; Provides Drastic Land Law Change." March 10, 1.

——. 1920j. "2 Whites Killed, Negroes Wounded in Race Rioting." June 21, 1.

——. 1920k. "What Hawaiian Commission Did at Washington." April 1, 1.

——. 1920l. "Wise's Efforts to Excuse Commission Branded Ridiculous." March 18, 1.

——. 1921a. " 'California Will Settle Japanese Question on Her Own Terms,' Kahn." January 1, 1.

——. 1921b. "Exclusion Body Refuses Aid to Ban upon Alien Land Ownership." January 5, 1.

——. 1921c. "Filipino Tide from Hawaii to Mainland Irks Coast." January 5, 1.

——. 1921d. "Japanese Issue to Come before California Law Makers Monday." January 2, 1.

——. 1921e. "Likely That Harding Will Appoint Man Backed by Delegate." February 2, 1.

——. 1921f. "Rehabilitation Bill Will Not Be Passed at This Session." February 6, 1.

Palmer, Albert W. 1924. *The Human Side of Hawaii: Race Problems in the Mid-Pacific.* Boston: Pilgrim Press.

Pang, Gordon Y. K. 1995. "Land You Bought May Actually Be Home Lands." *Honolulu Star-Bulletin,* February 17, 1, 4.

Parker, Linda. 1976. "Federal Management of the Native Hawaiians." *Journal of the West* 15, no. 2: 92–101.

——. 1989. *Native American Estate: The Struggle over Indian and Hawaiian Lands.* Honolulu: University of Hawai'i Press.

Pukui, Mary Kawena, E.W. Heartig, and Catherine A. Lee. 1972. *Nānā I Ke Kumu.* Honolulu: Hui Hānai.

Pukui, Mary Kawena, and Samuel H. Elbert. 1986. *Hawaiian Dictionary,* revised and enlarged ed. Honolulu: University of Hawai'i Press.

Ralston, Caroline. 1984. "Hawaii, 1778–1855: Some Aspects of Maka'ainana Response to Rapid Cultural Change." *Journal of Pacific History* 19, no. 1: 21–40.

Roberts, Stephen H. 1969. *Population Problems of the Pacific.* New York: AMS Press.

Robertson, A. G. M. 1920. *The Hawaiian Rehabilitation Bill: An Argument against the Bill.* Honolulu: H. R. Union Calendar no. 269, 66th Cong., 2nd sess.

Roosevelt, Theodore. 1901. State of the Union Address to Congress. In *The State of the Union Message of the Presidents,* edited by Arthur M. Schlesinger and Fred L. Israel, 2407. New York: Chelsea House.

Rountree, Helen C. 1990. *Pocahontas's People: Powhatan Indians of Virginia through Four Centuries.* Norman: University of Oklahoma Press.

Sahlins, Marshall. 1985. *Islands of History.* Chicago: University of Chicago Press.

Sai, David Keanu. 2005. "Kahana: How the Land Was Lost (review)." *The Contemporary Pacific* 17, no. 1 (spring): 237–240.

Sapiro, Virginia. 1984. "Women, Citizenship, Nationality: Immigration and Naturalization Policies in the U.S." *Politics and Society* 13: 1–26.

Schlesinger, Arthur M., and Fred L. Israel, eds. 1966. *The State of the Union Message of the Presidents.* New York: Chelsea House.

Schmitt, Robert C. 1968. *Demographic Statistics of Hawaii, 1778–1965.* Honolulu: University of Hawai'i Press, 1968.

Schneider, David. 1968. *American Kinship: A Cultural Account.* Englewood Cliffs, N.J.: Prentice-Hall.

Silva, Noenoe K. 1998. "Kanaka Maoli Resistance to Annexation." *'Ōiwi: A Native Hawaiian Journal,* 1: 40–75.

——. 2003. "Talking Back to Law and Empire: Hula in Hawaiian-Language Literature in 1861." In *Law and Empire in the Pacific: Fiji and Hawai'i,* edited by Sally Engle Merry and Donald Brenneis, 101–22. Santa Fe: SAR Press.

——. 2004. *Aloha Betrayed: Native Hawaiian Resistance to American Colonialism.* Durham, N.C.: Duke University Press.

Smith, Andrea. 2006. "Heteropatriarchy and the Three Pillars of White Supremacy." In *The Color of Violence: The INCITE! Anthology,* edited by INCITE! Women of Color Against Violence, 66–73. Cambridge, Mass.: South End Press.

Smith, William Carlson. 1937. *Americans in Process: A Study of Our Citizens of Oriental Ancestry.* Ann Arbor, Mich.: Edwards Brothers.

Spaulding, Thomas Marshall. 1923. *The Crown Lands of Hawaii.* Honolulu: University of Hawai'i Press.

Stannard, David E. 1989. *Before the Horror: The Population of Hawai'i on the Eve of Western Contact.* Honolulu: Social Science Research Institute, University of Hawai'i.

Stanton, Ron. 2003. "Native Blood and Custom Clash—Some Critics Say the Definition of Hawaiian Should Include the Practice of 'Hanai.' " Associated Press.

Stauffer, Robert H. 2004. *Kahana: How the Land Was Lost.* Honolulu: University of Hawai'i Press.

Stiffarm, Lenore A., and Phil Lane Jr. 1992. "The Demography of Native North America: A Question of American Indian Survival." In *The State of Native Amer-*

ica: Genocide, Colonization, and Resistance, edited by M. Annette Jaimes, 23–53. Boston: South End Press.

Sturm, Circe. 2002. *Blood Politics: Race, Culture, and Identity in the Cherokee Nation of Oklahoma*. Berkeley: University of California Press.

———. 2004. "Bill Clinton's Cherokee Grandmother: The Racial and Cultural Politics of Claiming Indian Kin." American Studies Association Annual Meetings, November 13, Atlanta, Georgia.

Tamara, Eileen H. 1994. *Americanization, Acculturation, and Ethnic Identity: The Nisei Generation in Hawaii*. Urbana: University of Illinois Press.

———. 1995. "Gender, Schooling and Teaching, and the Nisei in Hawai'i: An Episode in American Immigration History, 1900–1940." *Journal of American Ethnic History* 14, no. 4: 3–26.

Tanji, Melissa. 2003. "Ruling Threatens Hawaiians: Kamehameha Decision Implications Spark Concern." *Maui News*, August 25, 1.

Teaiwa, Teresia, and Joanne M. Barker. 1994. "Native InFormation." *Inscriptions* 7: 16–41.

Territory of Hawaii. 1919a. *Journal of the House of Representatives*. Tenth Legislature of the Territory of Hawaii, Regular Session. February 19–April 13. Honolulu: Paradise of the Pacific.

———. 1919b. *Senate Journal*. Tenth Legislature of the Territory of Hawaii, Regular Session. February 19–April 30. Honolulu: Honolulu Star-Bulletin, Ltd.

———. 1921a. *Journal of the House of Representatives*. Eleventh Legislature of the Territory of Hawaii, Regular Session. February 16–April 27. Wailuku, Maui: Maui Publishing Company, Ltd.

———. 1921b. *Senate Journal*. Eleventh Legislature of the Territory of Hawaii, Regular Session. Honolulu: New Freedom Press.

Trask, Haunani-Kay. 1993. *From a Native Daughter: Colonialism and Sovereignty in Hawai'i*. Monroe, Maine: Common Courage Press.

Trask, Mililani. 1993. "An Interview with Mililani Trask" by Ho'oipo DeCambra. In *He Alo A He Alo: Hawaiian Voices on Sovereignty*, 113–24. Honolulu: American Friends Service Committee.

———. 1994. "The Politics of Oppression." In *Hawai'i Return to Nationhood*. International Work Group for Indigenous Affairs–Document 75, edited by Ulla Hasager and Jonathan Friedman, 68–87. Copenhagen: IWGIA.

"Trial of a Queen: 1895 Military Tribunal."1995. The Judiciary History Center. Hawai'i.

Tuttle, E. P. 1920. "Rehabilitation Bill First to Come Up at Next Congress." *Honolulu Advertiser*, June 23, 1.

Twombly, Alex. 1902. "The Native Hawaiian of Yesterday and Today." In *Proceedings of the Annual Meeting of the Lake Mohonk Conference*, 1–13. New York: Lake Mohonk Conference.

United States. 1849. "Hawaiian Islands, Friendship, Commerce and Navigation." In

Treaties and Other International Agreements of the United States of America, 1776–1949, comp. Charles I. Bevans, 8: 864. Washington: Government Printing Office.

——. 1862. "Treaty with the Hawaiian Islands, December 20, 1849." In *Statutes at Large of the United States of America, 1789–1873*, 9: 977–83. Boston: Little, Brown and Company.

——. 1871. "Treaty with Hawaii: Postal convention between the United States of America and the Hawaiian Kingdom; Concluded, May 4, 1870." In *Statutes at Large of the United States of America, 1789–1873*, 16: 1113–14. Boston: Little, Brown and Company.

——. 1875. "Hawaiian Islands, Commercial Reciprocity." In *Treaties and Other International Agreements of the United States of America, 1776–1949*, comp. Charles I. Bevans, 8: 874. Washington: Government Printing Office.

——. 1884a. "Convention between the Post-Office Department of the Kingdom of Hawaii and the Post-Office Department of the United States of America, concerning the exchange of money-orders." In *Report of the Postmaster General of the United States*. 48th Cong., 2nd sess. H. Exec. Doc. 1, pt. 4: 584–95. Washington: Government Printing Office.

——. 1884b. "Supplementary Convention to Limit the Duration of the Convention Respecting Commercial Reciprocity between the United States of America and the Hawaiian Kingdom, Concluded January 30, 1875." In *Treaties and Other International Agreements of the United States of America, 1776–1949*, comp. Charles I. Bevans, 8: 878. Washington: Government Printing Office.

U.S. Congress. 1900. *The Act of Congress Organizing Hawaii into a Territory, An Act to Provide a Government for the Territory of Hawaii*. 56th Cong., 1st sess. C339, 31 Stat 141, April 30.

——. 1906a. *An Act Making Appropriations for sundry civil expenses of the government for the fiscal year ending June thirtieth, nineteen hundred and seven, and for other purposes*. 59th Cong., 1st sess. Ch 3914, Stat 34.

——. 1906b. *The Burke Act*. 59th Cong., 1st sess. 34 Stat 182, May 8.

——. 1920a. House. *Congressional Record*. 66th Cong., 2nd sess., May 21. Vol. 59, pt. 7, 7447–56.

——. 1920b. Senate. Committee on Territories. *Hawaiian Homes Commission Act*. Hearings. 66th Cong., 3rd sess., on H.R. 13500, December.

——. 1920c. House. Committee on Territories. *Proposed Amendments to the Organic Act of the Territory of Hawaii*. Hearings. 66th Cong., 2d sess., February 3–5, 7, 10.

——.1921a. House. *Hawaiian Homes Commission Act of July 9, 1921*. 67th Cong., 1st sess. C42, 42 Stat 108.

——. 1921b. House. Committee on Territories. *Proposed Amendments to the Organic Act of the Territory of Hawaii*. Hearings. 67th Cong., 1st sess., on H.R. 7257, June 9–10.

———. 1922. House. Committee on Territories. *Nonassimilability of Japanese in Hawaii and the United States.* Hearings. 67th Cong., 2d sess., July 17.

———. 1993a. Senate. *Congressional Record,* 103d Cong., 1st sess, October 27. Vol. 139, 14477.

———. 1993b. *100th Anniversary of the Overthrow of the Hawaiian Kingdom.* Public Law 103–150. 103d Cong., 1st sess., 107 Stat 1510. S.J. Res. 19, November 23.

———. 1997a. Senate. Committee on Energy and Natural Resources. *Hawaiian Homes Commission Act 105–19.* Report to Accompany HJ Resolution 32, May 16.

———. 1997b. House. Committee on Indian Affairs. *Proposal to Consent to Certain Amendments Enacted by the Legislature of the State of Hawaii to the Hawaiian Homes Commission Act of 1920.* 105th Cong., 1st sess., March 11.

———. 2007. Senate. Committee on Indian Affairs. *A Bill to Express the policy of the United States regarding the United States relationship with Native Hawaiians and to provide a process for the recognition by the United States of the Native Hawaiian governing entity.* S. 310. 110th Cong., 1st sess., January 17.

U.S. Supreme Court. 1999. *Official Transcript Proceedings before the Supreme Court of the United States, Harold F. Rice Petitioner v. Benjamin J. Cayetano, Governor of Hawaii, Case no. 98–818,* 1–58. Washington, D.C.: Alderson Reporting Company.

Utley, Robert M. 1984. *The Indian Frontier of the American West, 1846–1890.* Albuquerque: University of New Mexico Press.

Uyehara, Mitsuo. 1977. *The Ceded Land Trusts, Their Use and Misuse.* Honolulu: Hawaiiana Almanac Publishing Company.

———. 1982. *The Prophetic Vision of Keopuolani The Sacred Queen of Hawaii.* Honolulu: Hawaiiana Almanac Publishing Company.

Valeri, Valerio. 1985. *Kingship and Sacrifice: Ritual and Society in Ancient Hawaii.* Translated by Paula Wissing. Chicago: University Of Chicago Press.

Vause, Marylynn. 1962. "The Hawaiian Homes Commission Act, 1920: History and Analysis." M.A. thesis, University of Hawai'i.

Wagoner, Paula. 1998. "An Unsettled Frontier: Property, Blood and US Federal Policy." In *Property Relations, Renewing the Anthropological Tradition,* edited by C. M. Hann, 124–41. London: Cambridge University Press.

Waite, David. 1989. "OHA Asks Legislature to Settle 2 Disputes." *Honolulu Advertiser,* February 5, 3.

Wald, Priscilla. 1993. "Terms of Assimilation: Legislating Subjectivity in the Emerging Nation." In *Cultures under United States Imperialism,* edited by Amy Kaplan and Donald E. Pease, 59–84. Durham, N.C.: Duke University Press.

Wax, Murray L. 1997. "Educating an Anthro: The Influence of Vine Deloria, Jr." In *Indians and Anthropologists: Vine Deloria, Jr., and the Critique of Anthropology,* edited by Thomas Biolsi and Larry J. Zimmerman, 50–60. Tucson: University of Arizona Press.

Whitehead, John. 1992. "Hawai'i: The First and Last Far West?" *Western Historical Quarterly* 23, no. 2: 153–77.

Wilkins, David E. 1997. *American Indian Sovereignty and the U.S. Supreme Court: The Masking of Justice.* Austin: University of Texas Press.

———. 2007. *American Indian Politics and the American Political System.* 2nd ed. Lanham, Md.: Rowman and Littlefield.

William, Tyler. 1991. "Postmodernity and the Aboriginal Condition: The Cultural Dilemmas of Cultural Policy." *Australian and New Zealand Journal of Sociology* 29: 322–42.

Williamson, Joel. 1995. *New People: Miscegenation and Mulattoes in the United States.* Baton Rouge: Louisiana State University Press.

Wilson, Rob, and Arif Dirlik. 1995. *Asia/Pacific as Space of Cultural Production.* Durham, N.C.: Duke University Press.

Wirth, Louis. 1991 [1938]. *Urbanism As a Way of Life.* New York: Irvington Publishers.

Wolfe, Patrick. 1999. *Settler Colonialism and the Transformation of Anthropology: The Politics and Poetics of an Ethnographic Event.* New York: Cassell.

Wood, Houston. 1999. *Displacing Natives: The Rhetorical Production of Hawai'i.* Lanham, Md.: Rowman and Littlefield.

Wright, Theo. 1972. *The Disenchanted Isles: The Story of the Second Revolution in Hawaii.* New York: Dial Press.

Yamaguchi, Andy. 1989. "Change of Native Hawaiian Definition Tabled." *Honolulu Advertiser,* February 18, A5.

Yamamura, Douglas Shigeharu. 1949. "A Study of Some of the Factors Contributing to the Status of Contemporary Hawaiians." Ph.D. dissertation, University of Washington.

Young, Kanalu G. Terry. 1998. *Rethinking the Native Hawaiian Past.* New York: Garland.

Zack, Naomi. 1993. *Race and Mixed Race.* Philadelphia: Temple University Press.

Archival Materials

Kalaniana'ole, Prince Jonah Kūhiō. 1921a. Letter to Governor Charles J. McCarthy, March 7, 1921. Delegate Kūhiō, Territorial Depts. correspondence, 80 Governor, 1918–1921, box 7, M474, Hawai'i State Archives.

———. 1921b. Report to the legislature of Hawai'i: "Mr. President, Mr. Speaker, Senators and Representatives of the Legislature of Hawaii." Delegate Kalanianaole, subject correspondence, 41 Rehabilitation, box 4, M474, Hawai'i State Archives.

Lymer, Judge William B. 1928a. "In the Matter of the Application of Alfred Milner Stephen for Naturalization." *Before the Honorable William B. Lymer, Judge of the United States District Court,* Territory of Hawaii, at Honolulu, July 5, 1928. RG 21, U.S. District Court, District of Hawai'i, Honolulu, Naturalization Case Files, 1927–1959, 1466–1985, box 1, series 28.

———. 1928b. "In the Matter of the Application of Alfred Milner Stephen for Naturalization, No. 1515." *In the District Court of the United States in and for the Territory
of Hawaii,* July 10, 1928, RG 21, U.S. District Court, District of Hawai'i, Honolulu,
Naturalization Case Files, 1927–1959, 1466–1985, box 1, series 28.

McClellan, George. 1921. Suggested Amendments to H.R. 13500 by George McClellan.
Delegate Kalanianaole, subject correspondence, 41 Rehabilitation, box 4, M474,
Hawai'i State Archives.

New, Harry S. 1921. Letter to Prince J. Kuhio Kalanianaole, February 23, 1921. Delegate
Kalanianaole, subject correspondence, 41 Rehabilitation, box 4, M474, Hawai'i
State Archives.

Pittman, W. B. 1921a. Amendments to Hawaiian Rehabilitation Bill. Delegate Kalanianaole, subject correspondence, 41 Rehabilitation, box 4, M474, Hawai'i State
Archives.

———. 1921b. Letter to Senator Reed Smoot, January 10, 1921. Delegate Kalanianaole,
subject correspondence, 41 Rehabilitation, box 4, M474, Hawai'i State Archives.

Robertson, A. G. M. 1921. Letter to Senator Reed Smoot, January 10, 1921. Delegate
Kalanianaole, subject correspondence, 41 Rehabilitation, box 4, M474, Hawai'i
State Archives.

Wood, Sanford B. D. 1928a. "In the Matter of the Application of Alfred Milner
Stephen for Naturalization, No. 1515." *In the District Court of the United States in
and for the Territory of Hawaii, Exception,* United States Attorney, District of
Hawaii, July 16, 1928, RG 21, U.S. District Court, District of Hawai'i, Honolulu,
Naturalization Case Files, 1927–1959, 1466–1985, box 1, series 28.

———. 1928b. "In the Matter of the Application of Alfred Milner Stephen for Naturalization, No. 1515." *In the District Court of the United States in and for the Territory
of Hawaii, Notice of Appeal,* United States Attorney, District of Hawaii, July 16,
1928, RG 21, U.S. District Court, District of Hawai'i, Honolulu, Naturalization
Case Files, 1927–1959, 1466–1985, box 1, series 28.

Index

Abelove, Henry, 203n15

Adams, Romanzo, 202n5

Afong, Chun, 136–38

African Americans, 17–24, 200n19; disenfranchisement of, 129, 207n6; hypodescent rule of blackness, 15, 50, 90, 199n13, 200n15; Jim Crow segregation laws, 21; one-drop rule, 21–24, 199n13, 200n20; racialized conception of property and, 21–22

ʻAhahui Kālaiʻāina, 28, 60, 203n17

ʻAhahui Puʻuhonua o nā Hawaiʻi (Hawaiian Protective Association), 68, 79–81, 84–85, 205n10

Akaka, Daniel, 31, 172, 184, 201n1

Akaka Bill, 171–75, 184–89

Akana, Akaiko, 81, 123, 128, 165, 207n4 (ch. 4)

Alexander, W. D., 205n7

Alexander and Baldwin Ltd., 69

Allen, Riley H., 135, 206n17

Almon, Edward B., 100, 157, 159–61

aloha spirit, 109, 134–35

Aluli, Noa, 81

ambilineal descent, 201n4

American Factors Ltd., 69

American Indians. See Native Americans

Ancheta, Angelo N., 200n18

Andrews, Lorrin, 118

Apology Resolution of 1993, 31, 35, 174–75, 190, 192

Arakaki v. Lingle, 183–84

Arctic National Wildlife Refuge (ANWR), 186, 201n1

Arctic Slope Regional Corporation, 201n1

Arista, Noelani, 58

Ashford, C. W., 27

Asiatic Hawaiians, xi; anti-Asian policies towards, 19–20, 68, 74–75, 91–97, 168–69, 200n18; citizenship of, 33, 74–75, 91, 94–96; Congressional consideration of, 107–8, 112–13, 133–38, 207n3 (ch. 3); demographics of, 95–96; immigrant status of, 91; racial categorization of, 93–94

assimilation, 91; goals of HCCA, 86–87, 89–90; through racial mixing, 13–15, 18–19, 21–25, 124, 168–69, 199n11, 200n16; usufructuary rights, 24–25

Baer, John M., 206n2

Baldwin, Harry, 152–54, 156

Ballou, Sidney, 157

Barker, Joanne Marie, 89–90

Bayonet Constitution, 27, 122, 143, 205n7, 205n12

Bennett, Judith, 82

Ben-zvi, Yael, 17–18

Big Five businesses, 34; influence on legislation of, 100, 122–23, 146; monopoly of, 69–70; oligarchic structure of, 146. See also sugar industry

Biolsi, Thomas, 90

Bishop, Bernice Pauahi, 13

Bishop Estate, 69

blackness. See African Americans

Blaisdell, Kekuni, 189

"Blood Quantum" (Losch), vi

Dawes, Henry, 206n14

Dawes Act. *See* General Allotment Act of 1887

Deloria, Vine, Jr., 206n14, 206n16

demographics: of Asiatic Hawaiians, 95–96; from census of 1910, 101–2; of Hawaiian ancestry, 41, 171–73; showing racial mixing, 56, 101, 126, 202n9, 202n11

Department of Hawaiian Home Lands, 4, 174; *Arakaki v. Lingle* and, 183–84; breach of trust charges, 177–78; *Rice v. Cayetano* and, 178–84

Desha, John R., 157, 208n3

diasporic Hawaiians, xi

Dillingham, Walter F., 71, 204n2

Dippie, Brian, 17–18, 50, 86–87, 200n17

Dismembering Lāhui: A History of the Hawaiian Nation to 1887 (Osorio), 58

Doe v. Kamehameha, 13–14

Dole, Sanford Ballard, 28, 78, 122

Dominguez, Virginia, 20, 168

Dowell, Cassius C., 100, 110–12, 114–15, 157

Drewry, Patrick H., 157

Driver, William J., 157

Duncan, Rudolph M., 165

Emma Naea, Queen of Hawai'i, 40, 58–60, 63–64, 78–79

entitlement, 9

equal protection clause of the Fourteenth Amendment, 113–16, 174, 178–79

ethnicity. *See* racialization of indigeneity

Faludi, Susan, 177

family relationships. *See* genealogy and kinship practices

Farrington, W. R., 157–58

Ferris, Scott, 206n2

Fields, Barbara, 200n15

Fifteenth Amendment of the U.S. Constitution, 179, 182–83

Forbes, Jack, 55

Fourteenth Amendment of the U.S. Constitution, 113–16, 174, 178–79, 182–83

fractional measurements. *See* blood quantum rule

Frear, Walter, 83

Fuchs, Lawrence, 69

GAA. *See* General Allotment Act of 1887

Garroutte, Eva Marie, 55

Geary Act of 1892, 200n18

Gemmil, Faith, 41, 201n1

genealogy and kinship practices, 3, 31–32, 196, 200n22; adoption, 202n8; bilateral descent, 38–39, 201n4; contemporary practices, 40–43; elevation of status, 49–50; European-American system, 53–55; gender-based status, 48, 132; inclusivity of, 12–17, 41–42, 53, 130, 194, 201–2nn4–5; incompatibility of, with blood quantum rule, 38–42, 64–65; inheritance of lease lands and, 5, 176–77, 197nn4–5; kinship relationships, 1, 47–49, 53–56, 202n8; matrilocal basis of kinship, 132; mo'okū'auhau, 37–38; 'ohana, definition of, 1, 55–56; origin cosmology, 43–44, 201nn2–3, 203n10; Papa Kū'auhau Ali'i and, 47; political empowerment of, 10; precolonial class hierarchies, 44–47; rank differentiation, 38–39, 203n9; role in political life and, 63–64; role of place in, 51–52; shifting notions of, 46–47, 58–65, 202n6, 203nn16–17; taro shoot anal-

Jacobson, Matthew Frye, 199n14
Jaimes, M. Annette, 88–89
Japanese, 19–20; anti-Japanese policies, 68, 83–85, 91–97, 108; as cognate race, 205n12; Congressional considerations of, 112–13, 136–37; demographics of, 96. *See also* Asiatic Hawaiians
Johannessen, Edward, 206n18
Johnson, Albert, 100, 157
Jones, Peter Cushman, 93, 149, 151
Jones, Wesley L., 123
Jung, Moon-Kie, 93–94

Kaeao, D. K., 84
Kaeppler, Adrienne L., 38, 202n6
Kahahele, Bumpy, 189
Ka Lāhui Hawaiʻi, 174
Kalākaua, David, King of Hawaiʻi: Bayonet Constitution and, 27, 122, 143, 205n7, 205n12; election to the throne of, 40, 58–60; genealogical claims of, 47, 63–64; Japanese migration program of, 93; pan-Polynesian unity plan of, 205n12; sugar industry under, 69
Kalanianaʻole Kūhiō, Jonah, 78, 204n3; ʻAhahui Puʻuhonua o nā Hawaiʻi constitution and, 81; anti-Asian proposals of, 107–8, 207n3 (ch. 3); on crown lands, 79–80, 110, 207n4 (ch. 3); definition of native Hawaiian by, 151–52, 154, 156, 159–61; efforts to obtain business support by, 146, 151, 156; failure of HR 13500 and, 142–43, 149–50; first Congressional hearing and, 71, 97–102; Hawaiian Homes Commission appointment, 165; opposition to full-blood proposals of, 140–41, 149–50, 167, 185; rehabilitation interests of, 72–73, 81; report on

Congressional delegation by, 146, 150–52; second Congressional hearing and, 116, 118, 125–26, 207n5 (ch. 3); third Congressional hearing and, 157, 159–61, 164–65
Kalauokalani, David, 60
Ka Makaainana (newspaper), 47
Kamakau, Samuel, 42–45, 203nn12–13
Kamalani, Keao, 58
Kameʻeleihiwa, Lilikalā: on *akua* (gods), 43; on elevation of status, 49–50; on genealogical practices, 38, 40–43, 46, 203n9; on land division, 76; on precolonial class hierarchies, 44
Kamehameha I, King of Hawaiʻi, 59, 202n6
Kamehameha III, King of Hawaiʻi, 26, 59, 73; Māhele land division of 1848 and, 74–80, 109–13
Kamehameha IV, King of Hawaiʻi, 78–79
Kamehameha V, King of Hawaiʻi, 78–79
Kamehameha Schools, 13–14, 199n12
Kānaka Maoli, xi–xii, 75; adoption practices of, 202n8; depopulation of, 2–3, 41, 67–68, 81–82; 1890 census of, 202n9; federal recognition of, 171–75, 184–89; Hawaiian ancestry of, 41, 171–73; inclusivity of, 12–17, 41–42, 53, 130; origins of, 43–49; racial mixing by, 13–15, 60–64, 101, 199n11; role of place for, 51–52; role of taro for, 51; sovereignty claims of, 25–32; vanishing Hawaiians theories and, 15–16. *See also* genealogy and kinship practices; racialization of indigeneity; rehabilitation movement
Kanaka ʻŌiwi, xi
Kaneakua, J. M., 60
Kapena, John M., 93
Kaulia, James K., 60
Kawaha, G. K., 155

Kawananakoa, David, Prince of Hawai'i, 61

Kealoha, Samuel L., Jr., 171–74, 190

Ke Aloha Aina (newspaper), 58, 60–63, 203n14

Ke'elikōlani, Ruth, 13

Kekaha Sugar Company, 83

Kim, Claire Jean, 75

Kinney, W. A., 133–34

kinship practices. *See* genealogy and kinship practices

Knight, Charles L., 157

Kūhiō. *See* Kalaniana'ole Kūhiō, Jonah

Kuhio Bill. *See* House Resolution 13500 (Kuhio Bill)

Kuleana Act of 1850, 77–78, 204n6

Kumalae, Jonah, 118

Kumulipo, 43, 47, 201n2

Kumulipo: An Hawaiian Creation Myth, The (Lili'uokalani), 201n2

Kuokoa (newspaper), 60

Laenui, Pōkā, 189

land: Big Five corporate ownership of, 34–35; colonial land acquisition projects, 18, 20; crown lands, 75, 77–80, 109–10, 113, 145, 207n4 (ch. 3); development rights, 29–31; Hawaiian ownership of, 140; homesteading proposals, 81–83, 87–88, 97, 117–19, 146, 148–49, 156, 161–62; honorary whiteness through usufruct, 24–25; Kamehameha Schools lands, 13–14; Kamehameha III's land privatization scheme, 73–74; Māhele land division of 1848, 33, 74–80, 109–13, 204–5nn5–7; missionaries ownership of, 76, 99–100, 109; precolonial land tenure system, 45–46; pre-Māhele land tenure practices, 76–77; racialized concept of, 20–25, 33–34, 168; sugar industry leases of, 7, 26,

34, 68–71, 83; transfers under the Akaka Bill of, 188–89, 195–96; U.S. annexation of, 28–30, 78, 85, 109, 111, 190, 205n8, 207n4 (ch. 3)

Land Act of 1895, 82–83, 103

land lease policies under HHCA, 2, 34; breach of trust and mismanagement charges, 177–78; citizenship criteria for, 108; of dispossession, 8–12, 34–35, 74, 166–70, 174–75, 194–96; eligibility based on blood quantum, 3–6, 11–12, 30–31, 34, 124–43, 165–70, 174–75, 197–98nn6–7; inheritance and succession requirements of, 5, 176–77, 197nn4–5; prioritized leasing of, 176; rehabilitation goals of, 68–74; revenue uses under, 30–31, 179; sugar industry leases, 69–71, 124, 154–55, 164–65; waiting list management, 4, 177, 197n3. *See also* Hawaiian Homes Commission Act of 1921

Lane, Frank, 117

Lane, John, 81

Lane, Phil, Jr., 88

Lankford, William C., 100–101, 157

LaVelle, John, 88–89

"Leaders Belong to the People and the People Belong to the Leaders, The" (Like and Nāwahī), 60–63, 203n14

Lee, Herbert K. H., 176

Lee, William Little, 76, 204n5

legal constructions of identity. *See* blood quantum rule

Like, Edward L., 60–63, 203n14

Lili'uokalani, Queen of Hawai'i: on Hawaiian people, xii; imprisonment of, 201n2; overthrow of, 27–28, 40, 60, 94, 174, 190; restoration attempt by, 71, 73; translation of *He Kumulipo* by, 201n2

Lind, Andrew W., 101

Lindle, Linda, 14
Lindquist, G. E. E., 206n14
lineage. *See* genealogy and kinship practices
Linnekin, Jocelyn, 39, 45–46, 76, 78, 204n6
Losch, Naomi Noe, vi
Lowe, Lisa, 200n18
Lyman, Norman, 99–100, 102–3, 108
Lytle, Clifford, 206n14, 206n16

MacCaughey, V., 133, 135–36
Mackenzie, Melody Kapilioloha, 205n8
Māhele land division of 1848, 33, 74–80, 109–13, 204–5nn5–7
Malo, Davida, 42, 45
Mashpee case, 24
McCarran-Walter Act of 1943, 200n18
McCarthy, Charles J., 206n1; first Congressional hearing and, 100, 102–3, 112; Kuhio Bill and, 116; SCR 6 and, 152, 154–55, 178
McClellan, George M., 122, 157, 208n3; definition of *native Hawaiian* of, 139, 147, 149, 158, 161–63; opposition to homesteading of, 142, 148, 161–63, 208n6
McFadden, Louis T., 157, 206n2
McGregor, Davianna Pomaika'i, 80–81, 198n7, 205n10
McKinley, William, 29
McLaughlin, Joseph, 157
McLean, George P., 123, 149, 151, 208n1
McQuaid, Ululani, 207n1 (ch. 4)
Merry, Sally, 6, 57–58, 63, 91–93, 198n8, 203n16
missionaries: education of, 128; female subordination by, 39; land ownership of, 76, 99–100, 109; official roles of, 61; overthrow of Lili'uokalani roles of, 73; paternalism of, 91–92

mixed race, definitions of, 112. *See also* racial mixing
Monahan, James G., 101
mo'okū'auhau, 37–38
Moore, Allen F., 157
Morgan, Lewis Henry, 17
Morris, Glen T., 88
Morrow, William W., 108
Morton v. Mancari, 179
Murakami, Alan, 198n7

Nā 'Ahahui Alaka'i, 60, 203n17
Naea, George, 59
Nationality Act of 1870, 95
Nation of Hawai'i, 189
Native Americans: assimilation goals for, 22–24, 86–87, 89–90, 200n20; blood quantum policies for, 24; Burke Act of 1906 and, 89–90; citizenship of, 87, 206n15; emphasis on welfare for, 208n8; General Allotment Act of 1887 and, 33, 74, 85–90; Mashpee identity, 24; *Morton v. Mancari* decision, 179; racialization of, 17–22, 50, 200nn16–17; racialized conception of property for, 22, 24
Native Governing Entities, 172
Native Hawaiian Education Act, 195
Native Hawaiian Government Reorganization Act (Akaka Bill), 171–75, 184–89
Native Hawaiian Health Act, 195
Native Hawaiians, xii; Apology Resolution definition of, 31, 174–75, 190; as census category, 13; as defined in the Akaka Bill, 186–89; inclusive definition of, 172–73; as political category, 9–10; 2000 census report of, 41, 171–73. *See also* genealogy and kinship practices

native Hawaiians, xi–xii, 30; compromise definition of, 154–57; eligibility for land leases of, 3–6, 11–12, 30–31, 165–70; Kalaniana'ole's definition of, 151–52; legal definitions of, 2–3, 9, 158–70, 195–96, 197n2; McClellan's definition of, 147, 149; OHA definition of, 176–77; in OHA trustee elections, 11–12, 173–76, 178–79; prevalence of racial mixing by, 13–15, 199n11; Wise's definition of, 119, 124, 152–53

Native studies, 10

Nāwahī, Emma 'A'ima, 60–63, 203n14

Neumann, Paul, 61

New, Harry S., 123, 149–52, 156, 160, 164

Newlands Resolution, 28–29

Noa, Henry, 189, 192

Noyes, Martha H., 16–17

Nugent, John, 123, 136–37

Office of Hawaiian Affairs (OHA), 30–31, 171, 195; *Arakaki v. Lingle* and, 183–84; definitions of native Hawaiian by, 176–77; legal mandate of, 175; *Rice v. Cayetano* and, 178–84; trustee elections for, 11–12, 173–76, 178–79

off-islanders, xi

'ohana, definition of, 1, 55–56

'Ōiwi: A Native Hawaiian Journal, 58

'Ōiwi Maoli, xi

Okihiro, Gary, 95

Omnibus Act of 1910, 206n16

Organic Act of 1900, 195–96; amendments to, 70, 105–6, 117, 154, 165, 168; citizenship provisions of, 94–95; public lands provisions of, 29, 84, 103; sugar industry interests in, 93

origin narratives, 43–44

Osorio, Jon Kay Kamakawiwo'ole, 27, 58–60

Owen, Robert L., 123

Pacific Islanders, 82

Paglaniwan, Richard, 176

Palmer, Albert W., 134–35

Papa Kū'auhau Ali'i, 47

Parker, Linda, 85–86

Parker, Palmer, 207n2 (ch. 4)

Parker, Samuel, 61–63

Parker Ranch, 122, 147–48, 158, 207n2 (ch. 4)

part-Hawaiian: use of term, xi

Paschoal, M. G., 155

Phelan, James D., 123

Pinkham, Lucius E., 83

Pittman, Key, 123, 136–37, 139–40, 145, 147–49

Pittman, W. B., 122

place, role of, 51–52

Poindexter, Miles, 142–43, 150

Polynesians, 121, 134–35, 148

Pro-Kanaka Maoli Sovereignty Working Group, 189

property. *See* land

Pukui, Mary, 45, 55–56

racialization of indigeneity, 194–96; anti-Asian policies, 19–20, 68, 74–75, 83–85, 91–97, 200n18; assimilationist policies of racial mixing, 18–19, 21–24, 124, 147, 168–69, 199n11, 200n16; through blood quantum classification, 42, 49–58, 119, 124; Brah's differentiated racialization, 20; census categories, 13, 173; colonial origins of, 6–12, 18–20, 49–58, 87–88, 91–92; in Congressional hearings on HHCA, 101, 110–13, 121, 125–43; in criteria for citizenship, 33, 74–75, 94–96, 108, 115–16; in eligibility for land leases, 3–6, 11–12, 30–31, 34–35, 124–43, 165–70, 197–98nn6–7; historical context of, 17–22, 67, 200nn15–19;

hypodescent rules, 15, 50, 90, 199n13, 200n15; Morgan's theory of cultural evolution, 17–18; of Native Americans, 85–90; paternalistic/welfare discourse in, 87–88, 91–92, 168–69; in rehabilitation projects, 83–85, 91–96; sexual boundaries in, 199n14; triangulation matrix of, 75, 91–97, 142; white property rights, 18–19, 20–25, 34. *See also* African Americans; blood quantum rule; Native Americans; whiteness

racial mixing, 13–15, 167–70; absorption considerations in, 207–8nn6–7; absorption debates on, 128–33; assimilationist goals of, 18–19, 21–25, 124, 147, 168–69, 199n11, 200n16; categorization of, 50, 57–58; census reports of, 56, 101, 126, 202n9, 202n11; with Chinese immigrants, 133–38; of colonial era diplomats, 60–64; the "grandfather's law," 129–30, 207–8nn6–7; hapa haoles, xi, 56–57; nationality as basis of identity, 57–58; in Queen Emma's genealogy, 59–60, 63–64; Robertson's Congressional testimony on, 124–38; as threat to whiteness, 147. *See also* Native Hawaiians

racial terminology, xi–xii

Ralston, Carolyn, 204n6

Ramsey, John R., 206n2

Rawlins, William T., 99–100, 102–3, 157

Raymond, J. F., 117

Raymond, J. H., 117–18

Raymond Ranch, 122, 148–49

Reciprocity Treaty of 1875, 26–27

Red Man in the United States, The (Lindquist), 206n14

rehabilitation movement, v, 2–3, 67–75, 80; anti-Asian policies of, 83–85, 91–97, 107–8; business efforts to limit,

124–25, 139; Congressional delegation of, 71–74, 99; funding proposals of, 145, 152; HHCA impact on, 7–9, 32–34, 164–66, 168, 198n8; homesteading goals of, 68–74, 81–83, 87–88, 97, 117–19, 146, 148–49, 156, 161–63; intermarriage with Pacific Islanders and, 82; Organic Act of 1900, 117, 154, 165, 168, 195–96, 205n8; racializing of, 83–85, 91–96, 124–33; repopulation goals of, 8, 87, 124, 132, 163–64; Robertson's Congressional testimony on, 121, 125–33; trial period for, 154–55; Wise's plan for, 118. *See also* Hawaiian Homes Commission Act of 1921

Reinstated Kingdom, 189, 192–93

reproduction, 199n14

Republic of Hawaii, 82–83

research methods, 6–7

Rice, Charles, 153–54, 157, 178

Rice, Harold (senator), 152–54, 156–57, 178

Rice, Harold F., 178–84

Rice v. Cayetano, 11–12, 35, 171–75, 178–84, 207n5 (ch. 4), 209nn1–3

Richards, William, 25–26, 61, 63

Rivenbaugh, B. G., 123

Robertson, A. G. M., 121–22, 207n1 (ch. 4); on absorption, 128–33, 164, 207n6; on Chinese-Hawaiian intermarriage, 133–38; opposition to HR 13500, 147–48; opposition to SCR 6, 156; on pure blood, 147; on racial mixing, 125–28, 207n5 (ch. 4)

Rogers, Puanani, 41

Roosevelt, Theodore, 86–87

Rountree, Helen C., 200n20

Russell, J. W., 153–54

Sahlins, Marshall, 46, 201n4

Sai, Keanu, 189, 191, 205n7

J. Kēhaulani Kauanui is an associate professor of American studies and anthropology at Wesleyan University.

Library of Congress Cataloging-in-Publication Data
Kauanui, J. Kēhaulani, 1968–
Hawaiian blood : colonialism and the politics of sovereignty and indigeneity /
J. Kēhaulani Kauanui.
p. cm. — (Narrating native histories)
Includes bibliographical references and index.
ISBN 978-0-8223-4058-4 (cloth : alk. paper)
ISBN 978-0-8223-4079-9 (pbk. : alk. paper)
1. Homestead law—Hawaii. 2. Hawaiians—Land tenure. 3. Hawaiians—Legal status, laws, etc. 4. Land tenure—Law and legislation—Hawaii. I. Title.
KFH454.K38 2008
346.96904′320899942—dc22   2008028477

CPSIA information can be obtained
at www.ICGtesting.com
Printed in the USA
LVHW052338091221
705810LV00006B/16